The Infiltrator

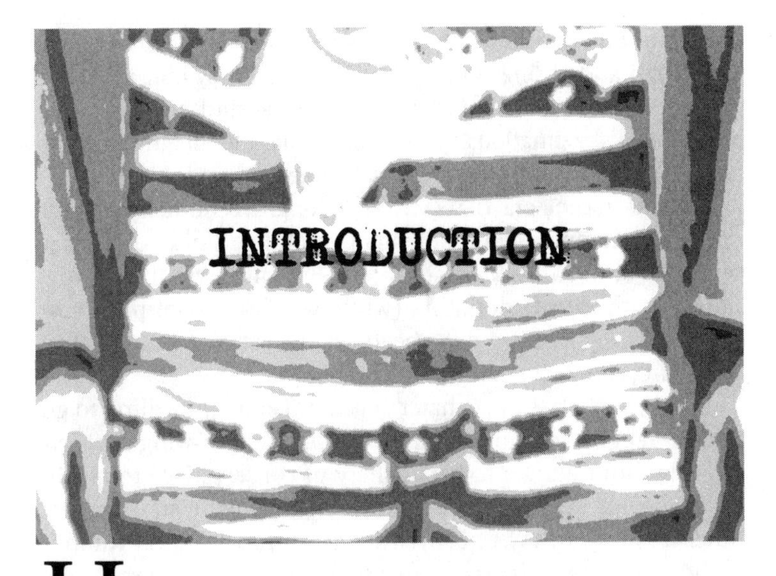

INTRODUCTION

Hi, friends! Welcome to the introduction of my latest book, *The Infiltrator: My Undercover Exploits in Right-Wing America!* To all you first-time readers, "What's up!" To all you old veterans, "Welcome back!" How have you been since the last time we were together? Did you get that tennis scholarship you were training for? I hope so!

First off, I have to say I'm very thrilled and surprised that the publisher asked me to write the introduction for this book. It's quite an unexpected honor that I would even be considered for the task. By no means is it because I wrote the damn book.

As I demonstrated in my previous books, my life's mission has always been to infiltrate and shake up the various institutions of everyday life in order to stand up for the underdog and, most important, STICK IT TO THE MAN! That's right, there's man-sticking involved in what I do (most often in a clever and cunning persona and/or disguise).

What to expect from this book: Man-sticking!

What *not* to expect from this book: Fun facts about celebrated French radiation theorist Madame Curie.

Have you ever wanted to see how the other half lives by going undercover and posing as one of them? What I'm willing to do for you—dear reader—is to throw myself into absurd, political, and potentially risky situations, yet manage to make it out alive in order to write about them in my singular, likable, and sardonic style.

In this recent era of WMD searching, freedom fry eating, civilian wiretapping, Iraqi prisoner pyramiding (and pointing at genitals), doing a heckuva good job (Brownie-style), and "Mission Accomplished" declaring (while wearing a cool pilot costume), my sights have now been set on extreme conservative right-wing American culture.

Yes, I, first-class playa-hater Harmon Leon, am willing to go to great lengths to understand the psyche of right-wing conservatives by infiltrating a rogue's gallery of conservative groups, in order to fight their repulsive ridiculousness with *my* repulsive ridiculousness. In my unconventional, anthropological romp, I shall become a regular *(chame)Leon,* if you will, letting you—the reader—live vicariously through my exploits as I venture into right-wing hellholes for sport, torture myself in some scuzzy swamps of spiritual and political horror, and try to eke out a living under this "no new jobs" regime.

While seeing how the other half lives (those who refer to liberals as "moonbats" and "commies"), I find that my conservative nemeses seem to love their God, flag, and country, and if your croissant-eating liberal ass doesn't love these things, too, then you can damn well leave! Then again, as a bleeding-heart, whiny-baby liberal who lives in godless San Franfreako and pokes fun at EVERYTHING THAT MAKES AMERICA GREAT, I'm just the man for this job!

Considering that Republicans control all three branches of government and have God's little born-again wonder boy in the White House, you have to question what the hell these fuming conservatives are *sooooo* pissed off about. Comedy is the weak taking on the powerful—that's why I've made it my mission to find out what makes right-wingers' blood boil, at a time when many liberals feel helpless against the continuing onslaught from the Right.

What are my chief weapons? Wit, cunning—and surprise!

Will there be satire? Yes!

Why? Satire is a sort of glass wherein beholders do generally discover everybody's face but their own. (OK, Jonathan Swift once said that.) But it should also be mentioned that one way to comprehend what's going on this country is either through humor or a moderate head injury. (Now that's something I once said!)

We will thus go on a journey through the conservative looking glass, as I, as your proverbial Alice, lead you on a journey down Bush's rabbit hole (whatever the hell that means). I shall go where few liberals have ventured—straight into the heart of the conservative beast, as I'm swallowed whole like Jonah inside the whale. You shall be introduced to a large cast of conservative characters that a sane few would ever get to encounter (or want to encounter).

I take to the Mexican border to spend a week with the vigilante group, the Minutemen Project. I brave rural Georgia in order to rub elbows with militant pro-war, patriotic skinhead bands, who are very angry and aggressive, not about stopping war, but about continuing it, while moshing to a three-chord thrash for George W. Bush. I'll spend three days at a teen-abstinence educators' conference using hand puppets and learning the ins and outs of our great leader's favorite method of birth control for kids—abstaining from sex. (No condoms allowed!) I go on crutches to a religious TV faith healer to be cured, since I can't afford health insurance. In order to become part of Bush's Illuminati, I infiltrate the Freemasons to expose their *reptilian agenda*. Attempting to make a living in this war-spending economy, I jump to such extremes as trying to land a job using a stack of fake resumes and answering e-mails from someone claiming to be a member of the royal family in Nigeria who needs *my* help! I even stoop to the lowest cultural rung by resorting to working with OJ Simpson on a prank celebrity reality show—you've been *Juice'd*!

What you have learned so far: That thing about *man-sticking*!

What I have learned so far: Maybe it wouldn't have been a bad idea to have Ryan Seacrest write the introduction.

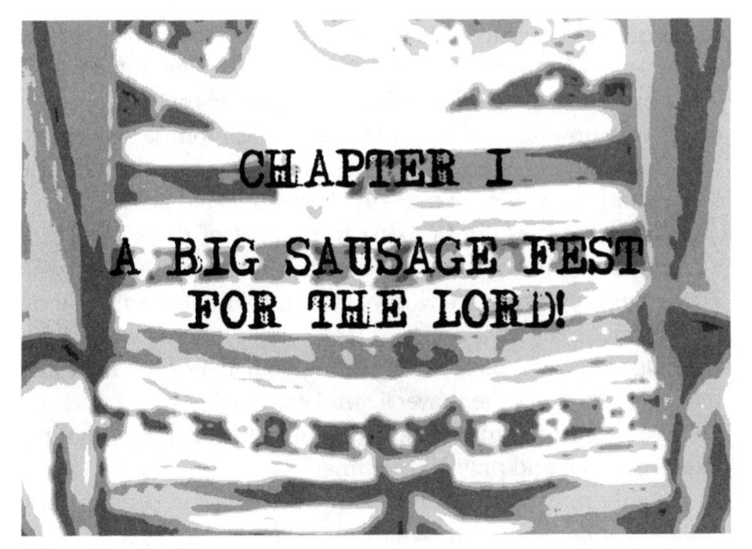

MEN. MANLY MEN.

The first thing one notices when walking toward the HP Pavilion in San Jose is lots of men—nothing but big groups of men. Not sissy-boy men, but manly men. The kind that go to big sporting events and watch play-off games with their buddies, not to mention men who are lovin' the Jesus. Tonight, the womenfolk are made to stay at home; it's guys only as the testosterone pumps in the large sports arena where the Sharks play hockey—all in the name of the Lord. Yes, "Calling Men to an Unpredictable Adventure"—as their saying goes—these are the Promise Keepers!

"If you want to truly change the world, change the men," states the Promise Keepers' literature. (Sorry, ladies!) This weekend is designed to "expose a list of lies of the world against their manhood." Holy shit, not only are people lying to men, but our very manhood is at stake too!

Who started the Promise Keepers in 1990? Why, the head

coach of the University of Colorado football team (a manly man doing a manly job). Touring twenty cities around the country, with ticket prices at eighty-nine dollars, filling larger outdoor stadium events with upwards of forty thousand people, Promise Keepers are holy big business. Yes, as far as filling arenas goes, the Promise Keepers are the AC/DC of men-only, Jesus-centered events.

What separates me (a man) from most of these men (not women) is I'm in the *inner circle* for this weekend's arena event. That's right, phoning a few days earlier, I volunteered to be on the Promise Keepers Prayer Team.

"Do you have experience putting your hands on men and praying for them?" the Prayer Team Leader asked.

"Yeah. This morning, as a matter of fact," I replied. "I put my hands on men and pray all the time!"

Highly pleased with my response, he put me on the team. "You're going to see some wild things," he added.

"What kind of things?" I asked, wondering if it would involve a big religious circle jerk.

"Transgressions, speaking in tongues, guys confessing to homosexuality, alcohol problems . . ."

"Cool! Bring it on!" I responded. Pause. "Woo!"

Some (we'll call them the whiny naysayers) proclaim that the Promise Keepers are a component of the religious and political right—a Trojan horse, if you will—for the advancement of an ultraconservative patriarchy. For instance, Promise #4 calls for men to reclaim their leadership role in the family. In a Promise Keepers' book, a section titled "Reclaiming your Manhood" reads: "Sit down with your wife and say something like this: 'Honey, I've made a terrible mistake. I've given you my role. I gave up leading this family, and I forced you to take my place. Now, I must reclaim that role.' . . . I'm not suggesting you ask for your role back, I'm urging you to take it back. . . . There can be no compromise here. If you're going to lead, you must lead." And what if "Honey" doesn't quite acquiesce to this change? Too bad! Manly men, according to the Promise Keepers, must take charge.

That's why I'm cunningly going undercover in the persona of a manly Promise Keepers volunteer. That will show that not only

I can be a pumped-up member of the Prayer Team but also, more important, I can also be a MAN or perhaps reclaim my manhood.

Persona
Name: Martin Manly.
Hobbies: Doing one-handed pushups.
Costume: Red, white, and blue patriotic tracksuit and a baseball cap.
Catchphrase: "Go Niners and Jesus!"
Goal: To high-five as many men as possible—in a manly sort of fashion for Jesus.

Inside the packed HP Pavilion, it's a big sausage fest, or pickle party, for the Lord. Ten thousand men, mostly big-bellied in sports jerseys and baseball caps, sit in the hockey arena's stands, shoveling down pizza and nachos. This is just like Comedy Central's *The Man Show,* but without the fun of women on trampolines (because it's men only). I expect the concession stand to sell big "Jesus is #1" Styrofoam fingers and beer hats for drinking red wine (the blood of Christ, of course). The crowd files into the stands that surround the large stage, with the same anticipation as those would arriving for the big game. To some, this *is* the big game. It must be really great for these guys to sit around, eat crappy food, fart if they want to, and learn about Jesus with their buddies.

"Git 'er done!" I hear someone yell from the stands.

Already checked in at the volunteer station, I've exchanged my patriotic track top for a manly baby-blue official "Promise Keepers—The Awakening" T-shirt and all-access badge that reads "Martin." Passing large men in sports-team shirts with their hands full of nachos and popcorn, I make my way toward an enormous sign that reads "Prayer Booth." Much like a kissing booth, the prayer booth is an area set up with several curtains, where those wishing to be prayed with can do so in privacy, led by us, the Prayer Team.

"I'm here to volunteer for the Prayer Team," I proclaim to an enthusiastic man. "Woo!"

"Great. We'll be having a briefing at six," he enthusiastically says, putting his hand on my back. I throw him a high five.

Roughly twelve middle-age to older gentlemen stand there, some looking like they've had hard living before meeting Jesus, others looking like they teach Sunday school. We, the Prayer Team, are brought into the bowels of the arena, corralled in a narrow hallway. One mustachioed man—who could easily be mistaken for talking to himself—is actually praying. All of us are adorned in matching blue Promise Keepers volunteer T-shirts. We, the Prayer Team, are the elite squadron that is on hand to satisfy the entire arena's praying needs.

"I volunteered for the Prayer Team just to get the free T-shirt," one of the men confides as I high-five him.

The Prayer Team leaders, who both seem absolutely giddy, give a briefing.

"Put your hand on them, but not inappropriately," the giddy leader explains, demonstrating by placing his hands on the other Prayer Team leader's shoulder, then his back.

"Can you demonstrate what would be inappropriate?" I ask.

"Should we have our Bibles with us to quote specific passages?" interrupts a man who's holding, well, the Bible.

"Let God give you the words," the Prayer Team leader offers to keep things moving.

"All right!" I scream eagerly, since this is the pep talk before the big game and I want to go to the play-offs. "You tell 'em!"

"When they make the altar call, that's when we're going to have the big rush," he adds. It'll be like Denny's hit with the hungry after-bar crowd.

"Should we put a time limit on our praying?" I inquire.

"Take your time with it," he says. "Most of all, have some fun out there."

"Yeah! Woo!" I yell, pumping my fist. "Take your time with it. That's right."

The hardened man next to me looks over, so I offer him a high five.

"OK, I want everyone to pair up, so you can give a little prayer for one another."

I look around. Should my prayer partner be the creepy guy with the mustache or the Sunday school teacher to my right? As I mull it over, I realize I'm the only one without a prayer partner. The others already have their hands on one another, heads bowed, and are getting down to some serious praying. I have a dejected look, like the last one chosen for kickball (except the stakes in this game are much bigger).

The two Prayer Team leaders, hands on shoulders about to pray, look over at me.

"Martin, come on over here," they say with big, aw-shucks goofy grins.

I scamper across the hall like a puppy about to get his stomach rubbed. With hands on each of our shoulders, we form a prayer threesome. We're each supposed to take turns and pray for strength. While the others do this, I've taken it upon myself to seize on random phrases and repeat them.

"Oh, Lord, please show Martin that we're a crazy bunch, but we follow your path—"

"Crazy bunch, oh, Lord, crazy bunch!" I exclaim. "Evil days! Evil days!"

When finished, we each take turns hugging each other. Why? Because we're men with men. Not gay men, of course, but men in the way God intended us, and because of that we're not afraid to hug. Then we high-five!

> **Promise Keepers Fun Quote:** "The demise of our community and culture is the fault of sissified men who have been overly influenced by women."

Lights! Visuals! Rock! Jesus!

With a multimedia array of large video visuals and lights in a manly U2-style, a Christian power-rock band called the Newsboys kicks things off, causing one of the volunteers to do a crazy, spinning, filled-with-Jesus, Grateful Dead dance.

"How many people here are pastors' sons?" questions the

lead singer with an Australian accent, and a few hands go up. "Security!" he adds in joshing fashion to gosh-darn chuckles.

Then, projected on a giant video screen appears tonight's master of ceremonies—the self-proclaimed "brother like no other": a large, black, hip-hop guy whose catchphrase, for some reason (I have no idea), is "Aiight!" But it rhymes with "All right," so maybe there's a connection.

"What's up! For how many of you is this your first Promise Keepers?" the brother like no other says, making a stage entrance.

Huge hoots and hollers!

"Aiight!" says the brother like no other.

"Aiight!" scream ten thousand men.

"Now you're talking black."

Big laughs.

"This is the Promise Keepers, men's men in the house!" explains the brother like no other, telling it like it is. "We're not looking for losers." Surprisingly, no, he explains, the Promise Keepers are looking only for winners.

Then, without much of a segue, "One of my favorite books as a kid was *The Lion, the Witch, and the Wardrobe,*" he continues, squeezing out applause. Confusingly, we then watch a five-minute trailer for the Disney film *Chronicles of Narnia*. I'm not sure of the connection, other than maybe sometimes Jesus needs a corporate sponsor, too.

"I tell y'all. That's the book I grew up with," says the brother like no other. "It's all about stories. How about that *Spider-Man*?" Huge thunderous applause, followed by a joke about a little white boy. "Or *Lord of the Rings*?" Bigger thunderous applause. Then, "But the greatest story ever written was written by God!"

A serious hush runs through the crowd of ten thousand men. One of the prayer leaders catches me by surprise, squeezing my shoulder, which scares the hell out of me. Momentarily forgetting, I give him a what-the-hell-are-you-doing-*that*-for look, as he moves on to squeeze other volunteers' shoulders.

"God has a plan in his hand to write about tonight," the brother like no other continues. "It's time to say, 'Wake up!'"

Judging by the noise, one would think the Sharks just won the Stanley Cup.

And then a manly *SportsCenter*-like update: "Eleven to seven, Angels are winning."

Huge manly cheers from the ten thousand men, cheers bigger than for the Messiah, though the Angels he refers to are not in heaven along with Jesus, but on the baseball field in the play-offs.

"I'm not messing with the Raiders fans. I got death threats last year." (Death threats are not very Jesus-like.)

"Raiders! Raiders!" I scream, throwing a high five to a guy wearing a T-shirt that says, "Break the Chains."

The game scores are followed by a man who tells of the pain of a life of drugs and alcohol. Finding Jesus caused him to break the chains. To symbolize this, he does some sort of interpretive dance/escape artist act with smoke machines and an array of lights. While wrapped in chains, rolling on the ground, he at one point dramatically puts a gun in his mouth.

"That's pretty wild," remarks the prayer leader, squeezing my shoulder.

Among the testosterone revelry, a lone woman (not a man!) walks through the crowd. What the hell is she doing here? There's nothing here for her—this is a men-only event! A guy wearing a black T-shirt that simply reads "God" on the back shoots her a strange look as she heads toward the exit.

"There's a prayer booth. There's brothers ready to pray for you. They're like dogs ready to attack," the brother like no other tells the crowd. That sounds enticing. "If you need someone to pray for you, there's about ten guys in back who make up the Prayer Team. Give a wave, guys."

We the Prayer Team wave to the crowd of ten thousand men. I pump my fist in the air, then high-five fellow volunteers.

After a confusing boxing sketch by the Awaken Drama Team, I take a break from the sweaty, pumped-up male adrenaline arena to explore some of the booths set up on the concourse. I pass the leather-clad, long-bearded "Harley Davidsons for Christ" booth, then encounter two elderly gentlemen who could easily pass for closeted queens.

"Sign our petition?" says one of the closeted queeny gentlemen under a banner that reads "Values Matter."

"What's this for?" I reply.

"It's to keep marriage between a man and a woman," he explains with a tight upper lip, explaining that men shouldn't be with other men—except in the case of the Promise Keepers, of course.

"It's so scary what could happen," I say, signing the petition with the name "Satan's Big Cock." For encouragement, I give a mighty finger snap. "You go, girl!"

He stands there for several seconds until I offer him a manly high five.

A crusty man in a yellow button-down shirt is running a booth adorned with logos from all the big television networks endorsing the "Media Leader Prayer Calendar." He explains: "You find today's date, and you pray for the media leader and the cultural celebrity listed. You pray for the cast and crew of TV programs or for music group members."

"Seriously?" I ask with bewilderment.

Grabbing their newsletter, I read: "Jennifer Aniston is turning towards faith. Unfortunately the faith is Buddhism. Becoming involved in Buddhism isn't going to fill the hole left by Brad Pitt. Pray for Jennifer Aniston."

"Each of these people are one miracle away from a vital faith in God," the crusty man says without a smile or irony. Clearly he believes that the praying will help these celebrities find their needed relationship with God. Nine different prayers are provided that can be used to clean up Hollywood for the betterment of the Christian good. Strangely, a large majority of the names are Jewish (hmm—heathens). As I look at the list, on this day we are supposed to pray for director M. Night Shyamalan as well as what's-the-deal-with-airline-flying? comedian Jerry Seinfeld.

"Can you mix and match which celebrities you want to pray for on any given day? Like could today I pray for the Wayans brothers and, say, Mel Gibson?"

The *Passion of the Christ* director, it's explained, doesn't need praying for. I look at the list again. On tomorrow's plate: Russell

Simmons and the Simpsons. Do they know that the Simpsons are only a cartoon characters?

"Does the praying work?" I ask about saving the souls of the Wayans brothers.

"We've been noticing quite an impact, quite an impact," the crusty man says with unflappable confidence, stating how they're trying to arrange to meet with such media leaders as uber-conservative Rupert Murdoch.

"Do you want to get on our mailing list?" asks the crusty man.

"Sure!"

Once again I sign "Satan's Big Cock" with the e-mail address satan@satansbigcock.org.

"*Who's this?*" I ask a woman (yes, a woman) running a booth with DVDs for sale, such as *Tolerate This* and *A Christian Unleashed,* featuring someone named Brad Stine.

"He's a comedian," the woman (not a man) replies with a snicker. "You're going to see him later tonight."

From inside the sweltering arena, the brother like no other announces, "If you think I'm funny, here's a guy who will rock your world."

Out comes Brad Stine—a blond, high-energy comedian who slightly resembles Denis Leary. My world isn't necessarily rocked as I watch him perform hacky material about the differences between men and woman.

"Girls yell. Guys scream," Brad Stine astutely points out to big, manly laughs, then hilariously relays how men, unlike women, love plasma-screen TVs.

"It's funny because it's true," I share with the Promise Keeper volunteer next to me, who agrees.

"God made man first so he can practice!" (So true! So true!)

More large, manly laughs.

"Guys love women," the Christian comic declares, suddenly getting serious. "That's what makes you a man!"

No laughs this time, just a big round of affirming applause, mixed with hoots and hollers. The logic might not be firm, but the clapping certainly is.

Then, strangely, the comedian segues into a bitter rant about being a Christian comic trying to make it in the heathen world of mainstream standup.

"I wanted to show that clean was cutting edge," he spews. "There's so much Christian bigotry in the country. But it's the only religion that would have me!"

Ten thousand big manly laughs once again, as the Prayer Team leader once again rubs my shoulder, which is starting to creep me out.

"Seventeen years in the business. I wanted a TV show. I wanted a recording contract. I wanted to do movies. I was doing the thing I was good at, which is standup comedy, and I was not at peace," he confides as the arena crowd grows silent. "I gave up my Hollywood dream to play for Christians." Why? "I wanted Christians to have the best there is!"

"Yeah!"

"Woo!"

So he's saying if the old Hollywood thing *would* have worked out, obviously Jesus might have taken a big backseat to hosting *The Family Feud.*

With building passion, he continues, "In these three years, I've had more mainstream media, major recording deals, a large agency sign me."

Jesus, it's implied, is a much better agent than William Morris.

"God said the reason I want you to put your dream out of the way is because it's too small!"

"Wooo! Wooo!" shouts the crowd of men at his self-serving comments.

"USA! USA!" I shout, erupting into a rapid high-fiving machine. "USA!"

Sure, he just got ten thousand men to applaud, but boy, Christian comedians suck. It's all hacky jokes, bitterness, and boasting mixed with a religious, serious message slipped in at the end.

As two paramedic women, totally uninterested, loudly converse, a man in an "Iron Sharpens Iron" T-shirt barks, "Can you ask them to be quiet?" venting his distaste for the gentler sex, almost blowing them away.

> **Promise Keepers Fun Quote:** "It appears that America's anti-Biblical feminist movement is at last dying, thank God, and is possibly being replaced by a Christ-centered men's movement."

Love of God and Country

The large men in the stands continue to wolf down greasy concession-stand food as two hardened-looking motorcycle gang members—scarred, covered with tattoos, and wearing "Messengers. Jesus Reigns." motorcycle jackets—make their way through the crowd.

"Has anyone needed the prayer booth yet?" I ask the Prayer Leader.

"It's been kind of slow," he replies, then squeezes my shoulder.

Next comes that weird meld of religion and patriotism with "The Epic Battle for a Man's Soul."

"I'm not over the hill, I am the hill," says a roly-poly man resembling comedian Louie Anderson in a video clip, pointing to his stomach. He's a Vietnam vet who's had half his face blown off in combat. It doesn't get more manly than a 'Nam vet who's fallen on a grenade.

A request is made for all the other Vietnam vets to stand up along with those who served in Iraq, harvesting a huge, loud, standing ovation. I didn't realize that Jesus was pro-war.

"Jesus and USA! Jesus and USA!" I chant.

The military man's shtick starts out funny, then segues into graphically describing what it's like to fall on an enemy grenade. And he sternly warns: "I might make some statements some of you might not like," regarding the 9/11 attacks and the Muslim religion. He then explains that he has the right to make these upcoming statements because he had half his face blown off in

Vietnam. I assume that the statements are going to be slightly racist. Ten thousand men grow silent.

"They don't have the same God as us. Their God says, 'Give me your son.' Our God says, 'Here is my son!'" he shouts.

A thunder of all-American screams and hollers echoes throughout, in a let's-kick-their-ass-screw-those-towel-headed-bastards fashion—because all their actions are obviously due to a blatant lack of Christ (and not because of US imperialistic foreign policies). Sure, George W. Bush said God told him to invade Iraq, then lied about the reason why we went to war, but it's OK as long as it's for the betterment of spreading democracy—and hopefully Christianity. Hell, it worked during the Spanish Inquisition. And think of the Crusades and what that did for civilization.

"We're not looking for soldiers; we're not looking for Marines," the war vet says in regard to our current situation in Iraq. *"We're looking for Jesus Christ!"*

"Woo! Woo!"

"Jesus and USA! Jesus and USA!"

"Are you ready for Jesus? LET'S GET IT ON," the war vet screams in a WWE are-you-ready-to-rumble fashion. Like General Patton leading the Third Army into the Battle of the Bulge, "FATHER, I'VE COME HOME!" he hollers.

Inspirational music builds. Men, and then groups of men, come down the hockey arena aisles, arms around each other. "There's an ex-wife beater here tonight, an ex-drug addict, an ex-homosexual. Come on down!" More men, hesitant at first, trek down the stairs and parade toward the front. They form a line and make their way to the altar normally reserved for the Sharks' home goal and the stage where Depeche Mode will be performing next week.

"As a man, I'm expecting you to do what's right before God," the war vet demands.

"If you're a man, start walking right now!" I almost expect him to call those who don't get up "big pussies." "Some of you came with a friend tonight. Well, you can leave with a brother."

A man of great girth, wearing a "Live To Die, Die To Live" T-shirt, chews tobacco, intensely listens, then spits into a cup. As the numbers start to dwindle, the war vet then relates another long, graphic story about having third-degree burns and about the nurse named Rosie who saved his life. He asks that everyone turn to the person next to him. "Look them in the eye and say, 'I'm your Rosie.'" Despite his best intentions, there's something creepy about staring into another man's eyes and saying, "I'm your Rosie." I turn to the prayer leader who's been squeezing my shoulder all night. "I'm your Rosie!" I say with assurance. (Again, my shoulder is squeezed.)

The music once again builds. "THE SECOND WAVE OF THE MIRACLE IS GOING TO HAPPEN!"

Another sea of men starts parading toward the front. It appears that more than three hundred men are coming forth to dedicate their lives to Christ. Each of the men receives a copy of a new joint publication by the International Bible Society and the Promise Keepers, *All about Jesus* (as well as a high five).

> **Promise Keepers Fun Quote:** "Don't you understand, mister, you are royalty and God has chosen you to be priest of your home."

After the Altar Call

The Prayer Leader was right. After the altar call, we, the Prayer Team, are slammed. Groups of men make their way over to the prayer booth area. Some have that desperate look in their eyes like they need that immediate prayer booth fix. One right after the other, men line up for the Prayer Team's touch, with the queue extending into the arena.

Looking at the newly formed line, I freak out and scream to the other Prayer Team members, "WE'RE SWAMPED!"

"Do you want to lead people on your own?" asks the Prayer Team leader, nervously looking at the large line.

"You know, maybe it's best if I pair up with someone so they can show me the ropes," I say, since I have no idea what to do.

I'm paired up with the tall, silver-haired man who looks like a Sunday school teacher. We're a team—like one of those crazy, mismatched buddy cop movies with the hardened veteran and the new rookie. A young, curly-haired man comes over to us as we escort him behind the Prayer Team curtain.

"What is it you want us to pray for you tonight?"

The curly-haired man is unsure how to express it in words.

"Is it pornography?" blurts the Sunday school teacher in a low voice.

"Yeah, pornography," I repeat more sternly, playing the bad cop in our Prayer Team situation.

"No," replies the curly-haired guy.

"Is it homosexuality?" I blurt in a more accusing manner, taking another stab at it.

"No!" he says in a louder voice, explaining he simply wants us to pray that he'll stay focused on school and stay clear of bad forces.

"Are you sure it's not homosexuality?" I repeat. It isn't.

The hands go on the shoulders; the eyes shut as we huddle up. Like freestyle rappers, we each take a turn at doing a spontaneous prayer for the curly-haired guy. When it's the Sunday school teacher's turn, I contribute by occasionally repeating his phrases, along with throwing in the intermittent "Yes! Yes! Yes!" and "Evil days! Evil days!" all in a monotone, while testing the limits of what would be an inappropriate touch.

When the Sunday school teacher hands over the mike to me, I simply start by plagiarizing his prayer, then throwing in a long mix about looking out for Satan. The mention of the word *Satan* causes the Sunday school teacher to convulse and sort of jump back, letting out an almost orgasmic verbal moan.

I stop and open my eyes to see what the hell is going on. I momentarily think he might have gone into *inappropriate touch* terrain. Thus I keep mentioning Satan to get this Pavlovian response.

"Beware of Satan's forces!"

"Uhhhh!"

The Prayer Booth area is buzzing with various raised voices and Bible quotes.

Next up for us: a father-and-son combination.

"What is it that you want us to pray for you tonight?"

"Tell them what you did." says the father (a man) to his son (soon to be a man).

"I got in a fight at school," the son says with lowered head, giving the reason for the fight was some other kid "smack-talking" him.

Since I don't know any Bible passages, I try to lend authenticity by attempting to speak in old faux English, so we huddle up.

"Oh Lord, protect-ith Trevor from the smack talker. 'Cuz blessed be he who turneth the other cheek to the smack-talkers. For the non-smack-talkers will inherit the earth over the smack-talkers, for blessed be he who is a non-smack-talker."

For good measure, I make sure to mention Satan.

"Uhhhhhh!"

"How was that? Should I change it up a bit?" I ask my partner after we all manly hug (and of course, high-five), and then they leave.

"Just look for God to give you the words," is his only advice.

Taking that advice, I'll see what God comes up with for me on our next prayer victim.

"OK, try to speed it up a little bit," the Prayer Team leader comes over and requests.

Thus enters a weaselly looking man with a thin mustache. Behind his back, the Prayer Team leader makes the speed-it-up sign.

"What would you like for us to pray for you?"

"My wife put a restraining order on me," the man proclaims.

Whoa. Is that something Jesus can fix? Is a restraining order in the Jesus jurisdiction? I really have to look for inspiration on this one. In this case, the words that God gives me are the lyrics from the Journey song "Open Arms": "So now I come to you/With open arms. . . ."

When finished, the guy with the restraining order starts crying. "You're my Rosie!" I whisper to him. The Sunday school teacher says, "Come here," and gives him a hug. He turns toward me for the hugging ritual. I, in turn, offer a manly high five. Hell, if any womenfolk found out about how I let him cry on my shoulder, it could seriously damage my reputation as the royal priest of my home.

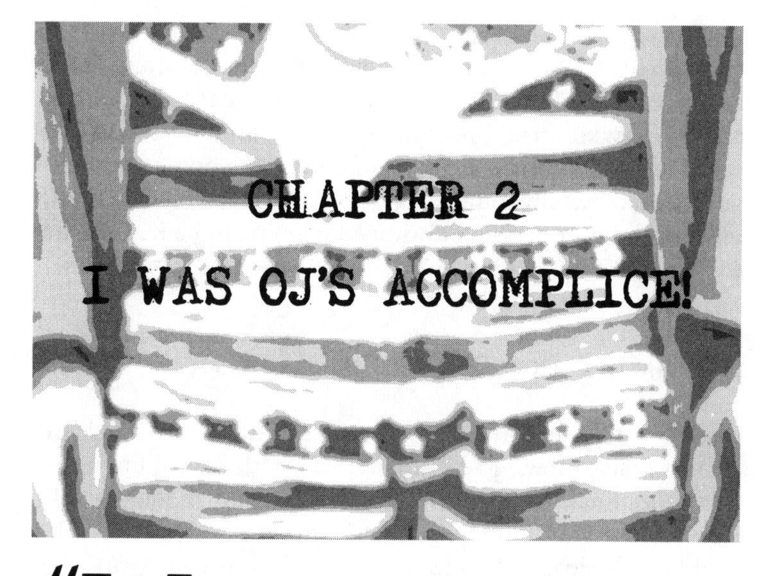

CHAPTER 2

I WAS OJ'S ACCOMPLICE!

"We really can't mention the murders," dryly explains the producer with utter seriousness. Sitting in a cluttered office, I take in the information, nodding my head vigorously. "No mention of the murders," I repeat (yet having a strong desire to mention *only* the murders). For this clause is a major consideration when one has just been hired to work on a zany, hidden-camera prank show with . . . OJ Simpson! You know, OJ, that guy from the murder trial of the century. The slow-speed Bronco chase; the subject of "If the glove don't fit, you must acquit"; the "not guilty" verdict that stunned America. OJ, as in holy-flippin'-cow-OJ-you-can't-be-serious-Simpson! That OJ.

"I heard he's gained some weight," the producer adds. Yes, some diabolical genius thought it would be a good idea as a comeback project for a man accused of a double murder to be on a hidden-camera prank show ("Gotcha!"). This straight-to-DVD affair, a *Punk'd* knockoff, is aptly titled *Juiced* (as in, "You've been *Juiced!*").

Some (let's call them *the sane*) would be apprehensive to work with OJ. But I couldn't pass up the gig. Jobs, especially acting jobs, are few and far between. And what better way to make a few needed bucks in this Republican no-new-jobs economy, and infiltrate the heart of asinine celebrity reality television, than by fully immersing myself in the inner circle of the most notorious celebrity in history. I'm going to be Kato Kaelin to OJ's OJ. Yes, I'm going to be OJ's funny second banana.

How the Hell Does One Become OJ's Sidekick?

I saw a listing for what was described as a "celebrity hidden-camera prank show." I sent my reel, the gods shined upon me, and I was hired. How exciting, my first celebrity hidden-camera prank show. During the phone briefing, the producer said he could not disclose the name of the celebrity but assured me, "It's going to be huge!" My mind wandered to all levels of celebrity possibilities. (Steve Guttenberg? The *other* Hilton sister?!) Still, I was not prepared when, right before production commenced, over the phone the producer told me, "OK. The celebrity is . . . OJ Simpson!" A long, stunned pause on my end, followed by, "Oh, my God! . . . You *can't* be serious? . . . Oh, my God!" The next thing I knew, I was on my way down to Los Angeles to begin a week of filming and hanging out with OJ Simpson.

OJ Is Dressed Like a Gangsta Rapper

Guilty or not, OJ is a man who once had it all and was banished from the Garden of Eden. In a 1998 *Esquire* article, OJ said, "I'm going to get it all back in spades." I question whether *Juiced* constitutes getting it *all back in spades* (or is even on the spades ladder).

In a nondescript recording studio in Burbank, we're waiting for OJ to show up, with the same anticipation as on the set of *Apocalypse Now*, when they waited for an overweight Brando. A weird hush comes over the crew as OJ arrives with his handlers while he talks on a cell phone, walking with an evident limp. I was expecting OJ to be Fat Albert fat. But he's not (though he has a really large head in terms of cranial capacity). A shady entourage surrounds him. Rumors fly that Warren G, OJ's bodyguard, just got out of jail, and his driver doesn't have a license, while some LA-type in a sports coat keeps saying things into his cell phone like, "I'm hanging out with OJ right now. I could sell this footage to *20/20* for twenty grand."

OJ has been made to dress like a gangsta rapper (ironically wearing—forgive me—a wife beater). The first thing OJ Simpson says to me is, "Why don't you push me!" I've just met OJ, and now he wants me to shove him. The setup for the first "funny" prank involves singers and dancers coming in blindly for an audition. All they know is that it's for a "celebrity's" music video. What these "victims" don't know is that the celebrity is actually, yes, OJ Simpson.

"This is my first audition," shares an enthusiastic eighteen-year-old. She has just driven an hour to get here, one of the dozens of hopeful performers who've taken time out of their day with big dreams (stupid people with their dreams), thinking they're here for an audition, only to be soon humiliated on camera. I feel bad. We're just wasting people's time. Later, one of OJ's victims screams, "When the ad says I'd make $750 per day, that pisses me off," clearly not happy with the reward of a free *Juiced* T-shirt.

While wearing a pink belly shirt and going by the name *Power*, I'm supposed to audition with a group of dancers, screw things up, and then get into a big argument with OJ Simpson. So, as requested, on cue I will shove OJ. (I think I actually scream, "Do you want a piece of me?!")

I expect that, when OJ makes an appearance, people will freak out and flee from the room. I expect people to react with horror—most likely even crying, thinking, yes, the devil himself now has a reality show. But that, as it turns out, is not the case at all.

"You've been *Juiced*!"

The would-be dancers are actually thrilled to meet OJ Simpson. (It's great he gets to show America his practical-joking side.) They instead react with celebrity worship. After all, OJ was innocent—at least at one of his two trials.

"Why don't you all dance around OJ," the director instructs a group of excited girls.

OJ, attempting to be the ladies' man, adds, "This is not working out, but if you want to have dinner later, or . . ."

Yes, OJ loves the ladies. Later, while wearing a disguise in a tropical-fish store for another *Juiced* segment, he tries to be suave with a girl: "If I were OJ, would you try to go out with me?"

"I'm only seventeen," the frightened girl replies.

OJ coyly retorts, "If you were eighteen, I'd try and go out with you!"

Golfing with OJ

What's an OJ hidden-camera show without golfing pranks? But there's soon trouble in hidden-camera paradise. The *Juiced* honeymoon quickly turns rocky; OJ is nowhere to be found. The crew impatiently waits. The producer is raving.

"He wasn't super-enthusiastic on the first day. He got there at nine. He was supposed to be there at eight," rants the ranting producer. "OJ just doesn't give a shit. OJ shows up late; he doesn't want to wear wardrobe. He says, 'I don't want to do that.'"

The earnest crew, who is putting in long hours for little pay, all for OJ's big comeback, is indifferent about OJ. "It's pretty weird, you know, because of the murders," comments the sound guy. "But he is pretty funny," he adds. Yes, humor trumps all.

"He was on the news last night," shares a cameraman. "Direct TV is suing him. He supposedly stole a Direct TV box when he switched houses. He's in a world of shit."

Finally, jovial OJ drives up in a golf cart. "I'm playing golf with the worst golfers," he says to the stressed producer, who passive-aggressively pleads to let the shooting begin. "I'm going to play a round of golf," OJ responds. "I need to warm up."

I get the strong feeling that OJ is not doing *Juiced* for the art of hidden-camera prankdom but rather only for the money. OJ continues to chat away with two of his lifelong golfing buddies, oblivious that roughly twenty people are waiting for him to start filming. After OJ vetoes the chosen wardrobe, old-time golfing knickers (the cap's too small for his melon-sized head), things get rolling.

We start by doing a few gags that clearly don't work. With a camera in hand, I pretend I'm a smarmy member of the paparazzi, trying to get OJ pissed off at me. ("OJ, will we see you later at the clubhouse, eating a clubhouse sandwich? *Celebrities Uncovered* wants to know!") Yes, I'm supposed to once again antagonize OJ Simpson. The humor here relies heavily on working off OJ's masterful improv skills. When I come running up to OJ, who's playing with a group of random golfers, he simply ignores me.

"People are always try to catch me doing something crazy on camera," he mildly comments to the golfers, who now want to pummel me silly. Once the producer quickly learns that OJ Simpson is not blessed with the Second City art of improv, for lack of anything else, the gag somehow ends (much to everyone's confusion) with me and the producer wrestling around on the fairway. Using a phrase that I've never thought my brain would formulate in all my life, I inform the producer afterwards, "OJ's really not giving me much to work with." We all watch as OJ keeps playing golf with the group of people we were trying to prank, now pretty assured this will be the last we see of OJ today.

Time to regroup. OJ has a plan. He knows how to really piss off golfers. I'm supposed to run on the fairway and steal all the golfers' balls after they're hit. All right!

"OJ! Mr. OJ! Will you sign a golf ball for me?" My arms are flailing as I run down the fairway to a group of golfers who emit pure venomous hate through their eyes. They're pissed off to, well, OJ proportions. "I'm a huge fan of *Towering Inferno*!" I cry, sprinting toward them.

One golfer, a very large and angry man, storms directly to his golf bag and grabs an iron. He cocks it back, ready to swing at my head. I'm depending on OJ Simpson, of all people on earth, for my safety. When things get too hairy, he's supposed to jump in and cry, "You're *Juiced*!" Except he doesn't.

"PUT DOWN THE FUCKING BALL NOW!" the large, angry golfer screams, turning increasingly red, rushing toward me.

"Not until OJ signs one of these golf balls." I insist.

"PUT DOWN THE FUCKING BALL NOW!"

"That guy's crazy," comments OJ, acting like he doesn't know me.

The large, angry man keeps charging at me. Worried, I think OJ, caught up in his golf game, has completely forgotten the whole premise of the show. Right before the club is to make contact with my skull, OJ nonchalantly decides to fill them in.

"You've been *Juiced*!"

OJ points to the hidden cameras. The large, angry golfer doesn't give a shit.

"I DON'T CARE WHAT IT IS. YOU DON'T TOUCH PEOPLE'S BALLS!"

Despite the prospect of a free *Juiced* T-shirt, the large, angry golfer doesn't calm down.

"YOU JUST DON'T GO TAKING PEOPLE'S BALLS!"

The producers jump in. He tries to smooth things over. The golfer instead storms away, pissed off, obviously with an afternoon of golf ruined. Afterwards, my eyebrow raises as OJ, in a reflective moment, shares to the camera, "That guy was mad. He was like OJ on alcohol." (Huh?!)

Life imitates art—or whatever the hell you would call this—when a golfer actually *does* ask OJ to sign his golf ball. "You made our day," gushes the Asian man with broken English and pure celebrity idolatry. "It was a huge honor!"

OJ THE SEVERE BURN VICTIM

I'm sitting in a motel room with OJ Simpson. Earlier, I accidentally walked in on OJ with his pants down. Boxers, in case you were wondering. OJ now sits in a chair and is having heavy makeup applied while the camera crew films *behind-the-scenes* footage.

"The lights are on me. I'm feeling like a star," OJ keeps repeating from under heavy, thick makeup. "I'm feeling like a star!"

OJ's supposed to look like an old white man (with a huge head). Unfortunately, he looks more like a severe burn victim. Later, OJ will be going to a very white Elks Club lodge for bingo night. Under a large American flag, he'll portray Carl, a very inept guest bingo caller with a stutter. I will be on hand to heckle Carl. Comedy mayhem will ensue.

Meanwhile, the TV's on. OJ's channel of choice is Court TV. (Of course, he can't get enough of trials?) OJ keeps talking to the TV as if it were a person who can hear him.

"That's such bullshit!" OJ says at certain moments to the TV.

It gets weirdly surreal and uncomfortable as a Court TV reporter goes into grizzly details about the Scott Peterson murder trial—you know, that *other* guy accused of killing his wife. "Of course they think he's guilty," exclaims OJ in white face to the TV. "They're prejudging him." About to add my two cents on why Peterson is so blatantly guilty, I stop dead in my tracks, look over at OJ, and figure maybe it's best to keep my mouth quiet on this one. Who knows? I might trigger something.

Court TV turns to Martha Stewart and other famous celebrity trials. OJ tells the TV he thinks Martha Stewart is guilty. I pray the reporter doesn't start talking about OJ. We're in a small motel room with the focal point of the biggest celebrity trial in history, and I'm within arm's reach! Everyone else gets weirdly quiet, as they awkwardly stare at their shoes.

"How are they going to work me into this?" OJ asks the TV, almost hoping for the notoriety. This is like watching a car wreck ready to happen—though uncomfortable, I can't look away.

The Court TV presenter asks, "How does celebrity play into this?"

The reporter replies, "If it's a good celebrity, they won't be convicted."

"So I was a good celebrity then," pipes in OJ. "You know, it's her lawyer's fault she got convicted," he then adds about Martha Stewart. "During my trial, my lawyers covered my ass."

The room stays quiet. This time I look at my shoes.

At the Elks Club, OJ, as stuttering Carl, executes the gag with the pure comedy finesse of a high-school gym teacher.

"If you didn't stutter, you'd sound just like OJ Simpson," a lodge member, clearly not getting it, exclaims. The weirdest part is, afterwards no one fills in the Elks Club members that their white clown–faced/burn victim/inept bingo caller was actually OJ. I guess the producers feared a riot. Venturing back to the motel, the camera crew stops a random guy and asks if he recognizes the identity of the large-headed burn victim. When finally told it's OJ, the confused man sympathetically asks, "Is this how you have to go around now?"

At the end of the evening, OJ, still in disguise, wants to pull one more prank.

"Let's go to the bar. I want to fool my wife," he slips, then corrects himself. "I mean, my daughter." (How many times will I end up awkwardly staring at my shoes during this shoot?)

The producer asks the Juice while still in character, "What do you think of OJ Simpson?"

"He's a very handsome guy," OJ modestly replies. "If I did guys, I'd do him." Then, adding with a laugh, "When I was incarcerated for seventeen months, I *did* do him!"

Before leaving, OJ tells me, "You're pretty funny. You really got your stuff." Always the people pleaser, OJ makes a promise to introduce me to some key showbiz people at a company that produced a TV series he was on in his heyday. "They'll probably put you in something," he adds.

Would it be a career boast, a fast track to the A-list, having OJ Simpson's stamp of approval? ("He comes highly recommended by OJ!") Should I be ready for my close-up? I find out later the production company he mentioned went out of business five years before.

The Return of the White Ford Bronco!

Due to OJ's uncanny performance ability ("It's clear that he has no talent," shared a crewmember earlier), I've been hired on for another week of *Juiced*. I'm not saying I'm that good; I'm saying OJ is just that bad. I have a growing concern that OJ is going to start taking personally all these gags where the premise is strictly to antagonize the Juice, with me doing the antagonizing. But hell, I'm unemployed, so I'll stay with the gig.

Added to the mix, we'll be filming in Vegas—a city of glittery facades, masking its true vile underbelly. My goal in Vegas is to go out drinking one-on-one with OJ and see if I can get him to confess to the murders—by telling him about all the murders *I've* committed. (What you say in Vegas, stays in Vegas!)

Earlier, we spent an afternoon at a used-car lot where OJ, one of the most recognizable faces on the planet, portrayed a used-car salesman. He really enjoyed the role. ("I like this. This is natural.") OJ tried to sell unsuspecting customers a used white Ford Bronco. At least he's got a sense of humor about that whole "incident."

"I tried to keep mine, but unfortunately they wouldn't let me keep mine," he said.

For some reason, this particular Ford Bronco has a large bullet hole on the side. OJ signed his autograph right above the hole, making it a limited edition collectors' model.

"It's OJ," a man exclaimed after being pranked.

"Just be glad he doesn't have a knife!" his friend laughed under his breath.

Between pranks, sitting in the lot manager's office, we learned more about the famous white Bronco from the slow-speed chase.

"Ford owns Hertz. They would give me new cars each year. I got a Bronco and a Town Car. I gave my father-in-law the Town Car."

OJ told the producer that the police had lied about finding $10,000 and had exaggerated about the amount of blood found in the Bronco. (Though he made no mention about the disguise kit and the passport.) Guilty or not guilty, one has to question the motivation of making light of a symbol that people widely associate with the murder of his wife (and that other guy, Ronald Goldman) and playing off the fact that in his white Ford Bronco, OJ once threatened suicide in a long police standoff. You'd think he *wouldn't* want any jokes about that. But it's nice to see he's maintaining a sense of humor about these things.

"One thing I can tell you, it has great escapability!" OJ chuckled.

Again, Americans truly love OJ. A crazy homeless guy, who'd just gotten out of jail that morning, wandered onto the lot. He got down on his knees and praised OJ. Then he looked at the Bronco.

"Oh, God! Oh, God! This is the car!" cried the crazy homeless man. "This is it! I can't believe it."

The executive producer has found an award-winning formula to keep OJ interested in *Juiced*. The idea is to constantly ply OJ with alcohol. OJ takes to the formula like a pope takes to a funny hat. OJ is now wearing a late-era Elvis Presley jumpsuit and is very drunk. We had to wait a few hours for him to show up after our last stunt because he wanted to show his outfit to his girlfriend back at the Palms. So we waited.

"Why does he drink so much?" questions a cynical cameraman, sarcastically adding, "Maybe he's trying to fight off some hidden demons?"

Upon returning, we find that OJ has fallen asleep in the motel room bed—passed out in his Elvis suit, snoring. Woken up, he's taken down to the motel lobby, where he's propped on a stool. OJ was supposed to play a wacky, inept motel clerk. But now OJ's too drunk. So I'm made to take on the role. I guess the idea now is if we can't have OJ pulling the pranks, at least we can have OJ *near* the pranks while they're being pulled. Like a puppy on a postcard wearing large oversized sunglasses, a drunken, Elvis-suited OJ is propped in the corner.

"What's that Elvis song I was singing?" slurs a confused OJ.

When a tourist comes in, I'm supposed to say his credit card has been declined and, while confiscating the card, threaten to rip it up, as drunken OJ strums on a guitar. (Yeah, I know, really funny shit!) So far, when the gag has been revealed ("You've been Juiced!"), this has resulted in people telling us to go fuck ourselves and storming out (despite the enticement of a free *Juiced* T-shirt!) Except at each attempt, OJ now fails to grasp the whole concept of the hidden-camera prank surprise.

"Hey!" drunken OJ whispers to a couple before I can pull

the cunning prank. "I'm OJ!" he slurs from behind Elvis glasses. "Hey! Do you recognize me?"

To others, he converses with them like he normally would. As I try to pull some hidden-camera "genius," OJ interrupts, "You're from Colorado! My daughter's going to school in Boulder next year."

But still, the most mind-numbing odd part of this whole scenario is that tourists go nuts when they find out it's OJ. Everyone loves celebrities. Everyone loves the Juice.

"Oh, my God! This is the greatest thing that's ever happened to me," screams a kid in a basketball tank top—who I'm pretty sure is off his head on ecstasy. He suddenly starts free-styling in order to impress OJ, high-fiving his buddy. "I just rapped for OJ! That's as big as it gets!"

Other tourists swarm in off the strip. Mothers and daughters requesting photos. It's bizarre celebrity worship.

"That was the man. That was the man, dude. There was no one else!"

It's no longer important if OJ is innocent or guilty—he's transcended that through the cult of celebrity; he's now seen as an institution, an American icon. Remember, this is no mere Kobe Bryant folks. It's OJ!

Bring on the Strippers

It gets really sleazy toward the end of *Juiced*—drunken OJ rapping, surrounded by topless strippers. Yes, strippers are thrown into the mix as we film OJ's rap video in a rented empty mansion—a formula for success! (Some might think this image signifies the end of the world.)

I became worried early in the day during one of our stunts in which I kept referring to OJ as Danny Glover over a dozen times, and he *actually* really did get angry. ("I ALREADY TOLD YOU I'M NOT DANNY GLOVER!") One more "Danny Glover" and I was afraid they'd find me outside a condo on Bundy Drive.

The guy who's letting us use the mansion not only is a

scumbag on many levels (he keeps bragging about how much money he makes) but has also invited over all his equally scumbag buddies. Large middle-age guys with big bellies all slam down copious amounts of Red Bull and vodkas, making them increasingly aggressive and drunk.

These horrible men, completely devoid of an iota of class, have their attention directed toward OJ's strippers. Ten years after the infamous trial, ten years after looking for his wife's killer. Who would've thought I'd find myself here? This is ancient Rome before its fall, the Dante level of showbiz purgatory one gets sentenced to when still craving fame but is banished from Hollywood paradise like a disgraced Fatty Arbuckle instead.

"Yo, coach, I'm a tiger on the loose. There's no stopping the Juice," OJ gestures with his hands, doing a bit of cocky rapping with the finesse of a Shaquille O'Neal. "People ask me how I made it to the top. I'm not a Simpson named Bart. I can't take credit, because God give-ith!"

The Red-Bull-and-vodka bunch keep uttering stuff I've never heard human beings mouth before without irony.

"Now what's the problem here? The ratio. Too many sausages," proclaims a horrible middle-age man among the Red-Bull-and-vodka-slamming group.

"Be careful for what you ask for—a five-foot-nine nymphomaniac—'cuz you might have to pay for it," snorts a crusty guy with a receding hairline.

"I'm the director of the guy trying to get that bitch's tit in my mouth," retorts his godawful friend. "Those bitches are used to the sixty-year-old guys who are loaded."

Bad energy's afoot. The only things missing from this volatile mix are loaded firearms and oily rags near open flames. The mansion's atmosphere gets increasingly aggressive. I know there's going to be trouble—I just don't know when.

While OJ raps and the strippers gyrate, I bond with his girlfriend of the last eight years (a heavy job title). We're both, as it turns out, originally from Minnesota. She's a former cheerleader and, for some reason, has a large bruise on her arm. I'm told OJ refers to me as "crazy boy," quite a compliment. (How crazy does one have to be for OJ Simpson to refer to you as "crazy boy?") As we talk, I suddenly start getting paranoid as I see OJ looking over because I remember what happened to the last guy in this same situation, and by no means do I want to see OJ's jealous side!

"Hey! What are you doing here?" barks the now-blurry-eyed guy renting the mansion with a tone that tests my manhood.

I tell him the reason I'm dressed in a cowboy costume is, obviously, I'm part of the video shoot.

"OK, I'll tell my friends," he aggressively slurs, swigging back his Red Bull and vodka. "They were wondering!"

Yes, you do the math: OJ + strippers + mansion + big-bellied guys drinking Red Bull and vodkas. How the hell do you think a night like this will end?

"THAT STUPID FUCKING BITCH CAN'T TALK TO ME LIKE THAT IN MY HOUSE!" the drunken scumbag screams from the bathroom where he just aggressively barged in on a stripper. The shoot abruptly ends as everyone is thrown out of the mansion. Unfortunately, OJ has already left (just when we may need him to throw down and go berserk for our benefit). During the mayhem, the sound guy and I quickly grab a bottle of vodka and jump in the limo filled with the strippers. So thus, the evening has a happy ending.

More Strippers and OJ

OJ is back to being very drunk. You haven't lived until you've heard OJ jokes right from OJ himself. "Who was the first Jewish guy to get a Heisman trophy?" asks OJ, spread out on a large chair. "Fred Goldman, because he got mine!"

I let out an uncomfortable noise as the joke's punch line is directed at me. OJ Simpson is once again dressed in an Elvis jumpsuit, with a midget in a little Elvis jumpsuit dancing around him. Both are surrounded by topless strippers, as the mansion melee has now moved to the VIP room of a Vegas strip club. This is a true sign of the Apocalypse. Locusts will soon be filling the skies as people run screaming from burning buildings, bleeding from every orifice.

"I've never gotten a lap dance in my life, and I'm not going to start now!" OJ lays down the law as a stripper tries to mount him and his girlfriend looks on. Yes, you've got to draw the line somewhere.

Our Vegas shooting schedule abruptly ends. The first thing in the morning, the producer informs me, "OJ's sick today, so we're going to pack up and go back to LA." Strange. The last I saw of OJ, he was shit-faced. Fortunately, the previous night we took advantage of the fact that we had access to a midget in an Elvis costume. After the shoot, three of us and little Elvis hit the Vegas strip to film drunken revelers at 2:30 a.m. on St. Patrick's Day morning. Maybe some of our filmed shenanigans could be used for *Juiced*?

"Look at little Elvis's balls!" shrieks a drunken woman pointing to that tight area in baby Elvis's jumpsuit.

"What do you think of OJ Simpson?" I inquire as little Elvis scampers about.

Unfortunately, none of the responses is quite right for the final cut of *Juiced*.

"Murderer!" screams one drunk man.

"It's a failure of our justice system," shouts another.

"They should put him in jail for life," shares a tourist from Iowa.

Not exactly the responses we wanted. "Well, what would you think about OJ putting out a rap album?" I ask.

"I'd think hell has frozen over!"

It seems like a one-sided picture here on the strip, but if these Vegas party goers happened to actually be Juiced ("You've been Juiced!") by OJ, I'm sure they would change their tune to celebrity worship. They would request photos and autographs. OJ would most likely be the most famous person they'd ever meet in their blah little lives.

The cult of celebrity has no boundaries. Only in America could scandalized OJ Simpson reinvent himself, for a new generation, as a zany prankster.

Epilogue

Maybe I've been Juiced. I wonder if the irreparable harm I've done my karma by participating in this will be worth it. Guess I'll just have to wait for the DVD to come out. People ask me if I was scared to work with OJ Simpson. I wasn't really scared. But since this book is out, now I'm scared! I picture OJ reading it, then screaming, "I'M GOING TO KILL THAT MOTHER-FUCKER!" Needless to say, I won't be co-starring in *Juiced 2—Electric Boogaloo.*

Gags of *Juiced*

What would be *Juiced* without all the classic pranks plotted for OJ Simpson to match his diverse acting skills? Here are a few actual planned stunts that were on the *Juiced* call sheet.

Religious Ruckus

OJ dresses up as an old white rabbi. Pranks include going to a delicatessen and ordering pounds of ham and bacon, going to the baseball batting cages, playing basketball at a local park, roller-skating at the beach, going to a shooting range, and eating a full slab of ribs. YOU'VE BEEN JUICED!

Abused Day Laborer

OJ pulls up in a white van to places where day laborers gather. He gets out of the van and opens the side door to reveal a very beaten and bruised day laborer. He kicks him out of the van, then solicits other workers to see if they want work. OJ also pulls over and has the abused laborer escape and chases him. YOU'VE BEEN JUICED!

Fast-Food Mayhem

OJ operates the fast-food window. Pranks include telling people to pull up and then reverse, making fun of them while they're at the window, getting their order wrong when repeating it, ask them if they want an egg roll, giving them an outrageous total, and trying to talk them out of whatever they order. YOU'VE BEEN JUICED!

INS OJ

We send in two Latino actors to portray day laborers. After they are in position, OJ and two other guys in green windbreakers portraying INS agents quickly pull up to the curb and grab one of the actors. The other actor will scream. Havoc ensues. YOU'VE BEEN JUICED!

Scandalous

The host will show a prank victim that he found out that the victim's wife or girlfriend has been cheating. We tell the boyfriend they are at a hotel nearby and ask if he wants to confront them. We then drive the boyfriend to the hotel and he confronts his cheating girl with OJ. YOU'VE BEEN JUICED!

Jehovah's Witness

OJ will just go door to door trying to get donations for the Jehovah's Witnesses. YOU'VE BEEN JUICED!

Unpredictable Personals

A woman will bring her mom to meet the new love of her life. It's OJ. YOU'VE BEEN JUICED!

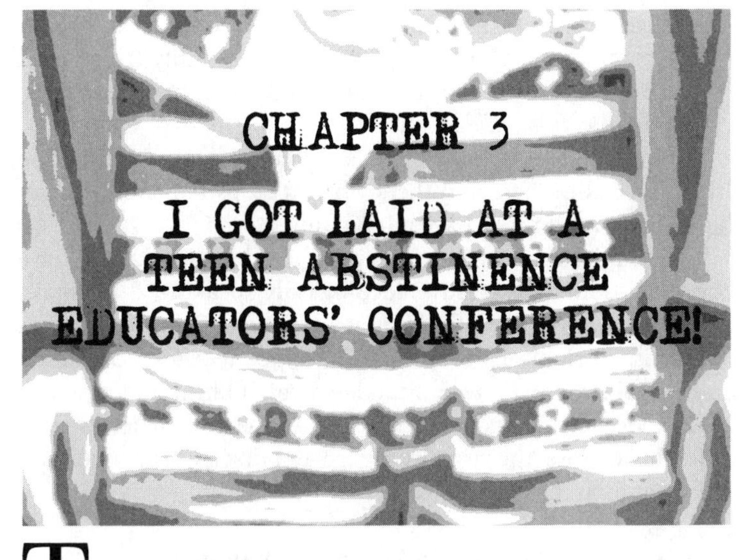

CHAPTER 3

I GOT LAID AT A TEEN ABSTINENCE EDUCATORS' CONFERENCE!

Teen abstinence is our great president George W. Bush's favorite method of birth control. Though abstinence has been preached for thousands of years, the Bush administration, thank God, has finally gotten it right. Over the past five years, the US government has spent nearly $1 billion to bring the message to the classrooms and to convince teens that condoms are ineffective and that the only safe form of sex occurs within marriage. They did it! Problem solved! Disregarding thousands of years of human nature, they know that the way to stop teen pregnancy and the spread of sexually transmitted diseases is for teens to simply not have sex. It's just that easy. Sign me up.

No, literally.

I'm going to attend a three-day conference sponsored by the group Life Choices. (Get it? They're cleverly one-upping "pro-choice.") There, I'm to be trained as a teen abstinence educator, learning the ins and outs of what's needed to teach kids in public schools how not to have sex. We've heard the whiny liberal rhetoric about teen abstinence programs, the complaints that they give erroneous information about health, sexuality, gender roles, contraception, and the prevention of sexually transmitted diseases—that they're full of medical and scientific inaccuracies, all under the guise of education.

Boo-hoo-hoo, whiny liberals. What's wrong with a little misinformation here and there when it stops kids from having sex—why should they have all the fun?

You might not know this about me, but my politics have become soooo conservative, ideologically speaking, that I make Jerry Falwell look like a fluff boy at a gay men's bathhouse. When did this ideological transformation happen? After I became a born-again virgin. (It's never too late.) Yes, if I'm attending a teen abstinence educators' conference, I want to practice what I preach. So I took the virginity pledge. But first a little preparation for attending the conference.

Born-Again Virgin Preparation

- 1 fanny pack
- 1 sweater vest
- 1 pair of dress slacks with tennis shoes
- 1 mop of hair tucked under a Kangol hat
- 2 hand puppets (to help further the cause of teaching teen abstinence)
- 1 pseudonym: Quentin Smalls

How do I look? Like a guy who never gets laid, of course.

My catchphrase: "Guns don't kill; having sex with unmarried people kills!"

One hour outside of Portland, Oregon, I journey to a secluded lodge in the woods near a mountain town of 1,190 people, where the weekend also boasts X-Fest—an "underground" Christian music festival. Yes, I'm in God's country.

Instead of attending Burning Man, the desert art festival with thousands of naked bodies (where I'd certainly feel the pull of the devil's pitchfork of temptation), I've opted to attend this long, very long, three-day abstinence conference. Good thing that I'm now a born-again virgin because there's one thing I think I know for sure: I'm not getting laid this weekend.

Walking by some trucks with American flag stickers, I make my way inside, passing tables with literature and posters; one placard says, "Abstinence—The Healthy Alternative" and shows an awkward couple wearing backpacks. The message is clear: instead of fornicating, go backpacking. Another sign reads:

A —affirming the power to create
B —body respect
S —sexual postponement until marriage
T —teen lifestyle training for fidelity
I —instant gratification delayed
N —no to premarital sex
E —energy focused on goal achievement
N —no conformity to media and peer pressure
C —confidence in the value of self and others
E —exercise self-control

Hmm, I never knew "abstinence" was really an acronym. If I remember correctly, when I was in high school, abstinence wasn't an acronym. It was just something called "not really getting any."

As I adjust my Quentin Smalls name tag, I start talking with other attendees. A man who runs a Christian bookstore, upon hearing my overly enthusiastic aspirations as a teen educator, pipes in: "It's good to see someone taking the initiative."

"I was really inspired by the Silver Ring Thing," I explain, referring to the Cirque du Soleil of teen abstinence programs, which uses rock concert theatrics and a high-tech style incorporating music, laser lights, humor, and skits in order to relay the message to kids, "Don't have sex!"

"I want to start my own big theatrical teen abstinence show." Pause. "I'm also toying with the idea of puppets," I explain, moving my hands to simulate just that, while talking in two different voices and introducing him to my teaching aid, Mr. Wait Until Marriage.

"You know the Silver Ring Thing is in a lawsuit right now with the ACLU," he says.

"You're kidding!"

It's true. A $75,000 federal grant to the Silver Ring Thing was suspended after the Bush administration was accused of using tax dollars to promote Christianity.

"I think the ACLU is just jealous over the cool mixture of laser lights, hip-hop, and the teen abstinence message," I reason.

Apparently I've misread the conference literature and showed up too early. So I kill some time by checking out some of the teen abstinence tables. "Abstinence—Because 100 Percent Matters" reads a poster showing a guy rock climbing. (I don't really see the connection, other than that's what you can do—climb rocks—instead of sex. I weigh in my mind, "Which is riskier?") A table set with pro-life literature, dolls, and gift items has a sign that says, strangely, "Support Our Troops."

Confusion is the message here: "Save unborn fetuses, but send our troops to a place where they can get killed." Color me stupid, but shouldn't pro-life include protecting people currently living?

"Everyone, this is Quentin," is how I'm introduced to the group of roughly eight people who head the conference. They consist of two humorless types, adorned with glasses, goatees, and button-down shirts, who eye me with suspicion. As questions are fired faster than bullets toward Keanu Reeves in *The Matrix* ("Quentin, what church do you go to?" "How did you hear about this, Quentin?" "Why did you come all the way from California?"), I compensate by overly smiling (mental note to self: have better back story prepared for next teen abstinence conference).

"I brought hand puppets!" I announce with pride to stunned silence, adding after a few beats, "As a teaching device." Sighs of relief abound as a brief discussion of the effectiveness of hand puppets commences.

Sitting in a conference room and eating fifteen-dollar box lunches (turkey with mayo on white bread, of course), we engage in shop talk. One topic: all public health websites should refer to the failure rate of condoms rather than to their effectiveness. Another: should extreme graphic slides be used when speaking to students about STDs (which condoms, of course, don't prevent)?

"We're kind of split on the effectiveness of graphic slides," explains a stoic woman who looks as though she'd advocate Prohibition in another era.

A bubbly lady, biting into her sandwich, changes the subject to her boss's daughter and his new son-in-law—both life virgins until marriage. Raising her eyebrows, she says, "I think they were ready for the wedding." She had teased her boss regarding the honeymoon deflowering process. "I said it to him: 'Guess what's been happening to her during the past week?'" the bubbly woman says. "He turned all red. That's my way of getting back at him for sticking his finger in my Reese's Peanut Butter Cup during lunch."

After the honeymoon, the new son-in-law supposedly commented about his new father-in-law: "I won't even be able to face him, knowing what I did to his daughter the past ten days."

"Did with his daughter," someone corrects.

"A bunch of women got together and threw her a party. She got a pair of lacy underwear as a gift. She held it up, then turned all red," she explains. "Everyone yelled out, 'That won't stay on long. That's going to end up on the floor!'"

The woman across from the bubbly woman changes the subject to her college-age son and his girlfriend, who made a pledge to a program called Master's Commitment. "They made a commitment they wouldn't date, so they could focus on their education," she says.

I look at my dry, tasteless turkey sandwich and can't believe this fucking thing was fifteen dollars' worth of food. The mood suddenly shifts.

"Have you seen the video?" the bubbly woman asks in the same manner as if someone did a bad smell.

"No. I haven't," I reply. "What video are you talking about?"

"It's put out by Golden Gate Planned Parenthood in San Francisco."

Since I'm the new kid on the teen abstinence educators' block, someone yells, "Show him the video!"

"This is what they think of us," the group's leader says with distaste verging on revulsion.

With the aid of a laptop, the Planned Parenthood promotional video is projected. An animated female superhero soon appears; a cartoon bubble reads, "It's Sexy To Be Safe."

The group watches with frowns and crossed arms.

"It looks like its time to take out the trash," proclaims the female superhero, grabbing a one-toothed, evil protestor wearing a black villain hat and holding an "Abstinence Education" sign. He is dumped in the trash. I let out an audible gasp.

An animated large condom is then put over the head of a large, cretinous abortion protestor. It explodes. The superhero declares she has the right to be pro-choice. Resentful heckles come from across the table: "Great! Why don't I choose to blow myself up!" The animated superhero adds, "You, too, can be a superhuman for a change!"

Lights on. Tense hush of silence. Unhappy faces.

"I just gave away my black hat last week," one of the abstinence educators sarcastically remarks.

I shake my head, disgusted. "What a load of a horse-hooey! What did you think of it?" I ask, directing my question to both the bubbly woman and my hand puppet Mr. Wait Until Marriage.

The bubbly woman momentarily is not bubbly.

"I was shocked by the violence. Are they saying it's OK to blow people up?"

"Yeah, and put very large condoms over people's entire bodies?" I add. (Then again, that would keep people extra protected.)

> **Abstinence Fun Fact!** Why not tell kids to try to abstain, but if you are going to have sex, use a condom? According to my new friends, that's an easy question to answer. Saying, "If you must, use a condom" is like saying, "Don't drink and drive, but if you do drink and drive, make sure you wear a seatbelt." Or saying, "Don't go and shoot a cop, but if you are going to shoot a cop, make sure to wear safety goggles and earplugs." So when we say it's OK for a teen to use a condom, it's like saying it's OK to shoot a cop! WHAT PART OF "WAIT UNTIL MARRIAGE" DON'T YOU UNDERSTAND?

Roughly a hundred folks are now gathered in a large conference room for the evening's events. The crowd is composed entirely of African Americans, Hispanics, Asians, and Jews—just kidding. It's not only very white here, it's *whiiiiiiiiiiiite*. Most of the people in the audience are poodle-haired old ladies in flower-print shirts—all with a similar small-town glow. The woman in front of me is quilting—no kidding. Those who are young already have families with several kids. A cell phone with a gospel music ring tone goes off.

"I want to applaud you, 'cause you're deep in the trenches, fighting the fight," remarks a cool pastor. (He makes references to Led Zeppelin and the movie *Zoolander*. Whenever he gives his abstinence state-of-the-union address, these references must really appeal to kids!) "What victories and struggles you face."

Watching this, I wonder what the fun people at Burning Man are up to at this very moment.

"When I was five years old, five, neighborhood children introduced me to *Playboy*," the cool pastor notes. "The way to prove my manhood was to pursue promiscuous behavior and pornography. The question can't be answered by porn and a promiscuous society."

For some reason, I'm reminded that there's pay-per-view porn in my hotel room.

"We are presenters of a message," the cool pastor intones, and soon other speakers take the mike and "present" away.

"Each of you are heroes to give lives to children that are here today," remarks a stern, gray-suited older man who's wearing glasses and a tie. (If this convention is about teen abstinence, why would teens be getting pregnant and having un-aborted fetuses?) Representing a foundation that's thirty years in the cause, he adds, "I'm thrilled to be with you today and say, 'You are my heroes. You are my heroes!'"

He then harks back to the good old days of 1860, when US abortion rates dropped, explaining that more abstinence education could bring things to that hallowed state once again. (Was he around then?)

"Change occurs because of heroes! I'm bringing the message

of history to you to say we can change it. If history repeats itself, and it does, we can create a culture where women are respected and babies are saved," the stern man says.

Then comes a series of TV commercials produced by his foundation, to be aired during Oregon State Beaver football games, showing the consequences of teens who don't practice abstinence. "This ad changes the English language by changing the view. We need to see the woman as a hero for bringing a baby to term."

The first commercial shows a hot-looking blond female firefighter (you see them all over the place) saving a tiny baby from a burning building. She mentions that her mother, who almost had an abortion, would be very proud today that her decision saved more than one life. "When you work with women coming to your clinic, they're heroes!" (Somehow they never show Jeffery Dahmer's or John Wayne Gacy's mother in these commercials.)

"The next commercial deals with selling abortion to blacks in inner cities," the gray-suit man dryly explains. "They [the blacks] usually have their first child, so we put the child in the ad." The ad has the feel of a Folgers coffee commercial. We see a smiling black woman in a middle-class house; she has a small child. With a huge, satisfied grin, she says she's decided to have her next baby as well!

There's more. A seventeen-year-old white girl clad in a nice running outfit is jogging. "You can't run away from your problems," she says. "I'm keeping it." She runs off. (I would guess back to her middle-class home, where she'll have the opportunity to jog off to college and have Mom and Dad share baby-sitting duties.)

But a question pops into my mind: Where's the TV commercial with the woman (or hero) who's been raped by her alcoholic stepfather and the words "Abortion—let's not have two victims!"

"Thank you again for being heroes!"

Though it is the week after Hurricane Katrina, there's no mention of praying for the people in New Orleans. I guess the focus should be more on saving children who, currently, might only be a drop of sperm.

> **Abstinence Fun Fact!** Planned Parenthood promotes abortion but discourages abstinence. Wake up! If teens didn't have sex, there would be no unwanted pregnancies. And, as we know, sex is caused by Barry White albums; therefore, we must forbid our teens from listening to Barry White albums. WHAT PART OF "WAIT UNTIL MARRIAGE" DON'T YOU UNDERSTAND?

Training Day

I decide to alter my look for the second day of the teen abstinence educators' conference. I'm now dressed real sleazy—tight shirt and jean shorts, cut really high. So high, in fact, that I run a risk of one of my nads popping out. Why? To take God's test on this whole born-again-virgin thing. I've also decided to talk in sexual double entendres to see where that leads, but, most important, I've brought my trusty hand puppets.

"There's just the three of us," says one of two overly nice ladies who are teaching the workshop. She looks a bit disappointed that I'm the only one who turned up for the hands-on training session that explains the abstinence curriculum taught in their public schools.

"A threesome," I mutter in a low, breathy voice, biting my lower lip. "That's more personal attention for me." I flash a mischievous smile.

"OK, here's something we teach," one of the overly nice ladies says, handing me a paper clip; this paper clip is supposed to give me something called a Life Lesson Analogy. "Make that paper clip as straight as possible."

I do just that, looking proudly at my handy work. Is that all there is to teen abstinence teaching? Will kids not want to have sex after doing that?

Oh. There's more. "OK. Now put it back," she insists.

Aaaah!

Using professional balloon-twisting skills, I bend the paper clip into the shape of a poodle.

"What would you need to put it back, to make it look identical?" she asks.

"Technology. Maybe tools," I throw out, spreading my legs wide apart. "Perhaps even an assist—from someone with . . ." Pause. "Beautiful eyes."

The paper clip symbolizes life's journey, apparently. "Don't give up; you're going to make mistakes," she says, implying that in life, as in bent paper clips, time is needed to fix things, for example, sexual promiscuity. "Stop and think before we charge on through. It's not hopeless." Huh?

"Through experience, I found that hand puppets are also effective in explaining this," I add to nods of agreement.

An overhead projector flashes the words "CHOOSING *NOT* TO DO SOMETHING EVEN THOUGH YOU HAVE THE OPPORTUNITY." Then the other overly nice lady takes over. "You decide not to take drugs," she notes. "Sexual abstinence is choosing to reserve sexual expression for marriage."

Just a choice? That's all. Problem solved. You just have to choose. This whole time I thought it had something to do with biological urges. But choosing not to have sex, for teens, is like, say, choosing Coke over Royal Crown Cola.

"Why do some teens choose to participate in sexual relationships?" the other lady pipes in. Several reasons are listed: "Drinking, friends, media . . ."

"Bragging rights," I congenially add.

"Girls, it just offends them." She says that when guys in her classroom mention the bragging. "Girls will say, 'Dude! Come on!'" She uses "today's" language.

"What if they want to be a gangsta rapper?" I inquire, running my hand down my thigh. "It seems to work for them."

"Is it a good enough reason to take this risk?" one of the women responds. "Is it worth the risk?"

"I dunno. It seems fun to be a gangsta rapper," I remark.

Besides, think about it—without sex before marriage, would we even have rock music or, for that matter, Italian cinema?

"What are the consequences of sex? Girls feeling really

exploited," the woman says. "Petting? That's just bad behavior. That's how rumors start."

Let's see, no petting. So hand under the shirt, over the bra is obviously taboo. And masturbation is likely out of the question.

"Hold true to your own dream, or life will be disappointing," she says. "Whatever that dream might be. I don't know, president of a big company maybe. It can happen." (Sure, except for company presidents who fuck their way to the top.)

"Look at your goals. Having an STD is going to impact your goals," nice lady no. 2 jumps in. "If they pursue relationship goals, each step that they take to get more and more sexual increases their chances of risk! Condoms will reduce risk of STDs, but not all STDs. They won't eliminate it. There's still a 20 percent chance." (A 20 percent chance. Damn, she surely got her statistics from a different source other than the mainstream medical community—perhaps it's the same scientists who confirm the world is only a few thousand years old?)

"They have so much they can put focus on! School, sports, what's really important to them," lady no. 1 says, putting forward a theory that, if correct, would greatly expand teen softball leagues. "It's taking that energy and using it for something else."

"How about origami?" I throw out, then take a hard look at the boundary chart the ladies have passed me. "Avoid arousal" is one of the key boundaries.

"What if dancing makes you aroused?" I ask. "Should we, as instructors, tell kids not to dance?"

"If you found that as a weak spot, then avoid it," nice lady no. 1 states. (The premise of the movie *Footloose* suddenly makes sense.) "Maybe they can pick a different kind of dance? Instead of freaky dancing, maybe try, I don't know, square dancing."

"Square dancing, yes; freaky dancing, no," I repeat.

"Pick a boundary at maybe holding hands; move it back a notch," she suggests.

"How about direct eye contact? What if that makes you aroused?" I say, making direct eye contact.

"You've got to train, like an Olympic athlete," she answers.

Yes, indeed, train like an Olympic athlete—an Olympic athlete with a big, insatiable boner!

It's an interesting theory. I've been a born-again virgin for two days now, and the crack of dawn is making me horny. (In fact, my hand puppet Mr. Wait Until Marriage is looking pretty darn good at this point.)

What other methods might curb the sexual libido?

"Use a keepsake as a daily reminder, such as a bracelet or ring."

"Like if you're trying to lose weight, put a picture of a tropical place you want to vacation at on your refrigerator as inspiration."

"Wouldn't people get married just to have sex?" I ask.

"People aren't going to get married just to get laid," she scoffs. Marriage, she explains, is about becoming a friend to your spouse.

"I have a younger son," lady No. 1 concludes. "He's made a pact not to date because he thinks dating is too much stress."

She explains he'd much rather focus on studying. "He keeps a honeymoon jar. He puts money into the honeymoon jar in order to keep focused on school." The money from the honeymoon jar will be spent on his future wife. Whom he hasn't met yet.

Pause.

I nod my head and repeat, "A honeymoon jar!"

The Case for Marriage

"What we think of marriage is not what the world around us thinks of marriage," the bubbly woman from earlier tells a room now 90 percent filled with gray-haired ladies attending the afternoon workshop, "The Case for Marriage." "This is the will of God that you should abstain from sexual immorality. We believe that human sexuality is a divine gift, a primal dimension of each person."

"No question about that. God is pretty clear where he stands on that!" says one lady.

I realize now that abstinence education goes deeper than telling high school kids not to have sex. It's imposing a code of conduct into our public schools directly from the Bible.

"Let me tell you. MTV started out bad and is only getting worse," says another.

Then the bubbly woman prescribes an easy solution: "Protect your eyes, protect the music you listen to!"

An effective method of eye protection, she notes, is a practice known as "look and drop." When a guy sees a woman and feels lust, he should train himself to immediately bounce his eyes away—look and drop!

"The mind works fast. This trains him to look away. He doesn't allow the visual image to take hold," she explains. "That's why pornography is so dangerous. Porn sets unrealistic expectations on women."

I do a quick look and drop around the room, but I wonder if she's including amateur porn in her analysis. After all, amateurs set some very realistic expectations.

"Great [that] we're getting our message out there: cohabitation is not the goal. Awesome [that] we're getting our message out there," she says, noting that marriage causes less disease, alcoholism, and depression than "living in sin." "We have the studies. We have the documents. We have science backing us up. But the message that society gives off, that's our battle."

Finally comes the opportune moment to utter my catchphrase. I raise my hand. "Guns don't kill; having sex with unmarried people kills!" I declare, looking and dropping at all the women in the conference room.

Abstinence Fun Fact! If God says you should save yourself for that one special person in your life, the one you're going to marry, then all bets are off once you get divorced. (Because God lets you sometimes save yourself for a second special person in your life.) WHAT PART OF "WAIT UNTIL MARRIAGE" DON'T YOU UNDERSTAND?

BRING ON THE SWAT TEAM!

"We're going to start out with a skit," announces a tall, lanky guy with glasses who helps coordinate the SWAT team. I don't think in this case that "SWAT" stands for "Special Weapons And Tactics," but something less exciting that involves not having sex. Instead, it's a group of perky kids (tall, lanky guy; chunky blond gal; and, correct me if I'm wrong, daddy's little girl, all adorned in matching SWAT team T-shirts) who go around to high schools and do skits about teen abstinence and get other kids to TAKE THE PLEDGE.

I'd have to say my favorite forms of entertainment (in no discerning order) have to be:

Bare-knuckle boxing.

Hand-bone.

And, of course, teens doing skits about abstinence.

"This skit is called 'The Pieces of My Heart' skit," announces the lanky guy.

A female volunteer is brought up from the audience. Blond chunky gal narrates as tall, lanky guy holds a paper heart. She says that he and his girlfriend decide to have *sex*. (Damn, this is not shown.) "She breaks up with him and breaks a piece of his heart."

Tall, lanky guy subsequently symbolizes this by tearing off part of his heart and gives it to blond chunky gal. This same interaction occurs again. More sex. More paper-heart-tearing.

"Now he has a really dinky heart," explains the chubby gal. Tall, lanky guy presents the paper heart remnant to the audience volunteer, who portrays the future wife of the now small-hearted man.

"So how does that make her feel?" asks chunky gal.

"Not good," admits the audience volunteer.

She directs her attention to the lanky guy. "How does he feel?"

"Like poop!" he blurts.

Here comes another fun teen abstinence skit.

"Does anyone want this twenty-dollar bill?" asks daddy's little girl, pulling out some currency. Assuming this is not a trick question attached to a moral lesson on teen abstinence, I quickly raise my hand and shout, "I do!" Some old ladies also raise their hands. (This better not be a trick!)

"How about if I crumple it up and step on it?" She does just that to perfectly good American currency! "Would you still want it?"

"Yeah!" I scream, waving my hand. "I'll have it!"

Then comes the lesson: "This is how we deal with born-again virgins. You're still worth the same. You can always start over. You can always change."

Ohhhhh! I get it. This is not about free money. She's simply making "an analogy." This is great news, being that I'm a newly born-again virgin myself. (Though I'm not entirely sure how that works, anatomically speaking, for women; do born-again Christians in lab coats, for example, cultivate laboratory hymens in petri dishes for reinstatement?)

But there's a more important message here: Those who decide to have sex are nothing more than something crumpled up under someone's shoe.

"Are you still giving away the money?" I ask.

No.

In steps the SWAT team's mom adviser. How does the adult adviser suggest that teens curb their libidos? "By setting boundaries!"

"As a couple, you should agree [that] at this point, we're going to go no further, and we're going to be safe," she explains. She looks at a handout titled "Progression of Sexual Activity" chart. It's divided into three sections: the Safe Intimate Zone (spending time together, holding hands), the Caution Zone (simple kiss, prolonged kiss), and, of course, the Danger Zone (not only sexual intercourse and petting, but also French kissing. Why? It explains: "He's aroused!").

"My boundary is tea-bagging," I solemnly state to the old woman next to me in a low, raspy voice.

"Convey to kids that they can start over, and they are very valuable, and they are important to society," the adviser explains. She looks at tall, lanky guy; chunky gal; and daddy's little girl. "I don't even want to know your boundaries. That's your choice."

According to the *Journal of Adolescent Health,* teens who take virginity pledges often remain technically virgins by engaging in oral and booty sex. It makes sense: if they're trying to preserve their virginity, oral and anal sex fit under the definition of not having sex.

Which is great because I like those two things way better anyway.

"Can I have the SWAT team take over again?" barks the mom adviser; the three perky teens jump into place.

"Why do we choose abstinence?" asks chunky blond gal. "Like the 'Pieces of My Heart' skit, I want to give myself to my husband. I don't want to think of another woman there."

(Ewww. That would be icky.)

Tall, lanky guy adopts a pirate voice and explains the three Rs—responsibility, religion, and respect.

Then comes daddy's little girl. "I got a lot going on in my life," she says, listing off a dozen activities she's involved with, concluding with the varsity golf team. "I feel I have so much going on right now that I don't want to risk getting pregnant or getting an STD. I want to go to college. I want to travel the world. I have trouble getting out of the house in the morning; I can't even imagine having to feed my kid."

She laughs, but there's more. "I have a boyfriend. He's pretty well known. He's a wrestler. He went to State." Woo! She tells everyone that she and her pretty-well-known-boyfriend (he went to State) choose abstinence. Hurrah for the annoying, over-achieving popular girl who doesn't put out and rubs everyone's nose in the fact!

"That's our choice," she says. "We choose to be abstinent."

(Besides, sex is totally icky!)

"Paul is on the SWAT team as well," the mom adviser pipes in, identifying the popular girl's pretty-well-known-boyfriend. (Ah, so it's Paul!)

"People out there say that teens have raging hormones and can't control themselves. I can. I'm not running around trying to make out with everyone, " says the popular girl (who most likely got a new car for staying a virgin).

The tone dramatically shifts to storytime. "The other side of this is the broken honor code," states the mom adviser. She makes a sad face. The SWAT team looks at their shoes. The mom, looking at no one in particular, says, "This young gal broke the honor code. And I said, 'You got to talk to her.'"

So the SWAT team spoke to the fallen teen about her lapse in following the code ("To honor my future spouse, I choose to save sexual activity for marriage!") and then betrayed that by dancing the humpty-hump.

"You can tell she was very, very broken," the popular girl says. "He was pretty proud of breaking her code, so it was all over the school. And we have a big school."

So what happened? Was a scarlet "A" branded upon her chest? Did she receive a good pelting with rocks? Were condoms provided, in case it happened again?

"She wrote a letter to the entire SWAT team and told them she broke the code and asked for forgiveness. She told her parents," the popular girl explains. Pause. "You know what? She's back on the SWAT team!"

Holy fucking shit! I let out an audible cheer, pumping my fist in the air. (Still, I have to wonder: Is there a limit to the number of times you're allowed to become a born-again virgin?)

"The parents called up and said, 'Thank you very much.' She knows what she did, and she won't go down that road again until she's married,'" the mom says with a firm, certain smile.

"You guys are very brave," an adult from the audience shares. "You're earning my respect."

"After you graduate, hit the colleges!" one of the gray-haired ladies says to the three perky kids, who are all high school seniors.

Tall, lanky guy points to a button on his shirt that sports a picture of a dog and the slogan "Pet Your Dog, NOT Your Date."

Hey, isn't that bestiality?

"That's the hot item to have right now," injects the mom adviser.

"That's so funny!" someone blurts out.

"How about 'Pet Your Pussy, NOT Your Date'?" I ask.

Abstinence Fun Fact! I don't want kids thinking they'll be protected by condoms, because it won't protect the most important body part of all—the heart. And isn't that the area of the body most susceptible to raging gonorrhea?

CONTRACEPTION

I'm one of two guys in yet another sterile conference room full mostly of old white ladies from small towns. To further test the sincerity of my born-again virgin pledge, I've decided to hit on some of the attendees at the abstinence conference.

I nudge my chair close to the seventy-year-old woman next to me; she has a button of George W. and Laura Bush on her purse. (There will be no worries about getting her pregnant.)

"Quentin, that's my cousin's name," she says after introductions, holding my handshake a little longer than usual. "What organization are you from?"

"Mimes for Abstinence," I reply, motioning as if I'm trapped in a box—of condoms that is, which I will be discouraged from using! I move in closer, licking my lips and making direct eye contact. "We try to slip in the message slowly, with hard facts, then pull out information, generating a gush of excitement."

Taking out my hand puppets, I explain why kids shouldn't have sex and graphically describe in detail the type of sex they shouldn't be having (tea-bagging, of course), which includes listing specific positions and a graphic, sexual hand-puppet demonstration, concluding with my theory that Popsicles promote oral sex. Before she can respond, I'm interrupted.

"We're trying not to make this a real controversial topic," explains the director, a soft-spoken woman in a cheery pink top. "What is our organization's policy on contraception? When I say this, I mean artificial contraception."

To help clarify, she asks people to raise their hands as she asks questions about who they think should use contraceptives.

"OK for singles, OK for married couples?"

No hands go up.

"OK for singles, not OK for married couples?"

Huge laugh. (Of course, no hands go up.)

With that, she launches into "A Modern-Day Fable about Holly and Steve." A slide shows Holly and Steve hugging and holding flowers, much as happy, married couples do. Trouble then enters paradise. "Holly began taking oral contraception—the pill. She gained ten pounds and felt tired and irritable. She couldn't maintain her full-time job. She soon felt resentful of Steve's sexual advances. No one in her circle of Christian friends had experienced this.

"Holly was being robbed of her happiness."

I look again at the slide of Holly and Steve hugging, holding flowers. What went wrong? They look so happy. To think it was all because of birth control.

We go next to the Bible, specifically Genesis 38:10, in which Onan spills his seed on the ground and is struck dead by God. The soft-spoken director questions the appropriateness of married couples using artificial contraceptives. "That's our objective: understand God's plan for marriage and families," she says. "The purpose of sex is procreation."

Apparently, once we separate sex from creating children, she explains, the door is open to a whole (pardon my French) hell of a lot of trouble: "Protestant church tolerance of birth control paved the way to the legalization of homosexuality, sodomy. And you know where we are today with gay marriage."

A murmur runs through the crowd. I wrinkle my forehead and frown. The old woman next to me wrinkles her forehead and frowns. Another old lady gets up and leaves, looking upset, moving her lips as they turn purple. Two court cases from the 1960s that found birth control to be in a zone of privacy protected by the Constitution are mentioned as precursors to *Roe v. Wade*.

"When we allow for contraception on demand," she says calmly, "we allow for abortion on demand."

The only acceptable solution is Natural Family Planning—NFP—or the so-called rhythm method, which, she explains, involves married couples not having sex during the time of the month when the woman is fertile. Yes, all that is required for God to smile upon married couples is sometimes abstaining from sex.

It's just that easy! It's just that fun! And, unlike condoms and birth control, it is approved from above. "The big difference," regarding other forms of contraception such as condoms, "is there's a violation of the natural law," she continues.

"It also cuts down on sensitivity," I say to the woman next to me with a wink.

Another big difference: "If a couple uses contraceptives, and it happens to fail, they are disappointed when the wife gets pregnant." In the case of NFP, however, God is part of the intimacy and decision making for the couple: "They know it could happen, and they totally surrender to it!"

To emphasize this, she calmly shares the story of a married couple's first time having sex. "When they were coming together, they could see the Lord," she explains. "They could see the Lord, they could see children. Do you not hunger for that kind of experience?"

Wow! I've heard of some freaky-ass shit, but a menage a trois with The Master? Oh, Jesus!

"There's a zero percent divorce rate for those who practice NFP," she says. (I didn't know birth control was one of the leading causes of divorce. But won't those who think birth control is a sin certainly think divorce is a sin?) "Birth control definitely affects relationships; I know that from experience!"

Now I fully understand why abstinence educators tell kids that condoms are ineffective. It's not a scientific or logistical issue; it's completely a moral issue for these folks. They think birth control correlates to something in the Bible (my favorite work of fiction next to *Battlefield Earth*). They're not thinking of kids' health; they have a moral agenda. It's like teaching creationism over evolution in the classrooms. It's religion over science, except here it's religion over facts and the health of kids.

"I want to ask her if it's OK to get a vasectomy," I later say to the woman with the George and Laura button on her purse. "Or if that will break up my marriage, since it's birth control?"

"I'd like to find out about that, too," she replies, then tags along at my heels.

When I ask about vasectomies, the soft-spoken director gathers her notes. "There is a high risk of prostate cancer," she says.

"Oh, so it's more of a medical thing," I remark, shaking my head. Unlike the tragedy of Holly and Steve, this surgical form of birth control is fine, except . . . GOD WILL STRIKE YOU DOWN WITH A HORRIBLE CANCER!

"What if I'm teaching a teen abstinence class and someone says they're going to have sex?" I ask next. "Should I tell them it's OK to use a condom?"

"Condoms send a mixed message," she says, straightening her notes.

"Yeah," I add. "It's almost like we're saying it's OK to have sex."

"Exactly."

"I could go on for hours about that," interjects the woman with the George and Laura button.

I throw out a solution that could possibly win me one of those Nobel Prizes.

"Know what they should do? Teach abstinence in Africa. That way it would completely wipe out the entire AIDS problem over there, because there would be no way to spread it!"

"Yes! That's right," says the soft-spoken director.

Pfffew! World crisis solved!

"And the best way to teach it is through hand puppets," I add.

"Quentin! Quentin! Quentin!" one of the organizers screams, as I walk by in a haze of misinformation, momentarily forgetting that's the name I'm going by.

Saturday Night at the Teen Abstinence Educators' Conference—Woo-Hoo, It's Party Time!

After my loooong day of workshopping, I begin to doubt my decision to remain a born-again virgin. It seems that this group is using abstinence as a vehicle, pretending to be concerned about public health when the larger picture is to advance a religious program and its agenda. It's a bit "One Nation Under God"-ish—a back door for Christian America to get into public schools and teach moral values quicker than you can say, "Scopes monkey trial."

That's why I've taken to putting large amounts of whiskey into my complimentary Starbucks paper coffee cup. Is there a term for having a hangover from an overdose of too much Jesus talk?

Grabbing my Starbucks whiskey coffee, I check out the Saturday night events, where I find more tables with more old ladies in more floral shirts. Strangely, no one sits at my table. (Could it be my teaching-aid puppets?) The overly friendly ladies aren't as friendly as before, the bubbly woman is less so, as I make it just in time for the SWAT team to do its "Pieces of my Heart" sketch once again. (I could never get tired of that.)

"We're not serving alcohol in here tonight," the waitress says when I order a double bourbon.

"There's the sound of the distant thunder, walking together, moving together," remarks the head of the conference, clad in an orange shirt and khaki pants. "The battle is getting greater!"

He goes on to speak of the beacon for the immoral agenda. "The gay newspaper protested our abstinence office." He's actually referring to Seattle's regular weekly alternative paper (I guess he's using *gay* as an adjective and not a noun), which did a story on the local pro-choice group who threw a Screw Abstinence party—to promote birth control. "The opposition has sent a plant," he remarks, saying he wants the plant to go back and tell them how it really is.

I give a quick look around the room to see who the hell the mole might be. Where is that sly, crafty bastard? I thought I was the only one infiltrating this conference. I'd like to meet this guy.

"To be strong, we must have God's grace, with this new wave of God's spirit," the conference head continues. "As God's spirit is sweeping America. Keep your eyes set on God, as we advance, 'cuz it's going to be a bumpy ride!"

Since the ride is going to be bumpy, I decide to get the hell out of there, sharply making my way toward the exit as eyes follow me.

While driving into Portland, my born-again virgin status is tested. The devil whispers in my ear, and I end up at a bar called Shanghai and notice a cute blond girl. I try to Look and Drop, Look and Drop, but it just doesn't work. All this talk of the evils of sex and abstinence has just made me horny. As an ironic twist, the cute blond works for a public access TV station and, for a freelance gig, once directed teen abstinence videos.

Our shared abstinence background breaks the ice.

Going back to her place, I end up severely crossing my boundaries (except for the tea-bagging part). I'm caught up in the moment. I'm about to break my born-again virgin pledge and fornicate (without a condom, of course, since I've been taught how ineffective they are and don't have any). Fortunately, the blond's prepared. (By no means would she have sex otherwise.) Thus, Quentin Smalls once again *becomes a man!*

Though I wasn't planning to have sex, and I made a pledge not to, the cute blond made me realize, whether teen or adult, you always have to be ready to protect the Johnson!

EPILOGUE

The days pass slowly now, as I dwell in permanent sin with a broken born-again virgin pledge, living in complete fear of ineffective condoms. Missing the old gang, a few days after I get back to San Francisco, I mysteriously get an e-mail from the head of the conference, the guy who eyed me with suspicion on the first day:

> Hey Harmon,
>
> I just wanted to see if you enjoyed the conference last weekend.
>
> When you are done writing your piece on the conference would you mind forwarding it to me? I would love to read it!

Huh? What the?! Was it my puppets that gave me away? That's not just creepy, that's creeeeeeeeeeeeeeeeeeeeeeepy!

In a paranoid world where we're all presumed guilty, easily spied on, and wiretapped, with some dragged off the streets and thrown into Kafka-esque jails, it's refreshing—even if it's the world of reality make-believe television—to turn the tables and beat the system.

The following ad appears on CraigsList.org:

> Has your parole officer accused you of doing something you haven't done? Could this put you back in jail? Then we want to help.
>
> Call us and we'll clear your name.
>
> We've got a show to help you prove who's telling the truth.
>
> If selected, we will profile your story on a new national TV show where guests are polygraphed to get the truth out.

I'm intrigued. My e-mail reply: "I am on parole!"

Going by the name Hank, I express how much, I, who is on parole, would love to be on this TV show (whatever the hell that might be). Immediately the TV producer e-mails back, thrilled to hear from "I, who is on parole." She leaves a phone number. Calling her back, I, who is on parole, weave an elaborate tale involving weapons and drug charges. This pleases her. I embellish further. I have something to prove to my probation officer. He said I flunked a recent drug test that landed me back in jail for twenty days. The producer is elated.

The next day, the producer phones back. She wants me on the show! That's right, Bubba, I'm booked on *Lie Detector* (Tuesdays, 8 p.m.), a show on family-friendly PAX TV that has a motto: "The lie detector holds the power to reveal the truth and expose deception wherever it might be found." My God, what a perfect TV show in the age of the PATRIOT Act and the Bush administration's frenzy for citizen surveillance—civilians hooked up to a lie detector. It would be perfect if those who fail the lie detector were scooted onto a no-name aircraft and then to an undisclosed blackout area for further interrogation.

But first, there's a question. "You said you were on probation," the producer says. "That's different from being on parole."

Whoops. How the hell am I supposed to know? All my knowledge of the parole system comes from watching two prison documentaries on A&E. Quickly, I recall: "Yeah, I'm on *parole*, but this is my *probation* period."

Then another monkey wrench is heaved into the mix: I, who is on parole, fax a copy of my police report from my latest arrest. "I believe you," she says. "The executive producer just wants to see a copy of it."

This presents a problem. I put her off. The producer calls numerous times. I put her off further. More phone calls. A friend offers a solution: I surf my way over to SmokingGun.com and, after an extensive archives search, download David Crosby's drug-and-weapons arrest report, along with the paperwork for Courtney Love's assault-with-a-flashlight charge. Using Photoshop software, I combine the two, making excellent use of the smudge tool. For consistency, I do a few rounds of enlarging and reducing the document at Kinko's. Randomly, I black out words, stating that on legal advice from my lawyer, I can't go into great detail about my weapons and drug charges, since the case is still pending. What you have to go through to get a rap sheet these days!

Hank now has an arrest report.

Faxing off the Crosby/Love document, I expect never to hear from *Lie Detector* again. There are about a thousand ways to figure out that I'm lying in ten minutes or less. Kids have done better jobs fudging their report cards. But lo and behold! The show's travel coordinator calls the next day to book my airline ticket to LA. I'll be put up for two nights at a Holiday Inn! Hot damn. *Lie Detector* awaits!

PREPARATION

To look the part of a guy on parole, I've grown a week's worth of bad mustache and wrapped an American flag bandanna around my head. To top off my look, I'm wearing a Jesus T-shirt, suggesting, as with many a con, I found JC while in prison.

Something's working here; when I get off the plane, a production assistant hands me an envelope full of fun cash to use while I'm in LA.

This is not the only time someone's lied on *Lie Detector*. I'm told about a guy who lied about trying to sell his kidneys over the Internet. After being on the show, it turns out he *was* trying to sell his kidneys! So thus the nature of the show is to vindicate people or catch them lying. I, who is on parole, is in the latter group.

WHAT AMERICA SEES ON HANK'S EPISODE OF *LIE DETECTOR*

The show opens with a bald, solemn man, wearing an orange prison jumpsuit, hooked to a lie detector. The screen flashes the words *Truth* and *Lie*. Graphics featuring numbers and colored lines demonstrate the program's high-tech nature. There's a shot of smiling host Rolanda Watts (known for *Inside Edition* and *The Rolanda Show*), with her arms folded, looking content.

"The lie detector holds the power to reveal the truth and expose deception wherever it might be found," a narrator intones.

Over the next hour, the world's foremost lie detector expert will use the world's most exacting scientific device, the Axciton polygraph instrument, to separate fact from fiction, truth from lie. (Well, fuck me sideways!)

My segment is cleverly named, "Up in Smoke."

Lie Detector host Rolanda Watts emerges from behind a piece of the set. Her personality can best be described as *highly outgoing*. "OK, you all, we all heard this one before, 'I didn't inhale. I didn't mean to get high. I was just in the room, and I got a contact high.'" She mockingly waves her arms around, using her fingers to put quote marks around the words *contact high*. "Yeah, right!"

"If you're Hank, a guy who's currently on probation and tested positive for drugs, this could be a major setback."

Then comes a photo montage, accompanied by generic speed-metal music, which uses the photos I sent in from my so-called parolee's life. These include random JPEGs found on the Web, among them a little kid playing the flute, some guy who has his back tattooed with the word *Santana* across it, and a street gang (of an ethnic group that clearly does not include me).

I also sent:

- A photo of the real me, taken when I infiltrated and wrestled with someone in the Christian Wrestling Federation.
- A photo of a random Christian wrestler.
- Me, wearing a stocking cap and gangsta shades, holding an Uzi and firing an AK-47, taken when I infiltrated a machine-gun convention in rural Kentucky.

"If you were looking to fill the role of party boy, some might say Hank looks straight out of central casting," Rolanda's heard in a voiceover. The screen then cuts to a shot of me walking in slow motion, in the style *Dateline* uses to make people look really sinister. It gets even better. There's a reenactment. (The word *reenactment* is posted across the screen, in case you don't get it.)

"Hank tried to play the part of peacemaker when a fight broke out at a party. The police mistook him for the instigator. They discovered drugs in the trunk of his car."

The reenactment is beautiful. *Lie Detector* actually hired an actor who looks slightly like me to portray me. (Try to think this one through: I provided work for a struggling actor—who most likely had to go through an audition process to get the part—to play me, all the while I am portraying a guy on parole.) Another reenactment: Hank hits someone on the head with Courtney Love's flashlight.

Another montage of me looking extremely psycho—as if I might eat babies—while I'm being hooked up to the lie detector. Then, after the montage, an extreme close-up of me proclaiming my mission statement: "I want to prove to my parole officer that I wasn't doing it. And lastly, I just want to prove it to myself!"

ONE-ON-ONE WITH ROLANDA

The *Lie Detector* set is basically two chairs and a table on a soundstage. My goal is to look as crazed as possible during the entire taping: never cracking a smile and keeping a psychotic, intense look in my eye, while under hot studio lights and surrounded by the entire production crew.

Rolanda goes back to a mocking tone, commenting on my fictional arrest: "I'm sure police hear this all the time, 'They're not mine. It wasn't me.'"

"Uh-huh," I grunt, looking like I want to bite Rolanda's head off. "Yeah, I had to take a drug test, and it came back negative."

From off-camera, the executive producer halts the taping and shouts, "Don't you mean *positive*? When you flunk a drug test, it comes back *positive*."

This is one of the numerous holes in my story. I clarify: "What I meant was, it was *negative* for me, because I ended up back in jail!"

Maybe the less I say the better.

"Here you were, having spent eight months for the original

offense," Rolanda says with a concerned look. "Now you have to spend twenty more days. What was that like for you?"

"It was like, 'Here we go again,'" I reply, trying to look especially nutso while at the same time suggesting that I am trying to be spiritual nowadays by subtly gesturing to my Jesus T-shirt.

"What's the worst part about being in jail?" Rolanda asks.

Pause. "It's just, like, really boring."

"It gives you a lot of time to think," she adds, coming to her own conclusions. "What did you think about?

I subtly gesture again to my Jesus T-shirt. "I just thought about reevaluating my life and my spirituality," I say meekly.

"You got an epiphany when you were in jail," she says with a pleased smile.

"Yeah, I got a little more spiritual," I agree and then start talking about my *pillar of strength*—my fictional girlfriend, Rochelle. "I couldn't have gotten through this without her and her support."

To illustrate my fictional girlfriend, I sent the producer a JPEG from a Google image search that used the words "big booty."

"Rochelle is my pillar of strength!" I repeat, hoping they'd flash the image of this large woman posing in a manner that shows off her best asset. Sadly, my talk of fictional Rochelle and her big booty didn't make the final cut.

Before meeting the lie detector, I get to plead my case. "I was at a party where they were doing the drugs. So that could have been the thing," I explain. "And I forgot to mention, I was getting dental work done, and I was on a pain pill."

Rolanda turns sarcastic, noting, "But a pain pill wouldn't come back reading marijuana."

"I don't know. I was thinking maybe it was secondhand smoke," I add with hesitation.

"What happens if you flunk this test today?" she asks, as if it would be the worst thing in the world.

Breaking my psycho stare, I laugh. It hits me how stupid this all is.

"Uh, I don't know?"

"If you pass the test, what will you do with this information?"

I regain my "I eat babies" composure and tell her that I'd like to be a positive role model. She smiles. She looks pleased. I wisely say how my other friends are serving life sentences on the installment plan! (Nice witty pun.)

"You've grown up a lot, haven't you?" Rolanda adds, shaking her head.

Pause. "I think so. Yeah."

"So you came here to clear your name?"

I nod vigorously.

"Are you ready to face the lie detector?"

"Yeah."

"Are you sure?"

With certainty, I reply, "Yeah, I'm ready to face the lie detector!"

"Let's get you hooked up."

"OK, let's do it!"

LIE DETECTOR LIP-SYNCH

Members of the crew spray the set with a smoke machine to create an eerie, netherworld effect. Home viewers see intense Hank hooked up to a lie detector machine; the test is to be administered by Dr. Ed Gelb, a man who never cracks a smile and who has polygraphed the likes of Jon Benet Ramsey's parents, Snoop Dogg, and Axl Rose.

"Remain still," the doctor proclaims authoritatively. "The test is about to begin."

The studio lie detector test is actually a shadow-play conducted for the cameras. The real lie detector test was administered early in the morning at Dr. Ed's intimidating office, which is filled with plaques from the Los Angeles Police Department. I tried to keep as quiet as possible around Dr. Ed, a man with an extremely dry sense of humor. I figured he probably knows more about the parole system than I ever will. At least I hope so.

After searching the Internet, I learn that the best way to beat a polygraph test is to put a tack in my shoe and poke myself when each question is asked. Which is what I do. I'm not sure if this helped during the morning session. But it was very uncomfortable.

For the faux test reenactment, Dr. Ed says, "The advice, Hank: the attempt at any countermeasures will invalidate this test." The accompanying screen graphics read: *Says he did not smoke marijuana while on probation.*

"Do you plan to tell the truth on this test whether you knowingly used marijuana while on probation?" Dr. Ed asks.

I stare straight ahead like I'm harboring disturbing secrets. I shift my eyes back and forth, taking in the information that Dr. Ed is providing as my forehead strains and my eyebrows make intense peaks.

"Yes!" I intone.

"Did you do marijuana while on probation last January?"

Extreme close-up. "NO!"

This is true; I wasn't on probation last January.

"This test is now over. Remain still for ten seconds, please."

Then comes the cunning teaser: "When we return: Is Hank really on the straight and narrow, or is Hank really just blowing smoke?"

The Results

After a big buildup, Rolanda slowly opens an envelope, as if this were the Academy Awards. I'm all prepared to freak out—extremely—when she says I failed, perhaps even storm off the set. Streaking might also be involved. What fun! Rolanda lets out a shrug and sighs.

"Hank, the lie detector has determined . . . that you . . . are . . ." She shakes her head. "Hank, you're telling the truth!"

The music turns triumphant.

I raise my arms in the air in victory: "HEEEEEEEEEY!"

I laugh. Rolanda laughs.

"I knew it, because I *was* telling the truth," I remark.

"You *were* telling the truth," Rolanda adds.

"Yeah!"

The music turns sappy and inspirational.

"Hank, this is a really big day for you because you've been vindicated. What do you want to say to your parole officer?"

I look directly into the camera.

"You're a motherfucker!"

The director asks for a cleaner version.

"You're a small little Mr. Potato Head!" I say. "'Cuz I proved myself right!"

Rolanda lets out an over-the-top laugh. I look pissed.

"So now that you've been vindicated, that must be a really good feeling."

"Yeah, it feels good—really good," I mumble with a blank expression. I once again state, "It just proves I've been telling the truth the whole time."

The sappy music builds. Rolanda looks at the positive.

"The good thing is you had a bad experience, but you found some good in it!"

I expand on her theme, explaining how I turned everything around for the positive and flaunting my Jesus T-shirt.

"Hank, you're amazing!" she says, touching my arm. (I'm a story of hope and inspiration for Rolanda and others!)

"Anything else you want to say? This is your big day." Rolanda says with a warm, bonding smile. "You say whatever you want."

I break into a smile for the first time, looking directly into the camera. "I'm just saying, when it comes down to it, stick to your guns, and the lie detector doesn't lie."

There's mention of sending a copy of the show to my parole officer. Rolanda goes up for a high five.

"Give me some loving on that one, babe," she says.

"All right!" I say. We high-five.

"You've been vindicated," Rolanda says. "Thank you."

"No," I insist sincerely. "Thank *you*!"

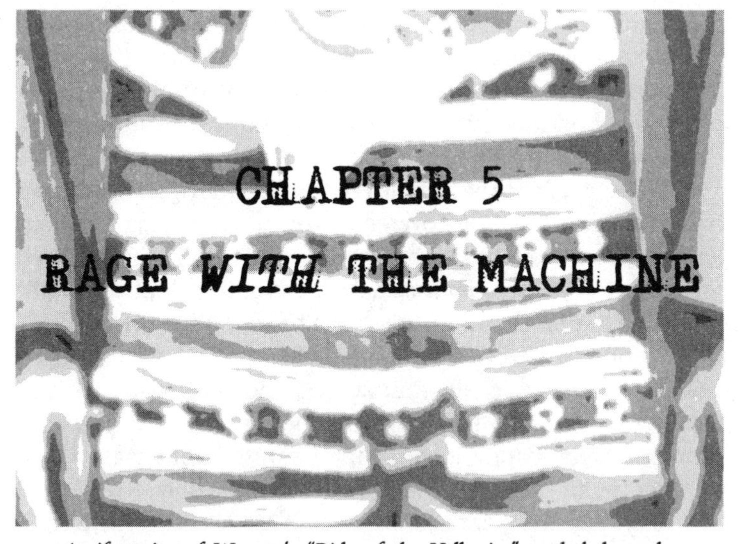

CHAPTER 5
RAGE WITH THE MACHINE

As if strains of Wagner's "Ride of the Valkyries" exploded on the landscape, suddenly a caravan of large vehicles swoop down upon a suburban home like military helicopters in a cloud of napalm. Emerging at once, roughly a dozen loud, rowdy skinheads, with that air of a long afternoon of drinking, pry themselves from the vehicles and fill the suburban yard. Yes, burly, heavily tattooed skinheads clad in bomber jackets blazoned with American and Confederate flags appear uniformly dressed, wearing jeans and laced shit-kicker boots. Here in the suburbs outside of Augusta, Georgia, I ponder what the hell I've gotten myself into and how will I be able to quickly escape.

In a city that hosts Fort Gordon—the largest training center for the US Army—it's not peculiar to see someone walking down the street sporting a jacket with the words "Kill 'Em All—Let God Sort Them Out" (without hipster irony, mind you). As businesses flash names like *Guns 'N Things* (selling both guns and ambiguous items), it makes sense that this is where I've come to cover the militant, patriotic, pro-war, right-wing skinhead scene. Once an arena for angry leftist punk idealism, the hard-core scene has taken a serious right twist and gone pro-war. Yes, it's time to salute a music genre where one can be very angry and aggressive about, not stopping war, but continuing it, as punks symbolically wave the flag and mosh to a three-chord thrash for George W. Bush.

It goes without saying that I'm heavily in disguise, with my hair in a bundle tightly covered by an American flag bandana and army-camouflage baseball cap, smartly hiding, what they would call, my true *commie* self. As the drunken skinheads walk toward me, I'm about to meet the band Nation of Suspects (NOS), not in a working-class neighborhood—which is traditional to skinhead ideals—but at their friend's house in a suburban subdivision with its preplanned streets and identical homes. They're happy to meet me because I told them I'm a reporter for an extreme right-wing music magazine.

How right-wing hard core is Nation of Suspects? The band's Web site posts photos of the band's NOS logo hand-scrawled on large bombs. Underneath a caption reads:

> Pictures provided by fans in Afghanistan. ". . . Their Nation Of Suspects bombs were dropped this morning on Taliban Forces setting up a mortar position. There was nothing left of the bastards but blood and guts stains. Another great day for their Jihad."

"We're relatively huge assholes," large skinhead and NOS front man Travis Lee greets me jokingly. Nation of Suspects, as it turns out, is actually the nicest right-wing, war-mongering skinhead band I've ever met. (Actually, they're the only ones I've ever really met. Good thing they don't know that I make my living satirizing conservatives.)

"We started the band to provide another perspective in the punk scene other than anti-war," adds Jim (who goes by "St. Pete's Jim") with a friendly smile, who seemed like someone you might buy insurance from, if he weren't a skinhead and was instead wearing a suit. He and Travis Lee (the John Lennon and Paul McCartney of patriotic right-wing skinhead hard core) formed NOS when they met at a junior college in St. Petersburg (Florida, not commie Russia), and, guess what? They've been *singing out for liberty and beer since 2000!* "It's fun, 'cuz there's a real reaction to the music," he mentions with a wide grin, regarding the whole patriotic angle in a relatively anti-Bush hard-core scene. NOS took its name from the book *Smoke and Mirrors*—a critical look at America's War on Drugs—which they say used the term *Society of Suspects*. "We thought that would be a little cliché, so we went with Nation of Suspects," recounts Jim. "Then, after 9/11, the name seemed to have gained even more importance."

How did the band's logo get plastered on bombs that later splattered the blood and guts? It turns out a friend's dad in the air force scrawled their NOS logo on the implement of destruction.

"How many bands can say that?" Jim boasts with pride. It's true. You don't see Jessica Simpson's name scrawled on any bombs dropped on the people of Iraq.

The band (including guitarist Austin and drummer Hari-Gari, who, strangely, is in a skinhead band but sports long hair) drove up for the gig late last night from the home base. "Tampa Bay is a right-wing stronghold. It's good for the scene."

Drunken shouts of "Oi!" (the skinhead battle cry) erupt from inside the house, and cans of Budweiser quickly fly open, as seven skinheads and I stand outside in the doorway, leaving me with an uneasy feeling. *What's wrong with this picture?*

"My theory is, if you don't remember it, it didn't happen!" blurts a skinhead staggering through, as I wonder how long is it going to take for me to get beaten up.

Nation of Suspects supports the war in Iraq. They also practice what they preach. After tonight's gig, NOS goes on hiatus because their large front man, Travis Lee, is reenlisting in the military, hoping to become an Army ranger in the Special Forces. Jim's taken the other route. Just graduating with a degree in political science, he aims to make the transition from right-wing skinhead band to working with the federal government in the Department of Homeland Security. (Great. And if he ends up reading this, I wonder whose phone calls will soon be wiretapped.)

"I've met several higher-ups in the military that are also skinheads. I've even met a drill sergeant for the USMC who is a skinhead," says another skinhead also named Travis (Travis II) who sports a prominent "Rock against Communism" badge. Not surprisingly, a good majority in the right-wing skinhead scene here have military backgrounds. It's not a huge stretch:

Military = shaved head, matching uniform
Skinhead = shaved head, matching uniform dress

Another similarity: they both KICK THE SHIT OUT OF THE ENEMY!

"I couldn't join the military due to a skinhead tattoo," Travis II professes with distaste, regarding an inked a pair of boots on his back. He adds with bitter sarcasm, "The USMC and Army are just *positive* they know what a skinhead means more than a skinhead does!" According to him, those ignorant of the subculture decipher the symbol to mean the notorious white power skinheads. Travis II claims that his faction, the American Skinhead Scene, is not racist—these skinheads just support the war, patriotism, and America! "I can never get into the military like I would have wanted to," he says with revulsion. A driving force behind the right-wing, patriotic skinhead scene, Travis II started American Defense Recordings, a label whose logo is a man rolling up his sleeves in front of the American flag. Besides Nation of Suspects, ADR (which sleeps near the enemy, based in ultra-liberal Athens) records other such patriotic, right-wing, hard-core bands as Lonesoldier, Working Class Soldiers, the Pillage, the Offensive, and Sons of Liberty, with a new compilation called *American Skinheads—Armed with the Truth!* The words on the back of his bomber jacket best sum up how croissant-eating, anti-Bush punks view his label: "American Defense Recordings—Hated and Proud!"

"We get a decent amount of orders from Iraq," Travis II declares as more beer is brought inside. (The five hundred pressings of the first *American Defense Recordings* EP—on red, white, and blue vinyl, of course—sold out.) Nation of Suspects also gets a hefty share of fan e-mails from soldiers in Iraq and soldiers' wives saying they're happy to see *music that supports the cause*, sharing things like, "It's good to see a band speaking what most service members feel."

The cover of a Nation of Suspects' single features the large words "Liberals Can Die!" Various images form a collage of leftist moonbat anti-war protestors who not only have the gall to mock patriotism and the mighty stars and stripes but, worse, seem to embrace those beret-wearing French. The other side has a shot of NOS standing in front of an Army tank. On the inside foldout of Old Glory are the strong words "WARNING: THIS AMERICAN FLAG LET *NO ONE* DARE BURN/U.S. SKINHEADS *DEFEND* YOUR FLAG AND COUNTRY!"

"In the skinhead scene there's an increase of right-wing bands in the US," Travis II says, as little kids frolic gleefully in nearby yards (dreaming of the day when they, too, will be old enough to mosh for their country). "So many bands that are patriots—US bands—haven't an outlet for putting stuff out."

"Once the 9/11 thing happened, that's when it really blew up," Jim adds, as the sound of glass breaking from inside the house punctuates his thoughts.

"I think kids are getting sick of having to go to school and work, and getting shit if they love their country," Travis II spews with disgust, as murmurs of agreement ignite from the rest of the crew. "The skinhead scene is good for that."

Since Southern skinhead bands are considered more militant, political, and right-wing, they feel they are unfairly treated when they try to play on the granola-eating left coast. Bands like Nobody's Fools (they're about *"drinkin', fightin', nationalism, and everything that makes you liberals squirm"*) often evoke conflict when they perform such songs as "Bomb the Taliban." Drinking beer in a circle, the skinheads all jump in with their opinion on this.

"People come there to shut it down or fight at the show!"

"We get labeled racist!"

"They're not allowed to play shows 'cuz people think they're Nazis!" spits a really angered little skinhead—once a ranger in Iraq who was discharged from the Army two years before, with 100 percent disability, when an RPG exploded and "messed up his brain," as he calls it. Now he lends a hand with the promotion of ADR records. "Intense" would be one way to describe him. "The people beating them up say they are anti-fascist, but they're the ones being fascist by shutting down the show." In Iraq the little skinhead's time wasn't spent rapping and lounging around Uday Hussein's pleasure palace pool, as shown in the documentary *Gunner's Palace*. "We didn't have time for that," he snaps with piercing stare. "We were too busy kicking in doors, shooting people in the face!"

I vigorously nod my head and sip my beer, not wanting either my door kicked in or my face shot.

To combat Nazi mistaken identity, the American skinheads formed their own scene (though a lot of venues get shut down). Skinhead Mike, a stocky guy with a large neck tattoo, recently promoted the Texas Oi Punk Festival in Corpus Christi, drawing a thousand attendees.

"It was the first show where we hung up the American flag behind our merchandise table and got applause," Jim remarks.

The festival went smoothly, except for one incident.

"This punk got up onstage and tried to stop the show," skinhead Mike recalls, explaining that the liberal punk started yelling, "You guys think you're tough 'cuz you're skinheads!" The situation was corrected by hitting him in the head.

"How did this happen?" I ask, pointing to the cover of NOS's vinyl single *Wages of War*, which shows front man Travis Lee; he, too, has a large wound on his head, blood dripping down his face.

"Somebody hit him in the head with an asp," replies the intense little skinhead.

"What's an asp?" I ask.

Mr. Kicking-In-Doors-Shooting-People-In-The-Face whips out a small black baton from his pocket and methodically demonstrates its proficiency. I ponder whether my turn will be next.

Take the Skinheads to Wal-Mart

Trudging through the parking lot of Wal-Mart—an all-American Wal-Mart —we're here to run a few errands before tonight's hard-core show. (St. Pete's Jim professes an affinity for Wal-Mart's argyle sweaters.) Most important, they want to get skinhead haircuts before the gig (leaving Hari-Gari behind, of course).

"Those guys back at the house from American Defense Recordings are more militant in their views. They're more anti-liberal," Jim clarifies, trying to distance his band from the kicking-in-doors-shooting-people-in-the-face crowd, as we past a Vision Center outlet. "They're more rough around the edges."

"Wearing anti-Communist badges in 2006 is pretty weird," Travis Lee adds with a laugh, as guitarist Austin is propped into a barber chair for a pre-show skinhead coif ($12.50 razor cuts), alongside big, puffy-haired Georgia housewives at Smart Style Family Hair Salon. (Yes, but who are the ones that are influencing them?)

Jim, a traditional conservative before attending university, says his views have softened after getting his poli-sci degree. "You learn how the world works and why, and you can't do that if you stick to one ideology," he explains as a large woman maneuvers a razor across Austin's head. Jim would even go so far as to describe his wife as a *borderline socialist*. "It's tough because she tries to like the band. I tease her and call her an 'American-hater.'" One rule to keep domestic bliss: "We don't talk about politics!"

As Travis Lee gets into the barber's chair, about to get a buzz cut similar to what he'll receive when reenlisting in the Army, Jim adds, "The biggest split in the hard-core scene though was with the Iraq war. We were very adamant in supporting it." The most overtly political statement at NOS gigs, he says, is a large American flag hung behind them on the wall. "We don't come off as preaching this or that; we come off as having a really good time."

The few tree-hugging liberals who show up at NOS gigs because they enjoy the music often have a drastic change of heart later on. "They read our lyrics and say, 'We don't like that!'" One song that might turn off the leftist, dread-locked, hacky-sack crowd would be, of course, their very subtly titled anthem "Liberals Can Die":

> Liberals can die!
> With filth and the slime
> Exploiting impressionable minds . . .
> Liberals can die!

"That song was written as a joke, to give the liberals a little joust," says Jim, as the puffy-haired beautician at the Smart Family Hair Salon razors the last remaining trace of Travis Lee's hair. "It almost feels like sometimes you created a monster."

Some of the monsters created are the rumors that pop up about the band.

Rumor #1: They're Nazis.

Rumor #2: Lead singer Travis Lee once punched a child.

Rumor #3: Lead singer Travis Lee once threw a flaming piece of wood through a liberal's window.

"People come to our shows and expect that. One guy at one of our shows, he was almost crying about it." As Jim tells it, the conservative punk, who saw NOS hanging out afterwards with some left-leaning friends, whimpered with extreme hurt, "I thought you said you were right-wing, and here you are hanging out with liberals!'"

The Love of Bush, Country, and Oi!

"Oi! Oi! Oi!" screams a girth-y skinhead with large mutton-chops, while a new goofy guy in a "Hate" T-shirt stumbles about, bumping into furniture. The suburban house is a much drunker atmosphere upon our return from Wal-Mart.

"You came all the way out here to cover a band of dumbasses!" questions a skinhead wearing a Brassknuckle Boys T-shirt, as we now stand in the garage by a keg of PBR and an accessible beer bong shaped like a skull. "There's dumbasses in every town."

"So, what's your angle?" says Skinhead Mike, who sports the neck tattoo and gets a little confrontational, claiming the media always tries to portray skinheads as racist rednecks. "They always try and put a horrible twist on it. It's all about standing up with what you believe in. They just try to spin it."

I nod my head as we're interrupted by a drunken Hari-Gari, who, with a big smile on his face, blurts to the only black skinhead at the party, "I don't like most black people. But I like you."

The black skinhead replies, "That's OK, I don't like most black people either."

Hari-Gari, not really helping Mike's argument, swills his beer, then slurs to his large front man, "Hey, Travis, I'm still drinking. We're going to suck tonight!"

"You're going to suck tonight," he clarifies.

"Travis, when he's not drunk, he sucks ass!"

"That's his last beer or else Mike will choke you out!"

"We should start a fight tonight," a friend chirps in, madly grinning like Private Lynndie England pointing at a pyramid of Iraqi prisoners.

The little drunk guy with the "Hate" T-shirt whips out a butterfly knife for my benefit. "I carry it around just to look menacing," he clarifies with a big belligerent laugh.

"Mike, where's your brass knuckles?" asks Muttonchops. "He's got the gold-plated knuckles!"

"Fuck that," shouts Hari-Gari, slamming down another beer.

To rally the troops, the little drunk guy in the "Hate" T-shirt starts screaming, "Crispy critters! Crispy critters!" (A cute nickname given by soldiers to badly burned corpses cooked to near cremation.)

"You got to check out the ZOG meter," someone else shouts. Not wanting to be like other members of the media who spin skinhead stories, I try to ignore hearing the term that refers to Zionist Occupied Government.

"We're really political, but we don't give a rat's ass," Muttonchops says as we finish the last of the beer in the kitchen. "But if you get political, then we *throw down*!"

"The main objective of any skinhead is to protect the values and things they hold dear and to defend it against anything they see as a threat," ADR's Travis explains. "We see the anti-American extreme Left as a threat to everything we hold dear and work for. That's what American Defense Recordings is all about."

"A left-wing band is on the bill tonight, but they are pretty passive," a skinhead remarks, as the member of the liberal Skuds, looking out of place with his overly pierced and tattooed gutter-punk look, proclaims he doesn't discuss politics with his right-wing skinhead friends. The reason? "I got a big mouth."

"I almost got fired from my fucking job for wearing an American flag." Travis II spews with distaste about an incident at a bar in Athens (a town he insists turns people into hippies or junkies). He says "leftists" (or "commies," as they're affectionately called) put up flyers announcing a boycott of the bar they work at because they wear American flags and military pants.

"We need to get the fascists out of Athens—all four of you," his skinhead friend pipes in, mocking their liberal antics for victimizing them for simply being patriotic.

"Bands come in from out of town and say, 'I know we're in the South and everything, but do you have to have guys like that to work the door?'" Travis II says, as the little guy in the "Hate" T-shirt now sways drunk, ends up passing out, but still stands up against the stove. "People come up to us and say, 'Who do you hate? Do you hate me because I'm Catholic?'" he says. "They just want to be a hard-ass in front of their friends."

The Athens skinheads then respond with the cunning: "'Bye, rich kid!" or "When you get out of college, why don't you get a fucking job!" Yeah! "All they are is rich kids whose parents have been paying for college." (Aren't conservatives the ones with all the money?)

"You can't do nothing in Athens to start a fight," a skinhead by the refrigerator remarks with a laugh.

Muttonchops recalls one time when he and his friends saw these two drunken guys pathetically crawling on the ground, yelled, "Hey, fags!" and walked away. "You had to see it," he says in order to understand the context. In his *Rashomon* tale, his skinhead friend, being the good Samaritan that he is, thought they needed help, went back over, and said, "'Are you guys all right?' Believe or not, the bastard threw a punch." So what did Muttonchops and company do? "We kicked the shit of them!"

RAISE THE FLAG

For tonight's right-wing skinhead gig, I contemplate changing into a "Bush Lied" T-shirt with my dreadlocks flying like Bob Marley's, while playing hacky sack in the mosh pit in order to see how quickly a brass-knuckled fist would be thrown in my general direction. Instead, I decide to highly humor the band by wearing their Nation of Suspects T-shirt, plastered with tanks, bomber planes, and the American eagle. (I do want to make it through the night without getting beaten up.) Following a truck with back window stickers promoting the merits of "Black Flag," "Oi!" "George W '04," as well as the American flag, we're led to Sector 7G, a small, converted concrete building that reads "Dry Cleaning Laundry." Inside is a little hole-in-the wall venue, filled with the energy of skinheads who've been drinking all day—in short, pumped-up testosterone. Drunken "Oi! Oi! Oi!" shouts fire continuously from the crowd that is almost entirely male. (There're very few, as they say in Army terms, "Suzy Rottencrotches.")

"You got to fight somebody," remarks a girth-y skinhead who holds up a camera, almost saying so for my benefit. "I'm going to get it right here."

"I'm incredibly drunk! I'm bouncing off the walls!" blurts a skinhead in a "Face the Aggression" T-shirt, as Nation of Suspects storms the stage, ready to lead the troops to battle. Wearing a German soccer sweat jacket, the normally soft-spoken Travis Lee unleashes an artillery blitzkrieg like a man possessed, an animal stalking his cage, wrapping the mike wire around his forearm. With that rapid hard-core vocal style that sounds not unlike wild wolves growling mixed with shells being emptied from an AK-47, NOS erupts into their first song, "Wages of War." Large, burly skinheads throw each other around with the impact of Scud missiles hitting a mosque, while a girth-y skinhead disturbingly shows some butt crack.

> Peace will come through mass destruction.
> You're dead next in World War III . . .
> Peace will only come through mass extinction.
> You can't escape World War III.

"I need a beer," the girth-y skinhead rants after accidentally spilling on himself then slamming into three twelve-year-olds on the peripheral, knocking over the liberal punk band's cymbals set against the wall. The liberal punk, like the liberal he is, tries to break things up when the swinging arms and slamming get too rough.

"Nation of Shit!" someone playfully screams.

After "Fight for the Right" (by no means is it the *right* "to party"), glossy-eyed Hari-Gari, suddenly and unexpectedly, falls off his stool behind his drum kit, landing like a bomb over Baghdad with a mighty *thud*. Who would have thought he'd be too drunk for the show? He remains unmoved for several minutes as the pro-war hard core comes to a standstill. Has Hari-Gari passed out?

"C'mon, Hari-Gari!" skinheads shout. "You shouldn't've went to the bar drinking a hurricane!"

The other Nation of Suspects members tenderly hover over their war casualty—motionless Hari-Gari. It's taking a long time for him to recover. After several minutes, Hari-Gari methodically makes his way back up to his stool, slowly rising, like an American flag over a used-car lot on the Fourth of July. The look in his eyes is lost, like one who could either vomit or pass out; those are the options—passing out or vomiting. With Hari-Gari back in the game, they kick into "Liberals Can Die."

"I just want to hurt people," screams the girth-y skinhead wearing a "No Holds Barred" T-shirt. Arms around each other, ten skinheads pump their fists in the air, as Muttonchops gets his friend in a headlock, giving him a more brutal punishment than a detainee in Abu Ghraib prison. One of the skins shrieks, "Yeah! They must die!"

Travis Lee suddenly grabs Hari-Gari's drumsticks and contorts his face like he's looking at the American Taliban on a gurney. "You're starting to piss people off!" he screams. Once again he instigates a slamming artillery attack by hitting himself in the head with the microphone, then punching the wall, firing back with "America 2/Iraq 0":

Beat 'em till they couldn't take no more.
Blood and teeth splattered on the floor.
Meanwhile, on our nation's soil,
The sheep cried, "No blood for oil."

The patriotic testosterone continues to pump hard as the drunken skinheads swing their friends around. The occasional two skingirls come out and do a cuter, feminine version of the slamming skinhead dance. "Know what, fuck off," the girth-y skinhead yells with the same fervor as if screaming at Cindy "bin" Sheehan, accidentally, again, spilling beer on his belly.

Just get out of bed with Saddam.
Just admit humbly you are wrong.
Empty protests won't change a thing.
But this strong nation will always win.

A fight breaks out with a large (in a baby-fat sort-of-way) redheaded guy wearing a green-hooded Guinness sweatshirt. I'm told this skinhead wanna-be tries to be part of the scene but just doesn't get it right. Travis Lee hurls his intimidating frame in front of him, not to head-butt the large (in a big baby sort-of-way) redhead guy but to spare him from being torn to shreds by the pack of hairless wolves and their *weapons of mass destruction*: butterfly knives, asps, and gold-plated brass-knuckles.

"Where's the bloodshed?!" Travis Lee screams after the incident, throwing his beer against the wall. The soon-to-be Army soldier then bites a can of beer in half, spitting foam everywhere.

Bloodshed on American Soil

"How did you do that?" I say to Travis Lee in the parking lot after the gig, noting blood smeared all over his face and flowing from his hand, forming a dark puddle at his feet.

"I have no idea," he replies, perplexed, glancing at the big wad of bloody tissue wrapped around his hand, as the blood continues to flow.

"You should check out the stage," Austin exclaims with a giddy tone. "There's blood all over the place!"

"I was expecting to punch through the walls and shit," Travis Lee admits, making an unhappy face, quickly learning that the walls of the old laundry were concrete. Theories abound; the group concludes that Travis Lee cut his hand open on an aluminum beer can.

"Do you need stitches?" I ask as life juice voluminously flows from the open wound.

"Probably."

A skinhead brother offers, "Do like the illegals do and just show up and get treated."

"I broke my hand," pipes in the intense skinhead Iraqi vet. Sure enough, his knuckle juts out like there's a small melon underneath the skin. "I break my hand a lot," he professes with enthusiastic pride on his battle trophy.

Suddenly, like Saddam Hussein being chased out of a spider hole, the large (but in a baby-fat sort-of-way) redhaired guy comes storming out of Sector 7G. A contingent of angry skinheads shouting abuse follows. The large baby-fat guy goes to his truck and opens it. He reaches in the trunk and pulls out a chainsaw. Those of us outside take a few moments to stare at each other, registering what we're seeing. The large guy, making angry grunting noises, revs up the chainsaw (this goes in the "I've never seen that before" column) in order to ward off the skinhead attack. Skinhead Mike, with his brass knuckles out, is held back.

Putting down the chainsaw, the large baby-fat guy grabs a long pipe. We stand there slack-jawed, watching the redhaired guy as he starts beating a parking sign. (He must not like the parking sign.) He then gets into his car, spins a donut in the parking lot, and speeds off as verbal taunts and garbage are thrown in his direction. After once around the block, here he comes again! What will it be this time? Mowing down the crowd, taking everyone out in retaliation like a suicide bomber in an open marketplace? Will he use other tree and shrub landscaping implements? Then, he comes around the block *yet* again! On the case, blurry-eyed Hari-Gari, awakening from his drunken stupor, reappears—this time brandishing a wooden ax handle.

"We wanted to replace the blood and shit and ridiculousness with the music-manship. This is the result of what happens!" Travis Lee holds up his bloody mess of a hand. "We practiced for this," he solemnly declares, still dripping the red—of red, white, and blue—down his arm.

Let's Toast to the Stars and Stripes

Like a platoon that's just stormed Fallujah, afterwards the skinheads storm a local hipster bar. Regardless of different political ideologies, I have to say, this is the safest I ever felt at a bar. (Good thing they think I'm on their side.) Patrons seem to clear a path for us, while the drunken revelry increases (This is what it must feel like to have a really big boyfriend.)

"I break my hand a lot," the intense Iraq skinhead vet again confirms. As we sit at the bar, he reflects on his time in Iraq. "You're not fighting for the war—you're fighting for your friends." I'm sure he applies these sentiments learned in Iraq back home with the pointless violence cherished among his skinhead friends.

The intense skinhead vet, slamming his cocktail, vents about liberals who criticize their music scene with anti-war sentiments. "They start trouble at shows," he grunts. "I'm fucking disabled for my country. I'm fucking fighting for my country, and you're telling me how worthless my country is?"

"We'd sell more T-shirts to liberals if we didn't have that," he says pointing to their slogan "Fight for the Right." He then gestures at the Blue-Eyed Devils sweatshirt worn by the intense skinhead Iraq vet. "The SHARPS [Skinheads Against Racial Prejudice] would beat someone up if they saw them wearing that."

"They're pretty white power," the intense skinhead justifies his Blue Eye Devil love, "but I just like the music." Sure, why can't one simply like a band and overlook such lyrics as:

Kill the Jew and cut off his head.
Destroy the enemy and his lies.
Send the filth to an early demise.

"When you first contacted us, I researched your e-mail address," the intense skinhead vet, Mr. Kicking-In-Doors-Shooting-People-In-The-Face, says with clenched teeth, leaning in closer with piercing, forceful kicking-in-doors-shooting-people-in-the-face stare. "I didn't know if you were part of the communist conspiracy!"

I sip despondently at my drink, wishing I were back in the land of puppies and ice cream. For some reason, the intense skinhead now occasionally screams, "Liberal Zionist Media." (Perhaps "Liberal Zionist Media" is the name of another white power band that is liked strictly for their music?)

Feeling the sloppy effects of too much beer—American beer—I abruptly move to talk to one of the skingirls. Another skinhead delightfully retells a *funny* tale about smashing a guy in the face with a cinder block for hitting on someone's girlfriend. ("His skin was rolling right off his face.") I figure it's well past time to hit the road. I'd hate if my conversation got misconstrued and the story ended with my getting the old cinder-block treatment. All and all, just a typical day when you *rage with the machine*!

CHAPTER 6
HOW TO GET POOR QUICK

It seems the American dream is to get rich quick. Hell, that's my dream—to be richer than an Enron executive or at least in the same financial category as an overpaid Halliburton contractor. Then maybe I'll get some of those much-talked-about Bush tax breaks.

We've all seen these ads in magazines, in newspapers, and on the Internet to get rich quick. But who takes them seriously? Maybe I do! It's my turn to get rich quick. How hard can it be? There are hundreds of these ads. Just think of it—this could be my ticket to escaping the nine-to-five wage-slave routine. I could join the elite of the Red State brigade and be invited for barbecue beef with Daddy Bush and Barbara!

A new life awaits me. I'll work at home, never get out of bed, and earn thousands each week in my spare time. Who actually wants to work for a living anyway? I want the easy way out. You might be skeptical. That's OK, so was I (chuckle). But even if only one of these ads we see is the real thing, that's fine. I'm not greedy. I only need to make one million dollars. I'd even contribute money to the Republican Party. So that's why I've checked out a few entrepreneurial companies.

Home Assembly

Assembling craft products at home is my first attempt at financial freedom and joining the elite. An ad in the back of a weekly paper says, "WORK AT HOME. Great Extra Income Idea! Assemble Products For Best Companies!" I call the 800 number and order the $40.99 booklet. Two weeks later, a large envelope arrives emblazoned with the words "Work at Home Directory." It also has a picture of a mom and a child sitting at a kitchen table. This kind of scenario must often occur when one "works at home." I wonder about child labor laws.

Inside the envelope is a small booklet called "Home-Based Income Opportunities." On the cover are pictures of an elderly couple hugging, a family on a picnic, a young couple laughing, and a man talking on the phone and holding a baby. Again, situations that were not possible before there were "Home-Based Income Opportunities."

Inside the booklet is a cavalcade of shit—shit that needs to be assembled. Adorable teddy-bear doorknob covers. Poorly designed stuffed lambs, dinosaurs, and rabbits. Baby bonnets. There's one curious item called "Dough Darlings"—create beautiful dough art in the comfort of your own home. Basically, it's dolls made out of dough. This craft is light years ahead of its time. At least it's putting Americans to work and not sending jobs overseas! At least now I'll become rich!

Hmmm, a few minor things are not mentioned in the literature. Almost all "assemble at home" projects require sewing skills. Not only sewing skills, but also a *sewing machine*. If you have neither, nearly 95 percent of the "assemble at home" jobs can't be done. And all assembly projects require a one-time starter-kit fee, which ranges from twenty-five to fifty bucks. And a "refundable" deposit is required for supplies, which can run up to a hundred dollars.

Not mentioning these factors is like not mentioning that you have to assemble the products naked, in a cage, covered in your own excrement. But I'm not going to let this prevent me from talking on the phone while holding a baby. I see big, BIG bucks on the horizon. I choose the craft-assembly project called "Angelic Creations." It involves "producing upper-scale country angels." This is much more prestigious than producing lower-scale country angels or down-and-out urban angels.

But the photo in the booklet shows something resembling a blob of fabric with wings. "No experience required." Great! Angelic Creations is how I'm going to make my first million!

I send a check for $34.95 to some place in Michigan. A few weeks later, I receive the ticket to my home-assembly fortune. I open the packet. There's a queer/creepy doll inside. It's a bunch of muslin cloth resembling a winged angel holding some sort of moss wreath. It looks like it might have cost eighty cents to make. It would be ideal for dusting. It's disturbing! The angel has no face. It's the kind of thing nightmares are made of!

The only other item in the packet is one page of instructions. "Please keep these angels away from children. They are not toys." Among other things, I'm told that I need to purchase more materials for constructing my own "upper-scale country angels" directly from the Angelic Creations company for an *additional sixteen dollars*. Glue is not included. Not to be discouraged from my millionaire path, I send in the additional check.

Once I receive those materials, I'll have enough stuff to construct five faceless angels. If my five angels are up to "upper-scale country angel" standards, the company will send me a check for twenty-five dollars. However, if Angelic Creations rejects them, I must pay three dollars to have the angels returned. The number of assembly orders is based on demand. But who would demand a creepy faceless angel? Only Satan himself!

Wanting to find out exactly what I paid for, I call the Angelic Creations home office. A woman who sounds like she's wearing a hand-sewn bonnet answers the phone. I say to her, "I recently paid $34.95 and received a package containing an angel and one page of instructions. I was wondering what my $34.95 went towards?"

"That is what you get. You're registered with the company and you get a sample angel and instructions."

"But how come there isn't any material to make the angels?"

"You can get supplies from us."

"But I don't understand what I'm getting for the money," I frown, looking at the sad pile of angelic rags.

Pause. "It's a one-time registration fee of $34.95. Then a sixteen-dollar deposit for supplies for five angels."

I could easily make this woman cry by criticizing her upper-scale country angels. Instead I order the materials. I will give this an earnest, sincere effort! I shall be the best!

Three weeks later a box arrives with the material to assemble five creepy angels. The woman in the hypothetical bonnet has told me that assembling each individual angel should take me about twenty minutes—once I get the hang of it. With the $34.95 sample angel propped up on the table beside me for inspiration, I consult the instructions:

> Step 1: Cut the selvage off the fabric. [OK, I'm already lost. What's "selvage"? Hoping this isn't important, I move on.]
>
> Step 2: Put batting into square of muslin. [What the *hell* is "batting"?]

The instructions keep referring to the angel as "her." This choice of female possessive bugs the shit out of me. My glue is spilling everywhere. The angel's arms fall off when touched. I improvise with a stapler to keep things in place. The flowers won't stick. I yell "Fuck!" often. Then it hits me! They have purposely made this hard so they don't have to pay me. The moss sticks to my glue-stained fingers like newly sprouted hair. There's braiding involved. How the fuck should I know how to braid! AAAARGH!

Three hours later, I finish assembling one creepy angel that looks like a rotting corpse. Only two hours and forty minutes longer than the bonnet woman said it should take. If the company accepts my beauty-challenged angel—which is doubtful—I will have pulled in $1.25 an hour. Three-quarters of the material is already used up. My creepy angel looks like the short bus–

riding little brother of the $34.95 sample. Glue stains the fabric. Parts are falling off. Things are uneven. My angel looks like "she" spent the night with the Hell's Angels. At least the thing will come in handy for wiping the mess off my table. I send everything back with a note saying, "Dear Smelly Angelic Bastards, Your dolls are the work of the devil. I quit!"

CHAIN LETTERS

I have not given up my dream of rubbing elbows with the Trumps over cocktails at the Trump Plaza. As I sit with my head in my hands, a thought occurs to me. What could be easier than making money through an elaborate chain letter? This has always been my secret wish. In the past, I've treated these letters as annoying spam e-mails when I should have been treating them as a *once-in-a-lifetime entrepreneurial opportunities.* It's time to take action!

One day I receive an e-mail from a gentleman—a rich gentleman—who claims he made $868,439 by sending a chain letter to two hundred people. Although he was earning a good living as a lawyer, he's since retired from his practice, and he spends his days playing golf. That, my friend, is the life *I'm* looking for. Cocktails at 4! Maybe? Accompanying his e-mail is a list of seven names with snail-mail addresses. If I want to cash in, I must send one dollar to each person on the list. My name then moves to seventh position and the first name is removed. Next, I have to copy the lawyer's e-mail and send it out. Sure, it's a pyramid scheme, but that doesn't mean I can't become as disgustingly rich as the lawyer. This is ridiculously easy—no muslin! no braiding!—and I vow to be the best chain-letter writer ever! I contact a bulk e-mail company, which also advertises via e-mail, and pay eighty-nine dollars to have them e-mail my letter to 150,000 people!

Maybe I'll become one of the richest people on the planet (right up there with the woman who invented Wite-Out!). One week later, I receive an e-mail from one of the people on the list: "Thank you very much for the dollar, please follow exactly as the letter tells you to do, IT REALLY WORKS . . . it will be slow at the beginning, but the post office will call for you to pick up the mail, because it is a lot . . . Thank you, GOD BLESS."

From the 150,000 e-mails I sent, I need only ninety-six responses—a return rate of less than 1 percent—to break even. I sit back and wait for the post office to call and ask me to pick up all my individual one-dollar bills.

Strangely, the call doesn't come. Weeks go by, and still nothing. Finally, I receive a letter from Pensacola, Florida. It's written in a grandmother's handwriting by someone who refers to herself as "Mrs. Hardy." There's a dollar bill inside. Out of 150,000 messages, only one response. That's it! I guess it's not the quantity but the quality. I'm sure she's a lovely person. This hasn't been a total loss. I am one dollar richer—despite the fact that I'm still ninety-five dollars in the hole.

Stuffing Envelopes

Maybe that didn't work out. Perhaps I've set the bar too high? I come across a flyer in a coffee shop: "Would you like to earn some GOOD MONEY to catch up on all your bills and be able to get through this year without going into debt?" Stuffing envelopes is a good, honest way to make a living, and better yet: "Earn $2,500 weekly *or more* stuffing envelopes at home!!! Honest home workers urgently needed."

All I need to do is send thirty-nine bucks. And there's no scam this time because there's a "REFUNDABLE DEPOSIT." The fee will be returned once I stuff my first 250 envelopes. Sounds completely fair! I'll earn two dollars per envelope stuffed. No supplies to buy, no sewing involved, no pyramid scheme—just good old-fashioned stuffing! (I'm overjoyed that I'm now on a mailing list and get ten such "opportunities" per day.)

Maybe the risk of paper cuts is high, but that's an occupational hazard when you work as an envelope-stuffing professional. Hell, how hard can it be? I've done this activity all my life. I'll be a rich man in no time—perhaps one of the richest!

Hello, Republican National Convention! And, just in case I'm dumber than a bag of mud, they do the math for me: "Stuff 250 envelopes and get paid $500. Stuff 500 envelopes and get paid $1,000. Stuff 1,000 envelopes and get paid $2,000. . . ." The best part is, "no previous experience stuffing envelopes is needed!" I'm already ahead of the game.

Simpletons are given practical advice on what they can do with their earnings: "When the check arrives each week, you can cash it and do whatever you want with the money, pay bills, make your car payments, go shopping, or even take a vacation. The money is yours to spend any way you want." Their target audience must be people who not only have trouble paying their bills but also need guidance on how to spend money. Why do I need them to tell me how to spend my new riches?!

I receive a small packet from Fort Lauderdale, Florida. Fort Lauderdale is to envelope stuffing what Ohio is to serial killers. Inside is a note that says, "Welcome Aboard!!! We're excited that you've taken the first step towards financial security by becoming an *Independent Home-Based Processor*." So that's what I am, an *Independent Home-Based Processor!* I thought I was merely an envelope stuffer! That'll look good on a resume (though I won't need a job after this) or sound impressive when I mention it down at the country club. There's also a "Certificate of Registration." I'll mount it on the wall so I can feel job pride in my new vocation! I will be my own boss! I'll be able to take vacations when I want and not worry about hiring babysitters or spending money on work clothes. All this from stuffing damn envelopes!

The packet contains twenty yellow flyers: "ATTENTION WORK-AT-HOME!!! Are you tired of living from paycheck to paycheck? Are you interested in Working At Home? In these financially stressful times, everybody is looking for a way to change their lives for the better. We can show you how!!!"

Hold on, Bubba! I'm supposed to strategically place these "highly effective" flyers around town? Huh? I thought the job was stuffing and licking—that's all. Now I'm supposed to sell other people on "being their own boss"? That wasn't in the contract, and, anyway, isn't that what *I'm* supposed to be doing?

Apparently, those interested in being their own boss will be sending me self-addressed stamped envelopes. Once the hordes of inquisitive work-at-home enthusiasts have bombarded my mailbox, my job is to "stuff" their envelopes with blue flyers advertising a thirty-nine-dollar directory called *Discovering Financial Freedom at Home*, which lists such opportunities as stuffing envelopes. It's only offered for a "limited time" at 25 percent off the regular price of fifty-two dollars. The stuffing company is clearly looking out for our best interests!

I place the twenty yellow flyers on bulletin boards next to others ads for things like yoga classes, diet secrets, and dog-walking services. The company suggests hanging flyers at gas stations, bowling alleys, car washes, motels, and RV campsites. These must be the haunts of the envelope-stuffing target audience.

"You would be amazed," the literature says, "at how some people use every imaginable trick in the book and send us envelopes with names and addresses taken right out of THE TELEPHONE BOOK!" Well, there goes that idea.

After one month, I find that I'm $2,496 short of my initial projected earnings. I receive only two self-addressed stamped envelopes. This yields me a four-dollar paycheck. One envelope is from myself. The other is from a man named Adamid Montanez. He writes, "I'm interested in working. Please if you help me. I need to work fast please." Adamid's note makes me feel really bad. What if this poor, desperate man spends his last thirty-nine dollars on a crappy list of sleaze merchants who'll ask for another thirty-nine dollars for materials to sew creepy angel dolls? The whole thing is a sad reflection of a desperate society.

I write a note on the back of a flyer: "Dear Adamid, By no means send $39. Again, Adamid, DO NOT SEND $39!!!"

I've had enough! Yet I'm in the hole—far, far from being vaguely rich. So what am I going to do? I'm going to take all the tricks I've learned and devise my own get-rich-quick scam: EARN $2,900 A WEEK TURNING DOORKNOBS!

Yes, that's right! We'll pay you $2,900 or more per week simply for TURNING DOORKNOBS for our company! The more doorknobs you turn, the more money you make! You'll be your own boss, set your own hours, and receive two dollars for every doorknob you turn!

If you turn 100 doorknobs, you get $200.

If you turn 500 doorknobs, you get $1,000.

If you turn 1,000 doorknobs, you get $2,000.

It's up to you how many doorknobs you turn! In these financially stressful times, everybody is looking for a way to change their lives for the better. We can show you how simply by TURNING DOORKNOBS! The secret to this revolutionary new doorknob-turning process can be yours for $39.95. The demand is so great that we are unable to fill all our doorknob-turning orders. That's why we're recruiting doorknob turners in your area. Complete money-back guarantee after turning fifty doorknobs!

My goal: Due to the current job-market crisis, I try to land a job using fake resumes. I am surreptitiously checking the quality of various companies' hiring systems. Given the few jobs that are available, what is the state of American business in making a hiring decision? I also plan to steal pens during each interview!

Preparation:

- 1 stack of fake resumes
- 1 white shirt
- 1 tie
- 1 pseudonym—Willis Drummond (from *Diff'rent Strokes*)
- 1 firm handshake (crucial for the interview process)
- 1 strong eye-contact ability (also crucial for the interview process)
- 1 minty-fresh breath!

Interview #1: The "Flaky-Guy" Resume

Job applying for: Management position for sports promotion company

Resume lies: All jobs last no longer than two months. One job begins and ends in the same month. My education background lists six different colleges in three years. There's also a mysterious five-year gap in between one job position.

I'm wearing a tie. People respect you if you wear a tie. It puts you in the category of "tie wearers." This is the perfect interview "costume." I walk into a sterile office with a loud radio playing bland top-forty music. This is the kind of working atmosphere that drives people to drink. The reception area is filled with nervous job applicants, all dressed similarly. Immediately, I steal a pen.

In groups of three, we are brought in for an interview. I wait for my fake name to be called. A perky woman leads a well-dressed man, a well-dressed woman, and me into a private office. The perky woman gives us the spiel. The position is a five-level managerial training program that promotes ski areas in Lake Tahoe. My mastery powers of strong and direct eye contact are utilized, occasionally with an attentive nod.

"The key to this job is being a 'people-person.' The kind of people we hire are the types who were class clowns and maybe a little cocky! How do you rate yourself as a 'people-person' on a scale of 1 to 10? Don't be modest."

The question is thrown at the well-dressed man. He answers with a modest 8. Then the well-dressed woman answers with a 10. No modesty here! The perky woman looks at their resumes, asking various questions about their work history.

"Willis, how do you rate yourself as a 'people-person'?"

I pause for dramatic effect. "Does the scale go higher than 10?" I let out the loud laugh of a casino pit boss. Can I push her buttons or what?! She eyeballs my resume.

"You sure worked many jobs in the last few months."

"Yeah, I like to jump around. It keeps things exciting." I

momentarily get serious and utilize my direct eye-contact skills. "I'm trying to find the right job, which I hope this will be, where I'll enjoy going to every day. A place where I get to work with people!"

This answer pleases her. She goes back to my resume.

"And what did you study in school, Willis?"

"I switched around *a lot*! I started in chemistry and ended up in history."

The perky woman wraps up the interview. First, she dismisses the well-dressed man, hinting at a prospect of being in touch. Then she does the same for the well-dressed woman. The perky woman waits till they both leave and leans forward in her chair.

"Willis, I like your attitude! I want to book you in for tomorrow! That way you can see the daily operation and decide if the job is right for you. Be here tomorrow morning at nine. Wear a shirt and tie!"

Conclusion: Well, fuck me sideways! My flaky resume got me hired! Being a master of direct, attentive eye contact must do the trick when a job requires being a "cocky people person." Maybe she thought I was a "class-clown" type, seeing that my resume was a joke! Unfortunately, the next morning, when the perky woman calls to see why Willis didn't show up for work, I tell her that he had left the country.

Was There a Good Pen to Steal?: Yes.

INTERVIEW #2: THE HINTING-AT-A-NERVOUS-BREAKDOWN RESUME

Job applying for: Salesman for a bakery-supply company

Resume lies: My education background says I graduated with a 4.0 GPA from Cambridge University in England with a degree in quantitative physics. My first job is listed as a computer software salesman for a fictional high-tech company in Silicon Valley. My work experience digresses to selling used cars, with a five-year gap between my current job, which is working at Kentucky Fried Chicken, where I'm responsible for "chicken sales."

The key to sales is selling *yourself* to the interviewer. The address given to me over the phone takes me to a doctor's office in the middle of Chinatown. There's nothing here even remotely resembling bakery supplies; only medical equipment. An old man, with his sleeves rolled up, points admittedly at his elbow, howling something in Chinese to the receptionist. Then he passes gas.

"Excuse me, I've come for an appointment concerning something nonmedical. Have I come to the right address?" I beg.

"Aah, yes, have a seat," says the lovely receptionist. I wait for a half hour, watching sick people come and go. Finally, a very tiny Chinese man wearing a stethoscope appears. He is no larger than a child!

"Be right with you."

Then he disappears. I wait another half hour. Finally, the tiny man reappears. I follow him into his office. I hope he doesn't make me get into a hospital gown or turn my head and cough. The tiny doctor explains he just started a business that he needs a salesman for. He studies my resume like it were a broken femur. He notes my Cambridge educational background.

"Aah, you're from England."

"Yes, I am mate," I say, conducting the rest of the interview in a fake British accent. Then he explains the nitty-gritty.

"The job involves selling cheesecake. We only sell cheesecake! Also cheesecake products."

I lose it. I'm openly laughing, then bite my lip while trying to stop by thinking about bad things.

"That's so funny because I used to have a job similar to that," I smirk, trying to cover up my giggling. Are cheesecake and cheesecake products like propane and propane accessories? Is this a joke being played on me? I'm sitting in a doctor's office in the middle of Chinatown, being interviewed for a cheesecake sales job by a very tiny doctor! What's wrong with this picture?

I use my powers of direct eye contact as the tiny doctor explains that the job requires selling cheesecake to hotels and restaurants. The doctor's eye skips my Kentucky Fried Chicken experience, glances over the five-year gap in job history, and asks about used-car sales techniques. He wonders how I would apply it to his cheesecake. I bring the focus back to my current fast-food experience.

"When I'm working at Kentucky Fried Chicken, I try to be a 'people-person,' gain the customers' trust, then suggest they buy *extracrispy* or a little bucket parfait."

"Aah," says the tiny doctor. Then he pulls out a piece of paper with four names on it.

"I have a few more people to interview, so I'll give you a call."

Conclusion: Having a 4.0 GPA from Cambridge University in quantitative physics doesn't cut it when it comes to cheesecake sales.

Was there a good pen to steal?: No, I never got to handle a writing implement.

INTERVIEW #3: THE PRISON RESUME

Job applying for: Selling window installations to random people over the phone.

Resume lie: San Quentin Prison, where I had three years' work experience in the tool shop.

Selling window installations over the phone must be one of the worst jobs known to humanity. Sounds like the aluminum-siding scam of the '00s.

I'm buzzed into the office, where many energy-saving awards hang on the wall. My interview is supposed to be with a woman named Virginia, but the receptionist says she is at lunch. She pages Virginia, telling me to take a seat and fill out an application.

"Would you like a Coke or something?" she asks.

"I'll have a mineral water."

"What?"

"A water is fine."

She goes in the bathroom and comes back with a stained coffee cup filled with tap water. I leave it untouched as I finish the application. There's a line saying, "Have You Ever Been Convicted Of A Felony?" In parentheses it says, "(This Will Not Affect Your Application)." I check the box marked yes. Let's see if former convicts are treated fair and square.

The phone rings. It's Virginia. She apologizes profusely.

"I'm sorry. I forgot we had an interview."

What! I need to be interviewed *now!* Right now, for one of the shittiest jobs known to humanity.

"We just hired a guy yesterday, but why don't you put your resume and application in my box, I'll take a look at it and give you a call next week if the guy doesn't work out."

Disgruntled by having the interviewer not show up for the interview, I scribble in the line asking to explain my felony charge, "Violent murder. Fucker was eye-balling my Bitch!" I could have been a little more subtle. I hand my resume and application to the receptionist and leave.

Conclusion: You should always keep job interviews with violent murderers.

Was there a good pen to steal? No. It was stained like the coffee cup filled with tap water.

Epilogue: A few days later, I get a message on my answering machine. "Willis, this is Virginia from the Save Energy Company. Could you give me a call? I wanted to talk to you to see if you still need work or if you found a job yet."

Fuck me sideways once again! Either she didn't read my resume or she believes in rehabilitation (or manslaughter experience is just what she's looking for).

INTERVIEW #4: BOASTING-TECHNICAL-KNOW-HOW-THAT-DOES-NOT-EXIST-IN-REALITY RESUME

Job applying for: Office worker

Resume lie: My office experience involves working with technology that doesn't exist in reality, especially the fabled "Crownwall 47 Tech System" and the Tele-Server1 Phone System.

Along with my resume, I fill out a form asking if I'm competent in such basic office-tech as Java Script and Microsoft Word. I answer no, but I write about my proficiency in "Crownwall 47." When finished, I'm corralled into an office by a pleasant, smiley woman.

"What attracted you to our ad?"

"The fonts. I liked the fonts. Was that done with a Crownwall 47 Tech System?"

She doesn't think so. Looking over my resume, the smiley woman asks about my office experience.

"I have a lot of phone experience with the Tele-Server1 Phone System."

She drops her voice to a whisper.

"What is that?"

I embellish on the Tele-Server1, employing my strong, direct eye contact.

"It's a software which works on your computer screen hooked to your retinas. If you're working on your computer, all you have to do is change screens and transfer the call blinking!"

"It's amazing what they can do now!" she says, impressed.

"The technology changes every day," I say, nodding my head.

"Do you have experience with Lotus or Java Script?"

"No, but I have plenty of experience with Crownwall 47, which also virtually does the same thing!"

Impressed by my knowledge of superior, fictional software, the smiley woman suggests that I'm overqualified for the office worker position, giving me the phone number of Mactemps, who hire people with high-tech backgrounds.

Conclusion: Never lie so much on your resume that you become overly qualified for the job!

Was there a good pen to steal?: I ended up stealing four pens!

Epilogue: Go figure: despite my limitations—and false resumes —I still landed two job offers in one week. So, next time you find yourself without work, fear not—there's always a future for an unskilled man from prison who can maintain strong, direct eye contact. It's a positive affirmation, given the few jobs available, that American business is stronger than ever.

I'm actually on my way to be HEALED! Yes, I going to be HEALED BY JESUS! HALLELUJAH! Since I can't afford good health insurance (who can in these dark Bush days?), what alternatives do I have in order to tend to my ailments? A wise choice would be attending a taping of faith healer Benny Hinn's (not Benny Hill's) TV show, *This Is Your Day,* which airs on TBN (or, as some refer to it, "the annoying God network").

Maybe now I can save tons of money by getting my illnesses healed without going through the medical community and, in turn, save huge amounts of money on costly doctor bills. Surely religious faith healers are legit and not just conning the poor, naive general public like the snake-oil salesmen of old. I could show others the way—so they, too, need not worry about being turned down by their HMO or paying for treatments. But in order to test the faith-healing waters, I have brought along some used crutches. (There's nothing more disgusting than the spongy armpit pads of used crutches.) I'm also wearing one of those vintage SARS hospital masks. (I could swear I'm coming down with that darn bird flu!)

Hinn Fact: Benny Hinn is a millionaire TV evangelist faith healer. He claims to heal people simply by touching them. When he was a guest on *Larry King Live,* Hinn said that if people touched their television sets while he prayed for them, they would be healed. Hurrah for Hinn!

On Your Mark! Get Set! Be Healed!

With crutches under arms and mask in place, I hobble toward the entrance of a big, gaudy building in the middle of an office park that might house government secrets, set in the heart of uber-conservative Orange County, California. Looking past a large man in an expensive suit standing by the door of the Hinn complex—perched under a sign that reads, "No Weapons Allowed"—I peer into the lobby full of burly security guards. It looks like a palace decorated by Michael Jackson's interior designer. The man standing under the "No Weapons Allowed" sign asks if he can help me.

"No," I mumble from beneath my vintage SARS mask. "Benny Hinn will take care of that. Does he heal everyone in the audience?" A woman standing beside a metal detector clarifies things for me: "*He* doesn't heal you! *God* heals you!" A sign above her head also reads, "No Weapons Allowed." (What is this weapons thing, and why do we need to be warned twice? If anyone gets shot, couldn't they immediately get healed?)

OK, fine, God heals you. So, if Granny falls over the minute that Benny Hinn takes away her wheelchair, then it's God fault (and at least Benny Hinn's ass will be covered for insurance purposes). I lift my SARS mask and ask the woman, "Do I need to sign up or anything so he can heal me?" Moving back slightly, she utters, "He'll pick people from the audience."

The metal detector goes off as I crutch through. "Oh, just go right on in," says one of the large security guards, leaving me safe in the knowledge that used crutches and a SARS mask will get anyone past security. Crutching on, I pass many photos of Benny

Hinn in action, celebrating the glory that is Benny Hinn. Some look like awkward Photoshop products. There's Benny Hinn with the pope, Benny Hinn with Mother Teresa, Benny Hinn lifting a small child toward the heavens, and various people weeping, weeping, weeping, all touched by the miraculous hand of Hinn.

A woman with big hair shows me to my seat. I accidentally step on several people's toes as I crutch along behind her. "Sorry," I cry, lifting my SARS mask. I flop into my seat and stare at the set with wonderment. Tacky fountains, Greek pillars, ornate chairs—the *This Is Your Day* set looks like what I'd imagine Donald Trump's living room to be or the set of a "how to be a millionaire" infomercial.

"Let me take those for you," says the woman with big hair. She walks away with my crutches. (Where is she going with them?) Perhaps this is Benny Hinn's first step toward getting me to walk on my own.

SHOWTIME!

People have their hands in the air, stick-'em-up fashion, and they're singing along with Benny Hinn. He's a swarthy man of ambiguous ethnic origin. His uniquely groomed hair defies logic. His suit seems *very* expensive.

Benny Hinn is excited. "I got some great news!" he announces. "We just got the building next door. They wanted $10 million, but we got it for $7.2 million!" The crowd hoots and hollers. "Now," Benny Hinn adds with what some might call a condescending laugh, "we got to start raising the money!" Then the taping starts.

"The following program has been made possible by viewers like *you*," announces, well, the announcer. He neglects to mention that viewers like *you* have also made Benny Hinn's private jet possible.

This Is Your Day's intro flashes onto the studio monitors: as inspirational music plays, we see a variety of crying people being healed (crying both before and after the healing).

Benny Hinn kicks things off by announcing his healing-tour schedule. He'll be playing Madison Square Garden–size venues. Wow, Benny Hinn is the Barbra Streisand of faith healing.

"Today, I want to show you what we did in Panama. Twenty thousand people were turned away!" he trumpets in sort of a patronizing manner. "Three deaf mutes were healed!"

"Amen!" praises the audience.

Footage of the Panama free-for-all is rolled. Hundreds of men, women, and children run toward Benny Hinn, the man with God's touch. Tears stream down their faces. There's a close-up of the feet of an old woman as she jumps up and dances around. As she does an ethnic jig, the announcer proclaims, "For two years, she had pain in her leg! Now it's gone!" HEALED!

A teenage boy jogs in place, his knees shooting high in the air. "Asthma for fourteen years. He could barely breathe. And now he's running around in a field!" HEALED!

"Praise Jesus!" exclaims the believer next to me, shaking her big-haired head, while wafts of hairspray make me queasy. I need my lungs healed. On the Panama tape we see another woman and hear the announcer say, "This woman came back to Panama to die. She's not going to die. She's healed of uterine cancer."

"Oh, it is *Jesus*!" howls Benny Hinn, in Jerry Springer fashion. "Yes, it is Jesus! God healed the people of Panama! Now . . . HE WANTS TO HEAL YOU!"

The crowd goes religiously ape shit. Benny Hinn closes his faith-healing eyes.

"Bone cancer has just been healed!" he announces. "Thank you, Jesus! I see someone healed of cancer of the spine. Thank you, Jesus! Someone's ears have been healed. Thank you, Jesus! Someone's leg has been healed. Thank you, Jesus!" Benny Hinn doesn't tell us who the afflicted people are, but we take his word for it that they're now healed among us. Clearly he knows what he is doing. Religious organ music builds. Benny Hinn stares directly into the camera. "I want to do more of these crusades like in Panama."

Gazing at the monitor, I feel as if he is talking to me and

only me. I'm mesmerized. "Partners, all you need to spend is less than a dollar a day!" he urges. I nearly reach for my wallet to pull out handfuls of money. There's not much money, but still, luckily, I'm able to shake off the spell.

GUESTS OF HINN

My vintage SARS mask is beginning to make my face itch (or else I've actually contracted SARS). I momentarily remove it, turning to the woman next to me. "It's the weirdest thing," I explain, breathing heavily on her. "Ever since I got back from Beijing—a few years back—I just haven't been feeling myself. I hope it's not bird flu and I'll be healed today!" She shoots me a look that could curdle milk.

This Is Your Day is not all about healing. There are also thought-provoking guests. The first is a Baptist woman with globe-shaped hair, author of a book called *Spiritual Housecleaning*. Some might find her to be the most uptight woman on the planet. She seems to have many issues.

"That magazine hidden under your son's mattress can affect your whole household," she stresses with extreme concern and a sneer. "It's spiritual pollution, and it can bring demons into your home!" Whoa! That's a big mind-fuck to lay on a teenager—his hidden *Playboy* can bring a plague upon the land! Surely they will be stricken with SARS, bird flu, and, of course, monkey pox!

"Sometimes people have arguments that only happen at home," the woman declares. "That's because they have demons in their houses!" She goes on to list other things that bring in the demons: antiques ("You don't know who owned them before!"), Christian books by *certain* authors, Pokémon ("They're little demons in your pocket!"), and, of course, Harry Potter. "There's something un-Christian about that book," she spits angrily. "Harry Potter is not Witchcraft 101. It's *advanced* witchcraft!"

She urges parents to go through their children's rooms while proclaiming, "Spirit of God, show me anything that needs to be removed from my house!" Then, she—whom some might consider a leading contender for the most-uptight-woman-in-the-world award—advises them to burn all the evil stuff in a big bonfire. (This woman who's concerned with spiritual housecleaning fails to mention that this could burn down your house!) "Or pawn anything of value and send the money to Benny Hinn," she adds with a laugh.

"I REBUKE THE ENEMY!" Benny Hinn interjects. The crowd goes Oprah to the tenth power, shouting, "Amen!"

The potentially most-uptight-woman-in-the-world continues: "You got to tell your kids that the rock-music posters on their walls and THEIR MUSIC bring demons into your household. If they won't take the posters down, you tell them it's your house so they have to live by your rules!" (Now there's an original concept.)

If you make a twenty-five-dollar donation to the Benny Hinn ministry, you get a free copy of *Spiritual Housecleaning*.

"I REBUKE THE ENEMY!"

Benny Hinn's next guest is a man who died—but didn't (because of Jesus). His two brothers are with him. If the show were an infomercial, this would be the testimonial part. "Can we hear you sing?" requests Benny Hinn.

The three brothers sing gospel. It's almost enjoyable. Then, one of the brothers of the guy who died but didn't starts talking. In a fiery voice, he shares how he once engaged in *homosexual activity*! The crowd gasps. Apparently, *Satan* led him astray, but now he's found the right path, thanks to—you guessed it—*Jesus*!

"TV doesn't show homosexuality as an alternative lifestyle—they make it seem like . . . a *normal* lifestyle!" he bellows. More gasps of disbelief. "They say people are homosexual because of their 'DNA.' It's more like their 'DEMONOLOGY!'"

I'm glad to see that someone is finally taking responsibility for his actions and putting the blame where it rightfully belongs—on Satan! Holding up the man's book (everyone has a book), Benny Hinn announces, "This is for anyone you know who may be struggling with the same demons."

"The feelings were gone, the demonic thoughts were

changed," the man continues in his fiery preacher-man voice. Again, Benny Hinn interjects: "People, I think we need to give the Lord a mighty hand!" Again, Benny Hinn stares into the camera: "Partners, because of you, I'm able to go around the world! I need you today more than ever! These crusades are very expensive, but when God calls on you, you'll do it!"

Time to Heal!

Over the next thirty minutes, the show seems to become a pure infomercial for a vast array of Benny Hinn tie-in merchandise. I'm starting to feel possessed by Satan, 'cuz I want to *scream*! I begin looking for my crutches (Where the hell *are* they?) so I can hobble out of here.

Finally, Benny Hinn goes wild with healing power. People are being healed left, right, and center! All with the touch of his hand! I've never seen anything like it. It's fucking weird.

"Those who are sick, place your hand on that part of your body and I will heal that sickness in the name of Jesus!"

Since I can't find my damn crutches, I place my hand on my little finger—I cut it while slicing a bagel. "There's somebody getting healed on their shoulder," Benny Hinn cries. No one fesses up. Regardless, Benny Hinn adds, in an uncanny display of telepathic power, "You feel warmth on your shoulder, and you're sitting to my right. Thank you, Jesus!"

Now I'm beginning to feel a little skeptical. It's quite a stretch to buy this healing act when all the "healer" has to do is look around for someone who's touching a shoulder. To the right of the stage is a group of people with wheelchairs and walkers. There's also a man in a neck brace. Why the hell doesn't Benny Hinn heal one of them? Huh? He doesn't have to play peek-a-boo games to see they need healing. Maybe God doesn't want them healed?

The whole thing now becomes like the flippin' *Price Is Right.*

"Lady in red! Do you have a problem with your lower back? Come here! Come here—God is healing you!"

The lady in red runs toward the stage. Benny Hinn touches her head.

"I REBUKE IT IN THE NAME OF JESUS!"

She lets out a shriek. Benny Hinn's power knocks her backward into the arms of one of his handlers. (How does one become a faith-healer handler?) He gently places her in a heap on the floor. Healing is very dramatic.

"Someone's skin itches! Come quickly!"

A man in a black-and-white-striped sweater trots to the stage.

"It's your right arm! JESUS, I REBUKE IT!"

The man also falls backward. He lies in a heap next to the rebuked woman. The people in wheelchairs look very pleased at Benny Hinn's stunts (yet they uncannily remain in their wheelchairs).

At last I find my crutches, under a row of seats. I wave them vigorously in the air in a "pick me" fashion. Benny Hinn doesn't "sense" me.

"Lady, right there! You have a pain in your chest? Get down here—the Lord is healing you! . . . You begin feeling a warmth. There! I REBUKE IT! Yes! Jesus is wonderful!"

Now, the power of suggestion is a mighty tool, but shouldn't these people be advised to keep seeing their doctors and taking their medications as well as experiencing Hinn's rebuking?

"Arthritis in the hand! Right there! Come over quickly! I REBUKE IT! You're healed! You will never have that problem again!"

That's quite a claim.

"Let's give the Lord a hand!" Benny Hinn insists, like he's in a Vegas showroom and has just pulled a rabbit out of someone's ass. A bunch of people are now lying in heaps on the stage, yet the man in the neck brace, the people in wheelchairs, and I, too, remain unhealed.

"People, raise your hands for what the Lord is doing here tonight!"

Again, everyone raises their hands stick-'em-up fashion and prays. Strangely, large, bulky security guys in suits eye me suspiciously, like I was a villain in a bad Bruce Willis action film. Perhaps the religious taping is just a front for a grand heist at Fort Knox. (That's why there were two "No Weapons Allowed" signs.)

Then Benny Hinn starts getting a little cocky.

"Lady—there, in the purple. What am I seeing? What am I seeing? Is it something with your skin?"

"It's my shoulder."

Benny Hinn addresses the audience: "Sometimes the word of knowledge is a bit foggy."

Oh, yeah, the old "foggy" excuse. I guess he can use the old "foggy" excuse to cover himself in any circumstance. Could it be that if someone doesn't get "healed," he can just insist that the person doesn't believe in Jesus strongly enough?

"You will not have that problem again, I promise you! What are you feeling now?"

"I'm shaking," says the nervous woman.

"That's Jesus!" Benny Hinn explains, giving the Lord credit for her stage fright. I wish he would make her bark like a dog. I'm growing increasingly testy about not being healed.

"There's someone with something on the end of her nose. What is it? What is it?"

"A pimple!" the audience answers.

"I know who you are. I won't embarrass you." He stares at a teenage girl who looks like she wants to crawl under a rock. I didn't know his healing extended to vanity problems. (Better he does it since today's lousy medical insurance probably doesn't cover it.)

"I REBUKE IT IN THE NAME OF JESUS!" he bellows yet again. "Isn't Jesus good?" Yeah, but her pimple still persists. Everyone stares at the pimple.

Benny Hinn goes on to rebuke whole families with the energy of a pyramid-marketing-scheme salesman (or George Foreman selling his grills—which actually work quite well). His victims lie in piles at his feet. One of the wheelchair-bound people, none too impressed, leaves early—in a wheelchair!

Why won't that religious bastard heal me? Is he putting me in the same ignored category as the wheelchair group? Instead,

Benny Hinn starts healing members of his production crew and then his wife. (Why can't he do that at home?)

"I'm sensing someone with a spine problem."

"It's me! It's me!" I scream, as one of the large security guards shoots me a look, then puts his hand on his earpiece.

Again, I vigorously wave my crutches. This is too much. I can't leave here without being healed. Healing time is running out. I bolt toward the stage. The woman next to me looks amazed that I can rush without my crutches. "Sorry, I have to be healed!" I blurt when I accidentally step on her foot. The security guards tense up in case this might be the moment of a James Bond–villain plot and they would need to fly into action in order to save the world in .007 seconds.

When I reach the stage, I scream, "Yes! It's me! I'm the one you were sensing with the problem with the spine! I am ready to be REBUKED!" The crowd is on my side, worked into a frenzy, feeding off my want-to-be-healed enthusiasm. Without missing a beat, the hand of Hinn touches my forehead.

"I REBUKE IT!"

Unfortunately, I don't fall backward. Maybe Benny Hinn didn't give me a big enough dose of Jesus. Instead, I'm grabbed by one of the handlers, who assists me, gently but firmly, to the floor, as I look out and witness a sea of delighted faces in the audience plastered with facial expressions one would have if they were witnessing a pure, unadulterated miracle. On the way down, I rip off my SARS mask and throw it into the crowd. "I won't be needing that anymore!" The crowd loves my display; Benny Hinn has cured my bird flu!

As I lie there among the other rebuked people—the newly cured now formerly arthritic, the pimple-sufferer, and the one who no longer has shoulder pain, the only thing I can do is giggle. I start giggling like a fucking madman. It's the kind of giggle you get when you realize that your parents are really Santa Claus and that man in the jolly red suit at the department store is merely an old guy with a bad beard who has booze on his breath and makes twelve dollars an hour.

"I REBUKE IT!"

WHEN THE HEALING ENDS

As the money-collection buckets are circulated, Benny Hinn tells a funny anecdote about casting out Satan while staying in a castle in Germany. I write "Satan Hates You!" on a piece of paper and place it in the bucket. My little finger still hurts. He hasn't healed it!

All around me people are pulling out their wallets and checkbooks, clearly impressed by the high theatrics and carnival atmosphere. I feel sorry for these gullible folks—they want to believe so desperately that they are ready to throw their hard-earned money at Benny Hinn, who will later likely be riding in a brand-new black stretch limo and dining on swan.

Leaving the building, I overhear another audience member snarl, "She always gets picked!" Apparently those who don't get picked can be a bit catty. I hand my crutches to the man who originally greeted me at the front door. "I won't be needing these anymore," I explain. He looks at my crutches, and then he looks at me walking in a normal fashion. "Praise! Praise! Praise!" he exclaims.

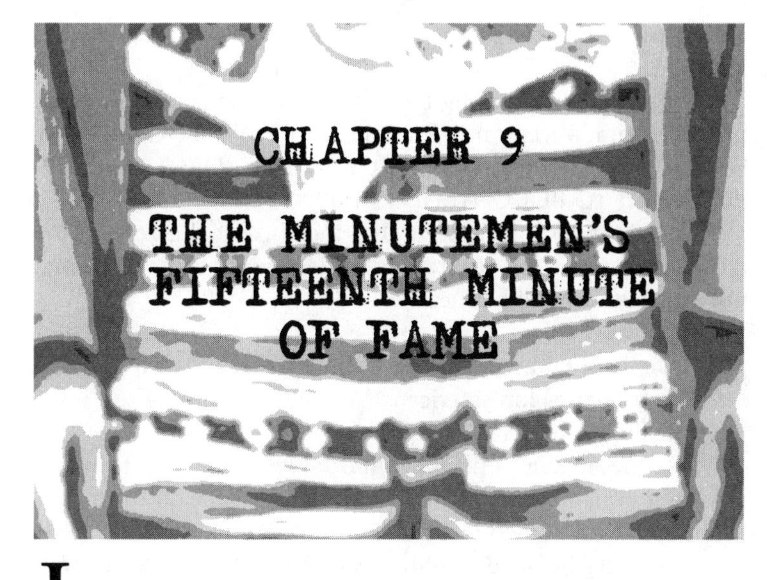

CHAPTER 9

THE MINUTEMEN'S FIFTEENTH MINUTE OF FAME

In front of a flapping American flag, screaming into the microphone, a hard-ass fireman from Southern California is angry. No, let's say he's foaming-at-the-mouth pissed off. He directs his attention to the press, with more passionate disgust than others had over the thought of illegal aliens invading their neighborhood: "It's the media that's the other half of the problem in this country for not covering the story THE WAY IT REALLY IS!"

Sitting in long rows of picnic tables are the Minutemen—the civilians who took it upon themselves to patrol the Mexican border ("The government's not doing their job!") in order to spot illegal aliens. In response to the hard-ass fireman, the crowd starts thunderously whistling and jeering—basically going ape shit.

The hard-ass fireman, from a third-generation Mexican family (his family "came in the right way!"), is vividly infuriated that the press ignored him as being among the faces in the Minuteman Project and instead focused on the majority of white participants, who were treated in some papers as racists.

Taking a quick visual inventory, with an impartial view, I'd have to say it's pretty fucking white here—mainly hardened elderly men with big pot bellies, some of whom brought their wives.

As I'm standing among the other journalists, the irate man points in our direction and screams: "SO WHY DON'T YOU FOLKS PACK UP AND GO SOUTH OF THE BORDER WHERE YOU WANT TO BE CONTROLLED!"

I'm not exactly sure what that means, but the very white crowd (plus one third-generation Mexican man) starts throwing out angry taunts and heckles.

"Traitors!"

"Like Bush said, you're either with us or against us!"

"Sorry excuses for Americans!"

"Media bye-bye!"

We, the media, shift uncomfortably from foot to foot, staring at our shoes. (I think they expect us to take off running.) I honestly think someone is going to yell, "GET THEM!"

Wasn't it the media who *made* the Minuteman Project? Wasn't the Minuteman Project, for these guys, in one way, a big publicity stunt to bring attention to their border concerns? For that I ask, Minutemen, where did the love go?

The Making of a Minuteman

Before the proposition of "going south of the border where I wanted to be controlled," I came to Tombstone, Arizona, in order to meet the men and women behind the Minutemen. (Surprisingly, there were no Minutekids.) Sure, I heard the news description of vigilantes hunting down illegal aliens like angry villagers chasing the Frankenstein monster. Sure, others said they were a bunch of harmless senior citizens spending their twilight years sitting in lawn chairs patrolling our borders—and backed by *beloved* Governor Arrrrnold Schwarzenegger (who also chased aliens in *Predator*). To me, it just sounded like a big three-ring, anti-immigration circus, with the Minutemen as the ringmasters under the big top of the Mexican border. Here's my minute-to-minute (OK, not every minute) recounting of my daring and dangerous descent into border politics.

ORIENTATION

With my photographer/drinking buddy Brad in tow, we arrive for the morning Minuteman orientation session on the twenty-eighth day of the Minuteman Project's (not to be confused with the *Alan Parsons Project*) monthlong jamboree.

"I'm going to ask you a pertinent question—are you armed?" a very large, intimidating man with a gun strapped across his chest questions us. This is before entering the office of the *Tombstone Tumbleweed* newspaper, some blocks away from where the historical gunfight at the OK Corral took place.

Though I'm dressed as a Minuteman—but even more so (aviator shades, matching Army fatigue shirt, shorts, and hat)—I do a quick body visual inventory. Firmly, I answer no!

After a short wait, they allow us into the backyard, where eighteen people, with serious, almost grim, looks are assembled (all men, except for a hardened grandmother and an unhappy woman who is part of an unhappy couple). Most are dressed like me, exuding an air of nervous uneasiness like those about to be shipped off to war—some of whom might not return.

As members of the esteemed media, we receive the same warm welcome one would grant to a fresh outbreak of genital herpes.

"Does anyone feel uncomfortable having members of the media here?" bellows the large, intimidating man, as a historic Wild West stagecoach clops by. Tense silence as future Minutemen, not sure how to react, turn their heads toward each other. "If anyone feels uncomfortable, raise your hand and I can ask them to leave!" I try to give my best "Hey, I'm on your side" look.

No hands go up. I take a lawn chair in the hot sun, behind an old guy whose T-shirt reads, "Retired—I Can Play With My Trains Anytime I Want."

Still not in the clear, the large, intimidating man questions with intense eye contact, "Do you have any recording devices on you?"

Letting out a nervous chuckle, I shake my head (hoping my tape recorder doesn't fall out of my pocket). The large, intense man has one other demand. "You can't quote me directly!" (The following quotes are paraphrased—sort of.)

"This is not about skinheads. This is not about the KKK," his orientation continues in weeding out trigger-happy fanatics. (I look to see if this disappoints anyone and note blank stares.) "We are here to observe and report."

The Minuteman mission statement is laid out: "The Constitution says protect our borders from the threat of invasion. We have the right to Freedom of Assembly."

The intimidating man points to the gun strapped around his neck. "If anyone has one of these things, no monkey business! We're not about this," he sternly states. "No rifles! No shotguns!"

Mustachioed Tex, wearing a cowboy hat and boots, speaks up. "Is that a Minuteman rule or an ACLU rule that you can't return fire if fired upon?"

"We want the operation to be clean."

"If I'm fired upon, isn't that imminent danger?" Tex questions. "I've been fired upon, and it's not a good feeling."

"I can't tell you what to do!" the large man barks as the wind flaps his green shirt, exposing his large belly.

Then comes a series of, apparently, *relevant* Minuteman questions.

"How about night visions? What's the visibility?"

"If I have an American flag, should I bring it?"

"Where's the FREQUS?" (At first I think he's referring to *freaks* and there's going to be hippie-bashing. Instead, he means radio frequencies.)

"Do you know how many contacts they've made on the border?"

"Ten per day. There used to be three thousands come around this area at night," our leader confirms.

The group's village idiot asks, "What's better, to have them see us and go around or shine a light and scare them back to Mexico? What's preferable?"

The answer: shine a light and let them know you're there.

"What if you shine a light on them and then they come after you?" the group's village idiot persists. He is quickly cut off when he segues into a pointless political diatribe.

"If you don't have a question, can you save it for later?"

The final rules. "No contact. Anyone has contact, they're gone," our large orientation leader stresses, explaining they've kicked out Minutemen for giving water to illegal aliens (who have traveled on foot for days through the hot desert). The reason? "You jeopardize the whole program."

So if some stupid illegal alien is about to die of thirst, it's better to let him fall into the dust than lose your status as a Minuteman.

"I'm going to look everyone in the eye, and I'm going to ask two questions, 'Do you agree to stick with the rules and what we're about, which is about the Constitution and securing our borders?'"

Everyone gets looked in the eye, then signs an all-important liability waiver. The final loyalty test for the Minutemen: "Please don't steal my pens. People have been walking away with them."

Stealing pens, who would do such a thing? How can they secure borders if they can't secure pens?

Tools of the Minutemen

- A walkie-talkie.
- A video camera. ("If you have a spotting, it's to prove you haven't done anything wrong.")
- The border patrol's number to speed dial on cell phones. (Why speed dial? "We've seen ladies get so excited when they spot nine or ten illegals.")

"When you call the border patrol, when they arrive, get out of dodge. You've done your job. You've done what you promised America what you will do," states the line supervisor, who sports a gray beard and green Fidel Castro hat. "If spotted, they will sit down. If they came with contraband, they will run."

At the last dusty outpost before the border, I stand among a group of concerned citizens in triple-digit heat, next to a burly guy whose T-shirt reads, "Be There In A Minute . . . Man!" Most, lone men who came out here from various parts of the country on their own, felt the call of duty. FOX News is filming with the attitude of the popular kids in this border-securing high school—for they work for the preferred network.

"The border patrol managed to seize seventeen bundles of cocaine!" (Or, as they playfully call it, "not pot.")

Clapping.

The night shift (10 p.m. to 6 a.m.) is the busiest time to patrol but clearly the least desired shift.

"You may get a bit lonely. You might have a few Mexicans to keep you company. The 'coyotes' sit on the hills watching us, where we don't have people," he says, referring to people who charge ($300 to $1,100) to guide immigrants from Mexico into the United States. "Since we've come out here, we heard the price has doubled."

There have been problems, though, with the Opposition—the ACLU (or, as called by the Minutemen, the "Anti-Christian Lawyers Union"). The Minutemen accuse them of causing problems with their "aggressive actions," purposely tripping border-patrol sensors or running across the border, pretending to smuggle immigrants. "We figure they were out there having Bible study," he says mockingly.

It's explained that the ACLU is getting desperate, writing on their Web site, "We will find human rights violations." The Minutemen accuse the ACLU's actions as being downright *un-American*.

"We got them smoking pot on camera," Fidel says with a sly smile as if he's got the ultimate goods on them.

The group is taken to Papa Bear—a line supervisor wearing tinted shades, slightly resembling Robert Duvall in *Apocalypse Now*—with a gun prominently displayed on his belt and various radio wires and military insignias on his vest. Strangely, this sixty-four-year-old, who was in the 82nd Airborne, drives a Miata.

"I have 165 paratrooper jumps," he boasts.

"I have more time in the latrine," jokes a fellow Minuteman.

With clipboard in hand, Papa Bear gives his briefing. (I expect him to say, "I love the smell of napalm in the morning.")

"Anyone armed?" asks Papa Bear.

The majority of hands go up.

"Be cool. If you have side arms, don't touch it unless you are certain that you're about to be killed." He points to a kindly old woman. "Phoebe assisted in a capture after midnight. Thirteen were captured."

Phoebe bursts into a proud smile.

Applause.

"We spotted a few coming under the wire. We called the border patrol. It was great for us to know that actually we got to assist in a tactical maneuver as opposed to hearing about how someone else did it." He adds, "Made my day," without irony. "All of us were calm, cool, collected during the operation. But when it was over, you had that prize, that package of eleven captured; *the adrenaline was flowing.*"

A young couple from San Diego is already bored. "There's sure a lot of standing around."

Papa Bear explains, "I'm not against a guy coming over here trying to make a buck. I respect that. I respect any man who walks fifty miles through the desert to feed his family. *But he's not doing that on our welfare system*!"

Papa Bear's concerned about the dope smugglers, the human flesh smugglers, and, of course, the terrorists.

"They found copies of the Koran and Arabic ID cards in the cleanup area," he confirms, stirring up some post-9/11 paranoia.

After the briefing, an old guy with a gray T-shirt blurts to Papa Bear, "I was in town today, and I almost wanted to catch some of the Mexicans who are already over here!"

"That's enough of that!" Papa Bear sharply shuts him down.

After he leaves, P.B. says, "You have to deal with fresh people every day, and some might be a little overzealous on how they want to protect America. And I have to calm them down and get them in line."

One overzealous member was a sixty-year-old pediatrician who laid in a gully every night in the dark from seven o'clock to ten o'clock.

"She wouldn't leave, and she was there unarmed, laying in that culvert with her cell phone and her radio, reporting what she saw and heard." Papa Bear flashes a smile, barring his lower teeth. "If that kind of group can capture or aid in the assistance of the border-patrol capturing, you telling me we can't close our border?"

To the Border!

Following a convoy of large trucks, we're eight people to seven vehicles going to the border checkpoint, the Naco Line. The bumper sticker on the truck in front of me reads, "Charlton Heston Is My President!"

"Are there a lot of rattlers out here?" asks the concerned grandmother of the bunch.

"Rattlesnakes aren't aggressive if you don't step on them," says the Naco line leader. "They migrate around the corner and they conceal themselves in the mountains." (Is he referring to rattlesnakes or Mexicans?)

"Please move the radio away from your mouth when you talk into it," the Naco leader then advises the old lady. "Don't get stressed. *Have fun*."

The Naco border is basically a barbed-wire fence, torn open at numerous spots, in such a way that a blind toddler could crawl through. In fact, I'm shown the now-famous "Hannity Hole," where FOX News poster boy Sean Hannity himself stepped through for his FOX cameras.

"Historically, this is one of the highest-trafficked areas," the line supervisor says, pointing to the large span of desert, with mountains off in the distance, as the strong wind embeds dust between my teeth.

What's the Minuteman relationship with the border patrol like?

"Superfriendly. Last night, they let me look through their nightscopes." On the other hand, "If you were to cross the border, the Mexican police would love to catch a Minuteman as a trophy—you won't get out of jail!"

The last advice before we're off on our own: "When you leave here, make sure you don't back over any migrants 'cuz they'll be right behind you."

TIME TO SPOT ILLEGAL ALIENS!

The group doesn't dramatically jump into action like the A-Team. Instead, we just stand around.

"It's actually been kind of boring because nobody has tried to cross since we've been here," remarks a Texas trucker with his rig parked in front of his tent. "But I like camping, so this suits me."

"We're not getting a lot of action, but we're making a lot of new friends," exclaims a couple from Michigan about to go on an ice cream run.

Hanging with the Minutemen is getting to be fun—it's almost like illegal-alien-seeking summer camp.

"I just love being here every minute," comments a friendly elderly guy named Ed (who shares homemade deer sausage with us in his trailer). Recounting his other experiences with the press, Ed warns, "If you misconstrue me, we'll have a chat." He tells the story as both a witty anecdote and a not veiled threat. "If they ask leading questions, we'll have a chat," he says again. (There goes asking Ed if he thinks all Mexicans should be put in zoos!). Ed also mentions how someone found copies of the Koran and Arabic flight schedules.

While downing the homemade deer sausage, he continues, "We know we didn't stop it here. We're not fooling anyone. But we proved it could be done. It's just to show if the government had the will, it could make an impact."

But not everyone has been thrilled about their presence. "This Vietnam vet with a big peace sign painted on his van drove by, 'Fuck you! Fuck you!' He even let go of the steering wheel so he could give the finger with both hands."

Ed segues back to the media, some members of whom he says staged phony photos to make it look like the Minutemen held guns to the heads of illegal aliens or pulled girls who were hiding by their hair. Again, the consequences if the press misconstrues him are mentioned. "We'll have a chat. We'll have a chat!"

THE MINUTE DUDES

"There's these two guys from San Jose in Army fatigues with guns on their belts—because they can—who caught a rattlesnake." We're apparently being told about a couple of "overzealous" types who might have slipped by during the weeding-out process, parading the poisonous snake around with a forked stick. "I was worried about those two."

Bypassing the much-anticipated Minutemen ice cream run, we search for the two unruly Minute Dudes, finding them sitting by their car.

"I said I want to touch a rattlesnake's tail. I never touched one before," retells the one with glasses, next to his buddy, who's wearing a Dead Kennedys' T-shirt (both a good forty years younger than your average Minuteman). "It feels like fingernails," he adds.

Taking time off from their other commitments (one's unemployed, the other's in the National Guard), the Minute Dudes came here because of what they read in the press.

"The newspaper said it was like a war zone down here, that there were militia men running around, there's firing squads and shit like that." The Minute Dude with glasses clarifies, "That's not what these people are about down here."

"Yeah," pipes in his Dead-Kennedys-T-shirt-wearing buddy. "Some people just see this as old people with guns and shit on the border. But that's not it. If you read the little pamphlet, it's all about protesting George Bush. If people knew that, I'm sure you'd have hippies out here. Hippies!" (Huh?!) "I don't want fuckers like Osama bin Laden, and fucking Mohammed Atta, the guy who crashed the plane into the World Trade Center, being smuggled across the border here," elaborates the one with glasses, who's been on what he calls "a guided tour to America for twenty grand."

Again, there's mention of someone finding a copy of the Koran. (What's with these terrorists who keep losing their Korans? Is this propaganda, or do they have trouble holding on to their holy book?)

"I think you catch them, stick them on a chain gang," he proposes. "Give them six months, then send them home."

Overall, the Minute Dudes have enjoyed their tour of duty.

"There's a lot of really cool patriots out here."

"There's some hot-ass ACLU chicks," adds the Minute Dude in the Dead Kennedys T-shirt.

"Yup!"

The ACLU chicks, though, for some reason, gave them weird looks, just because the two came fully armed. To demonstrate his attire, the Dead Kennedys Minute Dude excitedly puts on his Army flack vest and gun belt.

"See, we got the whole George Bush thing. We're going to be like, yeah, we hate George Bush, too. And everyone will be like, 'Oh, cool.'"

How awesome! I almost expect him to start air-guitaring.

The Opposition

Venturing off the border, for a much-needed break from the Minuteman, I enter a local Mexican restaurant, which, by sheer coincidence, is inhabited by a sea of ACLU volunteers—all adorned in ACLU "Legal Observer" T-shirts. So, this is the feared opposition despised by the elderly Minutemen. The ACLU comprises almost entirely zit-faced college girls. These are the antagonists? The Minutemen are letting themselves be picked on by a bunch of hairy-armpit college girls who most likely scribe their own poetry!

I shit you not, of the rare few ACLU men, two over-the-top effeminate guys are actually playing paddy-cake. Together they chant in a singsong voice, hitting each other's hands:

> One, two, three, four!
> We don't want no fucking war!

These are the people chosen last in gym class. This is a sheer battle of titans.

I try to make eyes with one of the few cute ACLU girls, flashing a smile, greeted with the same reaction as if I just did a bad smell.

Several more ACLUers also give me dirty looks. It hits me. I realize I'm dressed as a Minuteman (but even more so). Quickly, I get the hell out of there before explanations are in order.

Before departing, my photographer gets a chance to confront the low-key ACLU leader: "The Minutemen accuse you of setting off sensors in the desert, dumping garbage, and smoking pot."

With a shrug, he replies, "Ah, two out of the three."

Like the Minutemen, the ACLU also has a complete revulsion to the press. Tension is sensed back on the border, as we approach two frumpy girls in lawn chairs wearing "Legal Observers" T-shirts. To break the ice, I flash a friendly smile and wave, forgetting, again, I'm dressed like a Minuteman (but even more so).

"What's you experience been like with the Minutemen?" I ask one of the frumpy ACLU girls, who's reading Pablo Neruda, as I explain that I'm an *esteemed* journalist. They tense up even further. The other one, with the huge cold sore on her lip, remains close-lipped.

"It's been . . . kind of unremarkable," she mumbles, barely giving me the dignity of forming words. "We heard about the Minutemen, heard they were training people to be legal observers." (Ironically, her T-shirt reads, "Legal Observers.")

"What's your purpose out here?" I try to get their side of the story in true journalistic fashion.

The frumpy girls look at each, hesitant in responding.

"If there was any violation of the law, we would observe it."

"Have there been any violations?"

Pause. "No. . . . We say a boring day is a good day."

I ask how they feel about the situation on the border. The one with the huge cold sore sharply cuts in. "We have a policy not to talk about politics because we are here to observe!"

Strange, an organization dedicated to the politics of human rights has a policy about not talking about politics? At least the Minutemen shared deer sausage with us.

The head frumpy girl gets curt. "Guys, you're going to have to talk to Ray [the ACLU head] about that."

Before leaving, I ask what they do when not on the border.

"Uh . . . well . . . having a life . . . doing normal things."

I press further.

One finally confesses to being unemployed but is taking a Spanish class. I mention, before departing, what I was told about the rattlesnakes, gesturing to the frumpy girl's tennis shoes.

"They can bite through those, you know."

STILL NO ILLEGAL ALIENS

Driving down the border road, I find it fun to wave at the other Minutemen, who always joyfully wave back. This is like a big game of capture the flag. We park next to a van with two cardboard, hand-scrawled signs in the window reading, "Badges. We don't need no stinking badges! WE HAVE THE CONSTITUTION," and, in reference to Bush, "THEY IMPEACHED Nixon & Clinton FOR LESS."

"A boring day is a good day," remarks Minuteman Ken (hey, that's what the frumpy ACLU girl said), a likable guy, with a wry sense of humor and voice like Elmer Fudd. Ken's an ex-cop from Arkansas who looks like an old hippie dude with long, white hair and a thick mustache. Smoking a pipe, he points to the gun on his belt. "There's no rounds in it. This helped us get this press coverage. That's the reason why we're here, not to use them," he says. "'Oh, men with guns!' that's much better than, 'Oh, men with walkie-talkies—they might throw them!'"

"When the border patrol first heard we were coming, he said, 'That's great—all we need are a bunch of hillbillies out there, drinking, waving guns.' But after the third day, they knew that was not what it was. They thought we'd come out to get all the press and melt away by the end of the week. They had a pool going, guessing when the last Minuteman would be out there. And almost nobody was guessing past two weeks. Because we stuck it out, night after night, day after day, shift after shift, they came to have a lot of respect for us."

Ken thought he was going to lose it when the border patrol told him that for the first time, they felt this mess on the border might get cleaned up. "He said it was because of us."

There are still rumors flying that two hundred Mexicans are gathering to run across the border at once, to spite the Minutemen. Ken summarizes, "President Bush, if you don't secure our borders, we'll do it for you!"

Walking toward the gate of the Naco Hilton—a nickname for an abandoned ranch where Ken contacted the border patrol upon seeing forty pounds of "not-pot" coming across the border—another Minuteman, one that you'd describe as an asshole, drives up. He's irate at us for leaving tracks by the gate, and, in turn, he videotapes the license plate of our rental car, then drives away.

"Do you want to see some garbage left by people who have come by?" asks an approaching male nurse from Utah.

"Sure!" I answer enthusiastically. (Maybe there will be a copy of the Koran!)

We go to the spot. There's a plastic bag weighed down by a rock and one tiny shoe. We stare at it for several seconds. It's a plastic bag and a tiny shoe, all right.

The Utah nurse talks about the only major incident so far. "There was this guy. He called himself 'The Jokester.' He made a T-shirt that said, "I Caught An Illegal Alien At The Border & All I Got Was This Lousy T-shirt." The Jokester then found an illegal alien, made him put on the T-shirt, and took photos. Oh, the laughter!

NIGHT SHIFT, HUACHUCA LINE, 3:37 A.M.

The night shift is not unlike sitting in one's car extremely bored. I'm getting a little bit jittery, a little bit shaky, a little bit jumpy from drinking loads of caffeine, as I start seeing things in the dark void—which is the actual border. (Good thing I'm not armed.) Waiting and watching, watching the border—with my eyes! The Minutemen's job is not unlike that of UFO hunters. Comparisons: they both believe the government is letting them down or in a conspiracy. They are both mostly retirees, and both love to use cool night goggles.

Trying to get my car radio to work, I accidentally keep flashing my car's lights.

"There's someone flashing their lights towards the border," an urgent-sounding man called "Wisconsin" blurts over the radio, thinking we might be signaling "coyotes."

"Do you want backup?" answers base headquarters.

I push the talk button on my walkie-talkie. "I'M FREAKIN' OUT, MAN! I'M REALLY FREAKIN' OUT HERE!"

Finally, some action. We get a message over the walkie-talkie: "I'm going to move my car. Don't panic if you see some lights."

With a chuckle, another Minuteman replies, "I'll try not to get too trigger happy."

"CALL IN THE AIRSTRIKE! CALL IN THE AIRSTRIKE!" I scream into my walkie-talkie.

Silence from the other end. Then, finally, "Do you need some security backup?"

There're more potential sightings. "I just saw some lights. I'm going to go investigate!"

This time it wasn't me. Maybe we've actually spotted our first illegal alien of the evening! The radio transmits again: "This is Gooseberry Down, just south of you, I didn't see no lights, but I'm walking towards ya."

A few moments later, there're big chuckles over the radio concerning the light. "I just moved my position from in the trees, and it turned out to be the moon."

Seconds later, to create more drama, I scream, "MAN DOWN! MAN DOWN!"

At the Bible College

We pull our rental car up to the gate of a dilapidated local Bible college, used as the Minuteman command center and dormitory.

"Is this where the nine o'clock morning meeting is?" I ask a Waco Texan with a thick mustache and cowboy hat, who's drinking a can of beer.

"We can't give that information to the public," snaps his accomplice, a lady wearing a homemade macramé bonnet, while possessing an air of high-school hall-monitor authority.

I snap back, exclaiming that I'm an esteemed member of the press. Bigger apprehension. I list off the entire cast of Minuteman characters (large intimidating guy, Papa Bear, et al.) whom I've personally encountered. Warming slightly, the bonneted lady shares her frustration. "There's a flyer being distributed through Mexico by the Mexican government that says, 'Danger: Vigilantes.'" She sarcastically waves her hands around. "Big, scary people here!" Then, showing her Minuteman artistic side, "While here, I've taken pictures of ten types of birds, twenty-five types of plants. I have a songbird tape. Yeah, you should be scared of me!"

She digresses into a rant of insanity. "We really need to work on the diversity out here because we really haven't had the GLBT [Gay, Lesbian Bisexual, Transgender] community well represented. Neither have the African Americans shown up."

She's not joking. That's the craziest thing I've heard spewed this entire week. She's actually surprised the gay community hasn't come out in droves (but noting all the cowboy and military outfits, one might think otherwise).

"There were three black gentlemen from Tennessee who stayed for a week," clarifies the Waco cowboy, adding, "No Hispanics volunteered. Maybe they didn't want to seem like race traitors." He then animatedly shares his philosophy. "You always hear 'African American' or 'Mexican American.' How about loving America first? 'American-American.' 'American-Mexican.' Why is that?"

I shrug my shoulders.

9 A.M., Cafeteria of a Bible College— The Final Minuteman Briefing

"Don't wear full camouflage wear. We want to present a non-military, non-threatening image for the press," says a sign outside the Bible college cafeteria door. Since I am a member of the press, it's OK, then, that I'm head-to-toe in military fatigues.

With the morning briefing already in progress, several heads swerve with suspicion as I enter the cafeteria. At this meeting, there are fewer of the earnest, lovable Wilford Brimley–type Minuteman senior citizens and more of the hardened, older men in charge, among a sea of plaid and military green.

Jim Gilchrist, a salt-and-pepper-haired man in charge of the eight hundred to a thousand Minuteman volunteers (the number always seems to vary), takes to the center of the cafeteria.

"We are not common criminals," he declares, in regard to Minuteman leader Chris Simcox's recent trip to Washington, DC, claiming they were the talk of Capitol Hill. (They even signed autographs!) With a tinge of bitterness, he proclaims, "We are asking for an apology from the president about the Minuteman Project!" (Bush referred to the Minutemen as "vigilantes.")

Big applause.

There are specifics involved. "We are asking the president to meet with us and give a personal apology!"

Bigger applause.

Then, with major bitterness, built up from a month of presidential unappreciation, "I don't think we're going to get it!"

The Bible college cafeteria grows silent.

"If we stop now, we'll be seen as a thirty-day dog-and-pony show. We have to continue," he blares with voice rising. "We have just lit the fuse to keep this bomb rolling!"

The Minutemen eat this up, as a large, steely-eyed man with a Bowie knife on his hip moves next to me, standing over my shoulder, creating intentional intimidation, and eyeballing me as I scribble in my notebook.

"Anyone here with military background?"

The majority of hardened elderly hands shoot up in the Bible college cafeteria.

"This was a battalion-sized operation. In October, this has to be an army-sized operation!"

"Let's hope we don't have revelry!" an old guy quips.

Yes, the upcoming Minuteman project is to patrol four border states, with further plans to cover the northern borders (fucking Canadians sneaking over, taking our jobs!), with the grand overall Minuteman goal of citizens patrolling twelve border states.

Ha, ha, ha!

"This is going from a thousand-person operation to twelve thousand," he boasts, saying this current experiment is less aggressive and more passive (because of all the TV cameras probably). If they don't do this stuff, then, "You can kiss this country good-bye!" Gilchrist solemnly warns.

More night goggles will be needed. More infrared. With the Minuteman Project growing twelve times as large (the law of mishap probability raised by a factor of twelve), plans are also made to sweep the entire Huachuca mountain range.

"I'd do that twenty years ago," says a large, mustachioed man in green Army wear with a baby-fat face as he leans over. "Now I'd have to bring my blood-pressure medicine."

"Can we bring rifles up there?" someone asks.

"I don't mind one out of four people having a rifle," a supervisor confirms. (Hmm, the rules seem to have changed.)

The baby-fat-face man leans in again. "If Bill Clinton were president, he'd have Janet Reno send the FBI to shoot us out!"

In conclusion, "The media is not your enemy." I smile and nod. Then, with sinister disgust, Gilchrist curses the press who criticized the Minutemen. "It's dirty journalism! They will get theirs from their peers who will shun them!"

Didn't they get what they wanted—publicity?

"This is just an amazing cross-section of Americans," remarks Fidel, the line supervisor. I look around. It's practically all old white guys, the majority of whom have a military background. Is it dirty journalism to say such? Will I now be shunned by my peers? (I start biting my nails.)

"You're our Patrick Henry!" spontaneously exclaims a patriotic grandmotherly woman—referring to Gilchrist—to a round of applause. "A twenty-first-century Minuteman!"

"How about Paul Revere?" quips an old codger to significantly less applause.

The patriotic woman, taking his lead, puts her hands in the air, riffing, "The Mexicans are coming! The Mexicans are coming!"

Afterwards, the steely-eyed hard-ass man with a Bowie knife on his hip approaches.

"I don't think I met you guys," he states with intimidating strong eye contact. (Subtext: "I could kill you with one finger if you answer wrong.")

"I'm part of the media that isn't your enemy!" I crack, with my likable, ice-breaking wit. His leathery hands remain in a death-hold, gripping my hand a little longer than one should.

WHAT DOES MEXICO THINK OF THE MINUTEMEN?

Three visually angry Latino youths and one older woman in a brown beret, on the Mexican side of the United States Border Station, scream at the cars going into the United States.

"Fuck the Minuteman Project!"

"Chicano power!"

"Down with the Minuteman Project!"

After drastically changing my look and uncovering my dreadlocks, I approach.

"Can we help you guys?" asks the worked-up, shirtless protestor, gripping the metal border fence, noting our video camera. Mildly concerned I might be mistaken for a Minuteman, I ask what brought them to the border.

"We're here to push them away," proclaims the older woman, wearing a brown beret, not by coincidence; she's part of the Brown Berets, an organization founded in the late sixties—one of the most militant organizations in the Chicano liberation movement.

"We're just here to protect our people by any means necessary. With no weapons, with no guns. We come unarmed," the shirtless guy passionately remarks. "We're not here to start no violence. They're the ones who want violence. Not us." He adds, "They have weapons. They have guns and they're armed. They have permits to camp out here and hunt. So basically if they try to cover the whole border, they're going to try and hunt my people down."

I take all this in when suddenly we're overcome by a huge swarm of bees. I take off screaming like a little girl, "Ah, bees!"

When I gain my composure, the shirtless kid tells me, "We found this guy taking pictures of one of my people with a shirt saying, 'I Caught An Illegal Alien At The Border & All I Got Was This Lousy T-shirt.'" The Jokester! "He made him wear the shirt. That's messed up."

We're told of a peace rally going on in the local Mexican city's town square. When we get there, it's composed almost entirely of white ACLU members. Onstage a waif-y guy recites poetry to the crowd about his solution to the border problem: "The graceful way to jump the border is to fly over with golden wings."

A local tells me that a Guatemalan gang is also observing the Minutemen. If there's an incident where a Minuteman happens to kill an illegal alien, the Guatemalan gang will avenge, with three Minutemen paying the price.

"If they call themselves Minutemen, maybe they should be more concerned about their wives," theorizes a smiling, laid-back Hispanic guy with goatee and black hipster T-shirt. "They should put more effort into their personal lives and stop fucking around with people they shouldn't be messing around with."

Originally from Mexico, our new friend first came to the United States as an illegal immigrant. Now he has his residence card and feels the Minutemen are creating a bigger division and more tension within the people of the United States.

"What it's doing is creating stereotypes of people thinking now that everyone can be a border patrol and reporting everybody," he says. "What it does is it creates this ideology of superiority that they think they have the right to do this. They put themselves in a position where they think they are authorities at a place where they are not. It creates this mentality of 'We can stop this, we can do this, we can destroy them," he states, while in the background, little kids gleefully swing at an M&M piñata, hanging from a tree, with a large M across the front. (Or is it a Minuteman effigy?)

"They're dangerous," he adds. "Not dangerous themselves, but dangerous in the ideologies that they are creating." (It's true—by no means do I find the bonneted lady or those on the ice cream run dangerous, but I would if there were twelve thousand of them.)

"Most of them are veterans of war, right, and supposedly

they fought for this country. But at the same time they are people who don't have anything to do. If they can come for a month and sit around with binoculars and cameras, what does that tell you about them?"

The Last Minutes of the Minutemen

The Minuteman Project closing barbecue is a big clappity-clap fest, with many patriotic American flags waving, and the God blessing of America. The turnout is good, with scores of large trucks in the parking lot with bumper stickers that say profundities such as, "CNN Lies," "Don't Worry, the King of England Didn't Like the Minuteman Project Either," and "Hanoi Jane 1972, John Kerry 2004."

Like the last day of elderly, militaristic summer camp, there are continual handshaking, pats on shoulders, and thanks-for-coming-outs, as smug FOX News and various other news agencies point their television cameras.

A man with one of the bigger bellies among the group proudly proclaims to a guy wearing a "Tyranny Response Team" T-shirt, "I got an e-mail from some people in Australia who want to put together a Minuteman Project there 'cuz they got a big illegal problem. They want to secure the coast."

A rotund documentary filmmaker, who just had his camera pointed at someone, gets mad at me. "Don't film me without permission," he whines. Now even the media hate the other media.

Not surprisingly, the closing proceedings open with everyone standing up, putting their hands over their hearts, and reciting the Pledge of Allegiance. Then a pastor is brought up to give vindication in the name of Jesus Christ. (What about the Jewish Minutemen?) It's the frickin' love of God and country.

Some Teutonic-style cheerleading is kicked off by the Minuteman of the hour, founder Chris Simcox, wearing a red button-down shirt, looking like a thinner Jeff Foxworthy. But instead of uttering, "You might be a redneck," he proclaims, "We did this together. We the people. We all inspired millions of people to follow us and lead, so you're all leaders." (So I guess, like in the Special Olympics, we're all winners!)

If the American flag could smile, it would be grinning from ear to ear, as rows of lunch tables loudly applaud. Message to Congress: "We the people are tired of waiting for you to lead. We're going to lead our nation in an effort to protect our borders, to protect our families, our neighbors, and our way of life in this great country known as the United States of America!"

Huge "yeah!"s. Applause.

"I have almost twenty thousand new volunteers that will follow our lead and that will make sure we lead the way; as I said, the only honorable thing to do at this point is to relieve us of duty by sending out Humvees filled with National Guards to protect our borders."

Yeah!

A woman with a T-shirt that reads, "What Part of Illegal Don't They Get!" stands up, holding a round object. "Will you please sign the Minuteman family egg?"

Huge Minuteman laughs. There's more. Jim Gilchrist, the bad cop to Simcox's good cop, sarcastically proclaims in an in-your-face-Bush manner that *he's proud to be a vigilante*!

Yeah!

Fidel then shares, "I have stood shoulder to shoulder with heroes of America—you are it!"

Yeah!

A mustachioed guy adorned in a jean vest with red sleeves feels Bush should hold a press conference and say, "We expect all other countries in the world to respect our borders. Those who do not respect our borders shall be repelled by force if it is necessary!" There's more. "If he would do that, it would begin to change. But I'm afraid the president is not a Minuteman."

I think he's expecting a slow, building *Dead Poet's Society*–style clap turning to thunderous applause, but it doesn't really happen. Instead, he adds with wooden delivery, "People ask, aren't you afraid of getting killed? I tell them fear is for those who sit home and watch reality television. THE MINUTEMEN HAVE NO FEAR!"

Yeah!

Big-bellied men in baseball caps, with T-shirts reading "UN-PEACE THROUGH TERROR" and "Undocumented Border Patrol" wander about giving the thumbs-up. There are calls to go back to communities and track down employers and landlords hiring and renting to illegals. (Are they hiring al Qaeda as well, or were the Minutemen simply referring to Mexicans on this one?) We're told to bring pain to those employers in New York, South Dakota, and California—to *put the fear of God in these people.*

Yeah!

"You ain't seen nothing yet, we've just started."

Yeah!

"There's no telling how far this thing will go."

Yeah!

We're told, "This is the best cross-section of Americans I ever met, and there hasn't been one incident, no matter what the opposition says." (Those zit-faced college girls.)

A video camera is shoved in my face.

"What do you think of the situation on the border?" asks a cameraman from the Minuteman news organization.

"What part of 'illegal' don't they understand?!" I reply, reading my response off the woman's shirt.

An Arizona grandmother goes to the podium, leans into microphone, and starts screaming, "We want President Bush personally to come out and pick up every bit of illegal alien garbage!"

More yeahs! (Illegal alien "garbage" could be taken two ways, the second being very racist. What about those mentioned copies of the Koran?)

"Mr. Bush, we got your garbage bags, come pick it up!" She raises her arms triumphantly.

This is the part where it gets really ugly, and, with patriotic adrenaline pumping, everyone turns on us—the media. How utterly fucking strange! Who would've thought that my experience inside the Minuteman Project would end in a very tense incident, with me, momentarily, fearing for my safety in an angry crowd bonded together with what is becoming a lynch-mob mentality?

The oldest man here (so old he looks like he's about to fall over), a religious broadcaster since 1961 ("I've been battling the Left ever since!"), wearing an ill-fitting baseball cap, grabs the microphone, sternly raising his voice to the point where I think he might start clutching his heart.

"I went into religious broadcasting so I could TELL THEM WHAT I THINK OF THEM!"

Yeah!

"The left-wing media is the biggest problem we got in America. If it wasn't for them, our president and a lot of these other politicians would stand up and tell the truth, but they're afraid of these guys!" Adding, "But you don't be afraid of them!"

"Don't be afraid!" someone in the crowd repeats. "Don't be afraid!"

"Woo! Yeah!"

Angry, scornful looks from the entire tribe of Minutemen: Ken, Ed, Papa Bear, Phoebe, the Minute Dudes, as they vent their entire frustration with illegal aliens in our direction. The steely-eyed man with the Bowie knife and death-grip handshake shoots me a look; he never liked me to begin with. I slowly back away, hoping no one is reaching for a gun. Then I bump into a smarmy, well-groomed local Tucson reporter who takes flack from several Minutemen surrounding him.

"Aren't you that guy who had the hidden camera and walked around?" grunts an old man backed by disgruntled others around him.

The well-groomed reporter feebly defends himself. "I've been on this story since day one, and I've been nonbiased. We're the ones that said you were doing a good job."

It's not pretty when a well-groomed TV reporter loses composure and becomes unnerved. In a tizzy, he snaps, "I'm done with this!" He motions to his PA and storms off, his reporter panties left in a bundle. Before they turn their wrath on me, I hightail it to my car, passing the well-groomed reporter, who tries to gather his self-control. Poising himself to interview a random Minuteman with some by-no-means softball questions in order to get them on his good side, the reporter concludes, "It started out with protest. It ended peacefully," he says with big grin and almost a goofy giggle. "How good is that?"

The love is gone; the Minuteman, wanting nothing to do with the interview, storms off (I think to get a rope). Already, with my engine running and foot positioned to hit the gas, I quickly ask the well-groomed reporter why he freaked out earlier. He explains the depths he's taken to cover this story. "I came out here. I sat with the Minutemen in the lawn chairs!"

Looking at the desert dust beneath my fingernails, while glancing over my shoulder to see if the mob is heading our way, I swiftly ask, "What was your last story you covered?"

"The popularity of Texas Hold 'Em." He pauses uncomfortably, adding, "It's sweeps week."

I, as a journalistic peer, shun him. That, my friends, is some dirty journalism.

CHAPTER 10
A WASTE OF TIME-SHARE

One afternoon, the light on my answering machine is blinking. Why, who could it be? A long-lost friend? CNN reporter Wolf Blitzer? Hell, no—it's a prerecorded message from a woman with the ditzy delivery of an enthusiastic next-door neighbor. She wants to let me in on a little secret that only she knows about.

"Hey, you guys!" she says. "Listen—there's this RPM Promotion Center, and they're giving away, like, thirty trips to Las Vegas! They fly you there and you stay at the Stardust or Circus Circus. Anyhow, you just call them, and you can get some great stuff. So call them NOW!"

I play back the message several times. "Hey, you guys! Listen . . ."

On the fourth playing, my reaction is, "Oh, my God!" I can't believe what a lucky, lucky son of a bitch I am! Some strange company, out of the kindness of their hearts, has the sole intent of sending me to Las Vegas, *no strings attached*! Surely if they wanted me to buy something, they would've mentioned it in their damn cutesy prerecorded telemarketing message. Hell, if I could find a decent, good-paying job, I'd be able to afford my own Vegas vacation. But in this stifling Bush economy, a free vacation sounds like manna from heaven!

Vegas! Vegas! I'm going to Vegas!

Fumbling for the phone, I call about getting my "great stuff." (I like great stuff.)

"Reservations. This is Molly. How can I help you?" gruffly says Molly of reservations fame. Her phone manner is at best unpleasant.

"Yes, I'm calling about my free trip to Vegas. Vegas! Vegas!" I scream. "Can I leave right away?"

"No!" Molly of reservations fame exclaims, raining on my parade. Without explanation, she asks me if I fit certain criteria: "Does your household make over sixty thousand dollars a year?"

"Yes! As a matter of fact, I'm an eccentric millionaire! Can I go to Vegas now?"

"No. Are you married or single?"

"I'm married to a fine woman who . . . LOVES VEGAS! Vegas! Woo!"

"OK, all you have to do is come down and watch a ninety-minute presentation on vacation packages."

"Then can I go to Vegas?"

"Yes, yes," Molly affirms, using her at-best disgruntled phone manner.

I make an appointment for my girlfriend and me under the pseudonyms Ken and Kathy Baker. We're told to go to the Shell Vacations office on Sunday afternoon.

There's an air of mystery surrounding the so-called ninety-minute presentation. But who cares? Before I know it, I'll be eating ninety-nine-cent shrimp cocktails and playing nickel slots at Circus Circus. For some reason, it's mandatory that I bring a major credit card, which I'll need to show upon arrival. Hmmm . . .

Vegas Preparation

When Ken and Kathy Baker show up for their "ninety-minute presentation," I want to make it perfectly clear that they're all about *the Vegas*. In order to stress this, my girlfriend and I go to a local thrift store and buy matching Las Vegas Hard Rock Café sweatshirts. I top off my look with a Las Vegas visor, and I carry a used copy of *Fodor's Pocket to Las Vegas* (to flip through and spout random Vegas facts).

Ninety Minutes of Pure Annoyance

Sunday afternoon at two, we go to the Shell Vacations office. We're already chanting "Vegas! Vegas!"

Inside, we hear occasional clapping from another room. Balloons are tied to chairs. (What are the balloons about?) Hawaiian music is piped in. Other couples, a bit older than us and wearing fancy sweaters, are filling out questionnaires.

"We're here for the free Vegas vacation," I say to the receptionist with a bold I-wanna-go-to-Vegas smile. "Can we go right away?"

Three men wearing ties turn and give me dirty looks. The receptionist laughs.

"You mean, you're here for the vacation package presentation," she clarifies.

"But we get a free trip to Vegas, right?"

She mumbles something to the effect of yes. So begins the questionnaire portion of the afternoon. I put my finger on my chin and mark the box indicating that I make over $175,000 per year—which puts me within Bush's big tax-break area. I list the piece of fiction "Japanese toy designer, creator of *Bobomon*" as my occupation. My lovely wife, Kathy, claims that she is the owner of a string of beauty salons bearing her name.

Then it hits me. The balloons . . . the clapping . . . the couples with the nice sweaters . . . the mandatory presentation of my credit card. . . . This isn't about giving people "great stuff" and making sure they have a fun time in Vegas (Vegas! Vegas!)!

No! This place has a creepy hard-sell atmosphere one would expect from Scientology. This is all about vacation time-shares and the selling thereof. Bah!

They could have told me that straight up front, over the phone. Instead they merely mentioned free gifts and Vegas. I have as much interest in vacation time-shares as I do in contracting polio.

"Ken and Kathy Baker?" bellows our assigned time-share salesman. He has a firm handshake, a red face, and a greasy look. He goes by the name of George. He's going to play time-share hardball with us. I'll show him—I'm going to stand my ground and pressure him into sending us to Vegas, just like he's going to pressure me into buying a useless time-share.

Let's Tango!

Having someone talk to me about time-shares is equivalent to having someone talk to me about Our Lord Jesus Christ—it's something I could do without, but I know that no matter what I say, he'll be very persistent.

George takes us to the wheel-and-deal room (where the light golf-clapping came from). We're directed to sit at a small round table. Other people are sitting at other small round tables, animatedly discussing time-shares with their assigned salesmen. Our small round table doesn't have a balloon.

I launch into the conversation, steering it relentlessly on a collision course toward Vegas.

"Now, the Stratosphere—is that still in Vegas?" I inquire, firmly placing my Vegas Fodor's guide in the center of the small round table (without a balloon).

"I'm not sure. What's the Stratosphere?" George answers.

"It's a 1,150-foot tower overlooking Vegas," I reply with disdain, using some of my newfound Vegas trivia.

George tries to take charge, turning the time-share tables. He pulls out a long list of exotic vacation locations (Italy, the Caribbean, etc.).

"Do you like skiing?" he asks.

"No."

"Do you like swimming?"

"No."

"Is there anywhere on this list you would like to vacation?"

"Vegas!" I say with finger extended. "Vegas! Vegas! You're sending us there, right?"

"We got property in Vegas."

"No, I mean as our free gift."

George proceeds to show me a picture of a Hilton hotel and the inside of a suite with a large bed. "What do you think?"

I stare at it for a moment then say, "I really just want the free trip."

Red-faced George is a trained professional. He has experienced many rebuttals. He tells me that I could stay in a luxury hotel suite on *all* my Vegas trips. "It's like if you had a friend who drove a really nice Jaguar. He'd drive it one week, and you'd drive it the next week."

"I do something like that, except with my wife," I snort, giving an all-knowing chuckle and a poke in the ribs. Having a time-share is sort of like being a swinger. And, somehow, I think those two cultures *do* intersect.

George goes back to the picture of the hotel room.

"So what do you think?"

"How about, when I go to Vegas ON THE FREE TRIP YOU'RE GIVING US, I go check it out."

"Why do you need to go look at it? You've seen a Hilton hotel before, right?" snaps George (red face and all).

I see the whole time-share sales strategy. The salesman is not supposed to let people get away with just "thinking about it." The big cheese wants him to close the sale then and there—thus the need for the mandatory credit card check. Aha!

"Well, there could be loud construction next door," I reason. "Or the hotel could be haunted."

George laughs that salesman's laugh.

"This is Vegas. There's construction going on next door to everything."

Call me stupid, but I would want to see property I'm investing in before putting thousands of dollars down. I'm funny that way.

"Honey, when are we going to get our Vegas trip?" whines my fake wife, Kathy.

"Will you be quiet," I snarl through clenched teeth. "I'll handle this!"

It's time for another questionnaire, but a harder one. George leaves us alone as we answer such questions as:

Q: Where are you planning to vacation in the next twelve months?
A: Vegas!
Q: Where were your last two vacations?
A: Vegas and VEGAS!
Q: Which of the following areas would you like to visit?
A: Vegas!

Done!

George returns. He's now carrying colorful vacation magazines. He uses them as visual aids.

"If there was one place on earth you'd like to vacation, where would that be?" (Is this guy dense? Hasn't he been listening?!)

Pondering the question, I remove my Las Vegas sweatshirt only to reveal a T-shirt that says "Las Vegas."

"Vegas!" I scream.

I turn to my fake wife, Kathy.

"Vegas! Vegas!" we chant.

"OK, OK—besides Vegas, where would you like to vacation?"

I sit there in silence for a moment and reflect on places that aren't Vegas. Finally, when the silence starts to get uncomfortable, I pipe up with, "I guess there's nowhere else we'd really liked to go. We really don't like vacations."

"Nowhere?" George is shocked and angry.

"OK, I guess Moosejaw, Canada. Do you have any timeshares up there? That's where I grew up."

George is showing signs of frustration. He's offered us discounted vacation magazine subscriptions. (No go.) Inexpensive access to a health club. (Uh-uh.) More clapping comes from the other room. His already-red face is turning shades of scarlet.

"I tell you what, why don't we go to the big map in the other room and you show me where Moosejaw is? Huh?" he says, sounding like he's testing my manhood. "I want to see where Moosejaw is!"

I think he's trying to call my bluff. I have no idea in hell where Moosejaw is. I think George has snapped. They're going to find him later, stripped naked in the break room, sprawling in a sea of balloons and vacation magazines!

"Sure, I'll show you where Moosejaw is."

We parade into the other room (where there's more light clapping). Different people in different nice sweaters sit at small round tables (with other balloons). Sure enough, there's a huge map of the whole entire world.

George folds his arms. "Now, why don't you show me where Moosejaw is?"

I look long and hard at Canada.

"It's somewhere in here," I say, rotating my palm over a large portion of Canada.

As luck would have it, I spot Moosejaw out of the corner of my eye. "It's here!" I scream out like a girl. "Moosejaw is here!"

George is annoyed by my geographical prowess.

With the Moosejaw dilemma cleared up, we parade back to our table. Pulling out a pen and paper, George starts laying out what the down payment and monthly installments are for our worldwide time-share.

His plan involves us doling out eighteen thousand dollars, plus monthly payments, topped off with an annual renter's fee. Once that's arranged, we'll be able to enjoy time-share luxury hotel rooms around the world for roughly seventy-nine dollars per night. (And we'd still only have to pay airfare!) Wait a minute. This is not a good deal. This is not a good deal at all.

"George, I don't mean to pop your bubble," I state once again, "but we don't really want to buy a time-share. We just want to go to Vegas."

The Closer

"I'll be right back," says George, looking flustered. Moments later, he returns with Vince. Vince wears a black suit. Vince is the closer. Vince is *soooooo* smooth, he could slip right through your fingers when you shake hands, leaving a greasy residue. Vince is brought in for those hard-to-sell cases. I hate Vince.

"Now, when we go to Vegas, can we stay at Circus Circus?" I ask Vince, the closer, when he sits down.

"Vegas! Vegas! Vegas!" George says, like his sarcasm would somehow go over our heads. But Vince is smooth—he knows how to establish a common ground.

"I used to deal at Circus Circus," says Vince. He tells us about his blackjack-dealing past and how he once met Frank Sinatra. Then he tells us how great the time-shares are in Vegas.

"They want to make sure there isn't any construction going on next door," interjects George, once again thinking that his subtle sarcasm has surpassed the stratosphere of our intellect.

Vince, the closer, goes over the exact same payment plan that George has laid out for us, but he throws in a lower-payment option.

"So how do you want to pay—check or credit card?" he asks smoothly. He has the confidence of a blackjack dealer. (That's why he's the closer.)

I pull out my credit card. Then I immediately put it back. I repeat this process two more times.

I restate my mission statement: "We don't want a time-share—we just want to go to Vegas. Can we go to Vegas now?"

Vince, the closer, turns to my fake wife, Kathy, and asks, "What do *you* think of all this?" He's employing the classic divide-and-conquer technique. "Does he make all the decisions?"

"We just want to go to Vegas!" Kathy replies with a tired shrug, then she adds, "Vegas! Vegas!"

Vegas, here we come!

Vince, the closer, is so smooth—he knows when it's time to move on.

"Well, you can go redeem your vacation certificate," he grunts, like we're about to go and collect a big giant turd.

Vince and George leave. They're pissed that we didn't buy a pointless overpriced time-share (without the benefit of looking at it). But wasn't this all about getting "great stuff" and a free vacation as long as we listened to them babble on for ninety minutes? (And, yes, babble, they did!)

Yet another guy comes over. He, too, tries one last time to sell us the time-share at *an even a lower price*! This is like those Freddy Kruger movies where the monster just won't die! But the thrill is gone, gone, gone. And we get the last laugh, for we're going to Vegas *free of charge*!

"Vegas! Vegas!"

I swiftly fill out the mail-in claim certificate. As I read over the terms and conditions, I see that they've forgotten to mention that I have to pay eighty-nine dollars for hotel and airline taxes. What?

"They should have told you about that when you phoned," sneers the receptionist with a hint of a smirk. With a snotty grin, she adds, "Even on *Wheel of Fortune*, they still have to pay taxes on the prizes."

Bah! There is no such thing as a free lunch.

CHAPTER 11
HEAD-BANGING FOR JESUS!

It's always been a dream of mine to get booked on a Christian talk show posing as a guy who fronts a Christian speed-metal band. It's a personal dream right up there with becoming a lion tamer and winning a Olympic bronze medal in male figure skating. Thank Jesus—my prayers are answered (but not about the figure skating). I come across this:

> The show *Miracles Happen* features authentic, cool Christians whose lives have been transformed by the healing and saving power of Jesus Christ. Guests are invited to tell about their testimonies, healings, or miracles with a warm and inviting host. The show aims to glorify our Lord and plant seeds of hope to the viewing audience. Every story of transformation is good news, and yours is too. The only preparation we require is prayer.

Since my acting range extends to *cool Christian,* I send an e-mail. Immediately I hear back from the producer telling me the next *Miracles Happen* is to be shot on Saturday and asking me whether I'm available.

You bet your pink little ass I am! First, I need the right persona—so I explain that I play in a Christian metal band. What could be more ridiculous than head-banging for Jesus? It's right up there with other such natural fits as "vegetarians for meat" and "Klansmen for big, black booty." Think about it: rock, especially heavy metal, is the devil's music. That's what makes it fun. (If you've seen Stryper, you can back me up on that one.)

I call the producer, at which time I construct a tale of rock drug excess inspired by VH1's *Behind the Music*, most particularly the episodes on Motley Crue and Poison. ("I used to live in the house of whores, then it became the house of horrors!") Impressed, he books me on *Miracles Happen*, a public-access TV show, to tell of my Christian speed-metal transformation.

"Do you want to bring an acoustic guitar and perform one of your songs in the studio?" he asks.

"You know, what I would rather do is perform a spoken-word version of some of my Christian speed-metal lyrics," I offer, since I can't play guitar, adding, "That way it gets *The Word* across."

"That sounds great!" he replies.

Excellent! Not only do I get to dress up like a Christian metal-head, I also get to write asinine, junior-high school metal lyrics with a Jesus twist. First, a little bit of preparation is needed:

- 1 Jesus T-shirt
- 1 large black cross
- 1 studded wristband and belt
- 1 Axl Rose–style bandanna
- 2 fake tattoos that read "Jesus Rocks!"

Christian metal is a world unto itself, spawning bands with names like Armor of God, Bloodgood, Rage of Angels, and Crystavox, not to mention Tykkus. After much consideration, I decide to name my fictional Christian metal band Pray-er (rhymes with Slayer). The reason? It allows me to get indignant when people mispronounce it. ("It's not Prayer, it's *Pray*-er!")

Under the Christian metal stage name Chad Sin-No-More, I've recruited Johanna, an actress friend, to portray my speed-metal Christian girlfriend, Destiny. Dressed in slutty metal fashion, she, too, is wearing a Jesus T-shirt. Back story: Chad and Destiny met in rehab where they both found Jesus!

On the Highway to Jesus!

Saturday afternoon, hungover as hell, we show up at the studio. Upon entering, we're directed to the green room, which has a large bowl of grapes.

"Are you Chad?" asks the host, a very nice, very smiley, very well-groomed, very Christian lady who is slightly taken a back by our looks. "I didn't get any background at all on you."

I tell about my Christian speed-metal band, pumping my fist in the air a few times. ("*Prayer*?" "No, it's *Pray*-er!") The host, as it turns out, not only hosts *Miracles Happen* but also works as a third-grade schoolteacher.

OK, I start to feel a little bad about pulling this ruse, but there's no turning back now, so let's turn the knobs up to level 11!

"You're pretty much the only guest," the host asks in a third-grade teacherly way. (Huh?!) "So how do you feel about twenty-seven minutes?"

"Really?" I reply, mildly shocked. That's a hell of a lot of Christian speed-metal talk. It must be a slow week for *cool Christians* who've experienced Christ-centered, life-transforming miracles.

I learn the premise of *Miracles Happen*. "It's a show based on stories due to change in people's lives based on one event or multiple events," she explains. "What your life was like before, how the change occurred, and what your life has been like since."

"So I can talk about my band, *Pray*-er?"

"That would be great," she says with a big Christian smile.

"'Cause the producer said to bring in some of my lyrics to recite and stuff. And he told me to compare the positive message in my lyrics to mainstream metal bands."

"OK," she answers with mild apprehension. "Mind you, we air at six o'clock on a Tuesday night, so nothing too obscene."

I get defensive. "No, that's the whole point, that my lyrics have a positive message," I say. "They're made to inspire!"

"The set is just a chair with a black background. The point is it's all about stories; it's all about the journey that brought you where you are today. And the positive changes you are making in others' lives due to what you've been through," she explains.

"Uh-huh."

"We like to keep that in mind so that it's a story, not a lie, but a story," she adds.

I nod my head: "Yeah, no lying."

Besides Christian metal musicians, *Miracles Happen* has hosted such guests as a guy who works as a tree trimmer and who was woken up by a voice from God that told him not to stand in a certain spot. Low and behold, the next day a tree fell right in the very goddamn spot! Holy fuck!

Another guest went on a mission trip to India and was praying over a little deaf-mute girl. The little girl started moving to the music playing and then uttered the word "Jesus!" Both Destiny and I look at each other and exclaim, as if a dove had just appeared out of nowhere, "Oh, wow, that's amazing!"

"Can Destiny sit next to me while I'm being interviewed?" I ask, noting that she (along with Jesus, of course) is my pillar of strength.

My rock of Gibraltar, second-only-to-Jesus, is vetoed. "Destiny, you can watch on the monitor," snips the host. Wow, what a devout bitch!

"So we'll get you in, we'll hook up the mikes, and we'll pray. Then we'll get rolling!"

For Those about to Rock, Jesus Salutes You!

Two chairs sit next to each other in a small studio, surrounded by three TV cameras and an assortment of elderly crewmembers.

"Have you had any other Christian bands on the show?" I ask one of the three elderly cameramen.

"We had a band on the last show."

"Oh, really, what band?" I inquire.

He thinks for a moment. "They were singing Christian songs in Spanish," he says.

The third-grade schoolteacher/host situates herself in a chair close to me.

"Shall we pray?" she asks as the crew continues to set up.

"Hell, yes," I say. Then I quickly correct myself, excluding the word *hell*.

Our heads are bowed, our hands are clasped in a prayerlike manner, as the third-grade schoolteacher asks Jesus for guidance in Chad's sharing of his tale of transformation.

"Please help us to guide our minds, oh Lord . . ."

The praying goes on a little longer than I feel comfortable with. And then: "Amen!"

"Amen!" I confirm, this time without profanity.

Praying done, *it's showtime*!

"Quiet on the set," barks the floor manager.

We both sit staring with blank expressions as the opening credits roll. The combination of the bright lights and my hangover make me feel like I might pass out. Or is this a test from Jesus?

Then the host is talking into the camera: "I'm here with Chad, who has a very interesting story to share with you today. Hi, Chad, how are you?"

"I'm doing good, really good!"

"So Chad, tell us what you do?"

"I play in a Christian speed-metal band."

"Prayer?"

"No, it's *Pray*-er!" I then add the obvious: "You know, just because you're Christian, it doesn't mean you still can't crank out some butt-kicking metal!"

"Yeah!" the host says, with a confirming nod of her born-again head; I resist the urge to make the sign of the horns.

"But metal with a positive message!" I clarify, mentioning *Pray*-er's upcoming speed-metal CD. "It's called *Faster for the Master*!"

The host makes a happy face.

"Why don't you tell us how it all got started. What was your life like before?"

I throw out a little heavy-metal, meathead philosophy. "When I was little, I didn't go to church. Metal was my religion!" I explain, throwing my fist in the air. "Metal concerts were my church—except I'd drink a twelve-pack before 'attending services!'"

As the cameras roll, I recount my decadent past in my former, non-Christian speed-metal band *Skull Fuck!* "I gave into all of the devil's temptations. Satan was whispering in my ear." I retell about the exact moment (shortly after doing coke off a groupie's ass) when the Almighty turned my life around.

"I was in a motel in Bakersfield. I'd been up for a few days on crank. When suddenly I felt this tap on my shoulder. I turn around, and this voice said, 'Dude'?! . . ."

The third-grade schoolteacher/host interrupts me: "Wait, the Lord called you 'Dude?!'"

"Yeah. He called me 'Dude,'" I continue. "He said to me, 'Dude, if you keep this up, you're going to end in one of the Three Ds: death, drug overdose, or disease!'" I explain that "disease" refers to one of a sexually transmitted variety.

The host makes a sympathetic face. "What happened next?"

"I got rid of my guitar and burnt all my metal albums." Pause. "Except *Appetite for Destruction*, because the guitar on that really ROCKS!"

The host's smile somehow expresses that Slash's guitar work even transcends Christian values. Next I blow my own metal horn. "Then one day God came to me. He told me, 'You have a gift. Go use your gift in order to spread the word of the Lord! So I picked up a guitar again, and that's how I started my Christian speed-metal band."

"*Prayer*?"

"No, *Pray*-er!"

Our *Miracles Happen* host asks how the members of my old speed-metal band, *Skull Fuck* (not in those words), reacted to my spiritual transformation.

"They kind of don't understand it when I call them up and tell them to shield the dark forces and follow the path of Jesus."

I add, "Yeah, they kind of freak out." Pause. "They still got the devil whispering in their ear."

I elaborate the heights (or depths) to which I've gone to spread The Word! "I went to *Ozzfest* wearing a flowing white robe and assembled this large wooden cross and tied it to my back, in order to warn people about the evils that were going on inside. Those bands sing about fornication, drug use, how great it is to wake up lying in their own vomit," I explain as the host nods encouragingly. "Almost everybody looked at me like I was crazy. But a few people stopped and listened. One kid even ripped up his concert ticket. If I can reach just one kid, then it's worth it."

I make a proud face.

"That's very brave of you," the third-grade schoolteacher/host confirms.

But there was a price for my bravery. "Yeah, um, but I actually ended up getting arrested, 'cause with my cross and robe, someone thought I was part of the Klan," I add. "But if I could save one person, then going to jail was worth it!"

Changing the subject, the host asks, "What Christian metal bands out there do you like?"

Since I don't really know any Christian speed-metal bands, I use a little something I call *improvisation*. I say. "There's a great metal band out of Portland called Him/Hymn." I spell the name for the host to understand my clever word play then throw out the name of my other favorite Christian metal band: "Burning Bush."

"What is your goal with all this?"

"Pray-er just wants to reach kids with a positive, Christ-centered message." Pause. "Also, it would be wicked to have a number-one CD!" I exclaim, explaining how easily mainstream metal bands could change their lyrics to expound a Christian message. As an example, I use Judas Priest's "Breaking the Law."

"The lyrics give off a really negative message [law breaking]. All you have to do is change one aspect and it's a positive message."

To demonstrate, I maniacally screech out in a heavy voice my altered chorus:

I was praying to God!
Praying to God!
Praying to God, again!

Two more times the chorus is repeated. While I'm doing this, the host is making a sort of head-banging motion, in a poised, Christian lady kind of way.

"Do you want to recite some of your original lyrics?" she asks.

"I sure do!"

I pull a piece of paper and begin reciting in classic Dio tradition, the genre of metal that's all Dungeons and Dragon-y, that's full of juvenile, execrable junior high school poetry. It's my original, Christian metal composition, "Crush Satan's Skull!":

And the sin goblins come,
And I smite them down
With the magical saber of Christ.

And He delivers me to salvation,
As we ride together on the back of a beautiful winged horse
Named Malachi.

Capture!
Rapture!
Give your soul to the Master!

Smite the evil-doers. Smite them. Smite them.
Crush the skull of Satan! Crush it! Crush it!

The host has a fixed smile on her face; she looks mildly confused. I clarify my presentation: "Now picture those lyrics, backed by a grinding, head-banging, speed-metal guitar."

"Then, can you even hear the lyrics?" she asks.

I pause. In a perfect *Spinal Tap* moment of self-realization, I reply, "Um, well, not really. No."

Quickly, I elaborate. Even though audiences don't usually understand the lyrics, I still can use speed metal as my ministry. "I always give a little sermon right after we play 'Crush Satan's Skull.'" Pause. "It's usually really uplifting."

ROCK 'N ROLL THE CREDITS

The host seems to be running out of questions; it's toward the end of twenty-seven minutes, which just flew by. Falling into a staring contest, I ask her about what led to her own spiritual transformation. She seems momentarily flustered.

"Nothing really bad happened to me. I've been through a divorce," she explains, "but I was never addicted to drugs or abused or anything like that as a kid."

We momentarily grow silent. To keep some momentum in the show, I offer some more original lyrics, written to the tune of AC/DC's "Highway to Hell":

> Gay marriage, it's a sin.
> After all, you have to answer to Him.
> Prayer in school will do a charm,
> The Bible in the classroom could do no harm.
>
> I'm on a highway to Jesus!
> I'm on a highway to Jesus!
> I'm on a highway to Jesus!
> I'm on a highway to Jesus!

On completion, the polite Christian host says with a positive glow, "It sounds like you really turned your life around!"

"Yeah." Pause. "I guess I have."

"We need to keep talking because this is where the credits would roll," she remarks. We both sit in place with fixed smiles, and I'm certain I'll go to hell for this. But that's OK. Because rock is, and always should be, the devil's music!

CHAPTER 12
SAVE THE CUTE ANIMALS

It's time to give some equal time—or unequal time—to infiltrating the Left. If we want our message to be heard and to be effective, we've got to examine ourselves (at least just enough to say we did it) in order to point out why the Right calls us "moonbats" or, even worse, "the loony Left" when we present our protests like bad Dada theater.

That's why I've decided to become an animal rights protestor. Which animal protest is best? What's hot and what's not? If you had arachnophobia, all spiders would horrify you. Similarly, it would seem, if you were vegan, all types of animal food production would horrify you. (In fact, if you ventured into the back of a butcher shop, it might cause you to cry out for a war crimes tribunal.) But most people who come out in force show up only when the animal is really adorable rather than ugly. (Example: cats = cute, but cows = "Hey, that's a great vest!") And I'm all in favor of beauty.

Yes, it's time to protest the inhumane treatment of animals—especially the really cute ones.

Protest No. 1—South Korea's Illegal Dog-Meat Trade

The ad:

> Each year, two million dogs are electrocuted, strangled or bludgeoned to death in South Korea. Then they are boiled, skinned, browned by a torch, chopped up, and eaten. The Korean Government is even considering regulating and legalizing the consumption of these animals, even though the vast majority of Koreans don't eat dogs or cats.

This seems a good place to start. I honestly can say I would never eat a dog. Really. No argument there. (I heard it tastes like chicken though.)

Level of Adorableness of Animal Involved in Protest at Hand (out of 1–10): 10+

Saturday, I approach a large outdoor market by the waterfront in San Francisco. Among rows of jewelry and T-shirts stands one lone protestor. Given the number of dog owners, I was expecting a big turnout (perhaps a bullhorn or two). Yes, one woman talking on a cell phone stands in front of a disturbing sign (the key to a good animal rights protest).

Quality of Protests Signs: 4

There basically is only the sign, which reads: "Dog's Worst Enemy—Korea." I'm not a professional protester, but I really think this protest could benefit from a wider variety of protest signs. Though the disturbing image is very effective, I would suggest more signs and slogans, such as, "Korean dogs have something to bark about!"

Approaching the lone woman, I interrupt her cell phone call and play naive, pointing to the sign.

"Is this like in the circus and stuff? You know, like when they make them wear people clothes and jump through hoops."

"This isn't about the circus—it's about the millions of dogs in Korea that are electrocuted, strangled, and bludgeoned to death each year," she clarifies.

Pause. "Oh, that's a lot different."

She hands me a flyer.

Quality of Flyers: 8

Very catchy slogan: "Man's Best Friend—BETRAYED!"

The photo shows a dog looking sad. I assume I would be sad too if I were about to become someone's meal. Great font used on the word *BETRAYED*. It's in crimson red and sort of looks like it's dripping blood.

She explains, "They have them in cages at restaurants for people to pick out."

"Don't they do that with lobsters?" I ask, suggesting that this may just be a matter of cultural differences.

Her demeanor changes as if there is about to be an argument. "I don't approve of that either—I'm vegan."

I try to explain—lobsters in our country have it tough. They are the most popular creature to cook *alive*! But no one seems to have a problem with this. Supermarkets have tanks crammed full of these live crustaceans. Claws rendered useless by large rubber bands—lobster handcuffs! Shoppers tap on the glass, not even raising an eyebrow at what could be compared to an undersea Abu Ghraib prison. Animal rights protestors should break into supermarkets and liberate the lobsters! The reason they don't: Lobsters aren't that cute.

I'm directed to a very graphic video.

Quality of Protest Video: 3

Technically speaking, the production quality of the gruesome protest video leaves a lot to be desired. It could highly benefit from professional editing, a clear voiceover narration (perhaps from a celebrity advocate), stock footage, and a few different camera angles.

"What if the animals were killed more humanely?" I ask.

"Then I wouldn't feel so bad about it," she replies.

"I've eaten a dog before," I say with a serious expression, as a disturbed, tense look forms on her face. I break a smile. "A veggie-dog that is!" Oh, how we laugh.

Protest Extras: 7

Cards, preaddressed to the ambassador of Korea, await people to fill out. Roughly speaking, the card tells the ambassador that eating dogs is bad, and if the dog eating doesn't stop, I—the signer of the postcard—will boycott all products made in Korea.

Suggestions for a Better Protest

- Large papier-mâché dogs hoisted on sticks by protestors walking on stilts.
- Adorable dogs wearing people clothes and large sunglasses (awwww!).
- Placing dog poop into a brown paper bag, putting it on the doorstep of the Korean embassy, lighting it on fire, ringing the doorbell, then running away.

Overall Protest Rating: 4

Yes, we should protest Korea's treatment of animals because it's inhumane, but we should also protest because dogs are incredibly cute, especially when dressed in people clothes and made to pose for postcards. That, my friends, is adorable!

PROTEST NO. 2—ANTI–FOIE GRAS

Ducks or geese are force-fed until they are so large that they can barely move and can only waddle (kind of like Ralphie May of *Last Comic Standing*). They are crammed into a pen to wallow in their own filth (again, like Ralphie May of *Last Comic Standing*). Then their livers become so enlarged that they turn diseased.

Apparently, when made into pâté, these diseased livers are, according to gourmet chefs, an expensive delicacy and very delicious. (Ralphie May of *Last Comic Standing* must have a very delicious liver.)

Level of Adorableness of Animal at Hand: 8

The ad:

> Please join IDA, Viva! USA, Farm Sanctuary, and Animal Place at an educational outreach event outside of this "special dinner," the actual intention of which is to justify and promote egregious cruelty to animals.

I'm told via e-mail, "It will be a peaceful event."

Yeah, right. Foie gras protestors have been known to do such things as vandalize the cars of chefs, pour cement into restaurant sinks, and leave the water running at food establishments selling the product, as well as videotape the family of a known producer and then send it to him as an eerie warning.

This is going to be great. I love direct, angry protest confrontation. I imagine it to be like a modern version of an antidraft protest in the '60s, except instead of Vietnam, it's about foie gras. Dramatic conflict makes for a great protest!

Eighteen people, mostly kindly older women, stand outside a chichi restaurant in downtown San Francisco. Are these kindly older women the ones who poured cement into the sinks and vandalized a chef's car? Besides me, the only other guy in attendance looks like he's here because his wife made him come. Every five minutes he switches to a new protest sign.

Without fanfare, or an introduction, I grab a sign, start vigorously waving it, and file in.

Quality of Protest Signs: 10+

The signs are first rate. There's a wide variety—all mounted on sticks, all graphically gruesome, each offering different sayings:

"HOW MUCH CRUELTY CAN ONE SWALLOW?"

"WHY PET SOME AND EAT OTHERS?" (Good question, but it brings up others: *Why let some run around a racetrack and place wagers on them and eat others? Why ride some at a summer camp in northern Wisconsin and eat others?* Those would take one hell of a large sign, of course.)

"IT SUCKS FOR DUCKS." Nice use of rhyming.

"They're serving a twelve-course meal, consisting entirely of duck," explains the cute protesting girl next to me. "Even the dessert is duck."

"Like duck sherbet? Or duck-sickles?!"

Ducks made into dessert. That's going way too far. I start vigorously waving my "No Foie Gras" sign.

People drive by—some slow down, honk, and give the thumbs-up. Others flip us the finger, or *the bird*, if you will.

"I'd feel bad if we caused an accident," exclaims one of the kindly ladies.

A high school couple, dressed in prom formal-wear, walks by.

"I don't want to go by there," I hear the date say as she approaches. "It scares me."

They're handed a flyer.

Quality of Flyers: 9

"Foie Gras–Cruelty Revealed." This is good. The tagline sounds like a *Dateline* special investigative report.

Though killing ducks would be, in a way, worse than torture through overfeeding (think of six fat people settling into an all-you-can-eat buffet), this group has singled out foie gras. A Chinatown mainstay is the classic whole duck hanging in the restaurant window. To add insult to injury, the browned, skin-still-on, dead ducks are hung in the window on a hook, to be viewed like Uday and Qusay Hussein shoved in front of cameras on US television. But that form of duck abuse never raises a protester's eyebrow.

"There's so much violence in the world," one protestor tells a reporter. "This is one step against it you can personally take."

The reporter comes over for my comment on the restaurant serving foie gras.

"It's a delicacy of despair," I say in the perfect sound bite. She jots that down. I continue. "It's gourmet cruelty." She writes that down. "Foie gras leaves a bad taste in my mouth! It's a deadly dinner! A plate of hate!" She keeps writing. "Foie gras is for quacks! Go Niners!" I throw out for no reason.

I tell another reporter, "Not only do we have to boycott foie gras, but also Rocky Mountain Oysters for which farmers force the animal's testicles to swell to three times their normal size. Not to mention cow brains, which leaves the animal completely disorientated."

Quality of Protest Video: 9

Great video! It features hidden-camera footage, professionally edited with clean voiceover narration. The protestors from Korea's illegal dog and cat trade could take a page from the anti–foie gras group. Very artfully done in a cinema verité–style.

I think the best part of being an animal rights protester is not only speaking out for the cute, fluffy animals but also meeting an abundance of cute, flirty college girls.

"Do you want to share this with me?" says one with a newly issued leaflet, which is a foie gras disclaimer from the restaurant.

"Yes, I do. I do indeed. I'm against foie gras, too," I say and move in closer.

For really smooth players, I could easily see animal rights protests as a perfect place to pick up progressive women.

"Not only do I not eat meat or dairy," I tell another woman holding a sign, "but I don't even eat mock duck because 'duck' is in the name." She smiles with approval.

During the entire afternoon, I see only one well-dressed couple entering the restaurant. They are politely given a flyer. Maybe our protesting works? Or maybe . . .

"When does the protest last until?" I ask one of the kindly older ladies.

"It goes to 6:15."

I suggest that maybe it should run later, into the time when the restaurant actually has customers.

"We probably shouldn't stay later because it might make the restaurant angry," she replies with kindness.

I approach the reporter from earlier.

"I have one more for ya: 'Foie gras is a faux pas!'"

"You could be a copywriter," she says, still writing.

Suggestions for a Better Protest

- Large papier-mâché enlarged duck livers that could be hoisted on a stick by protesters on stilts.
- Blowing up large, liverlike balloons, then dramatically bursting them.
- Hiring children's theater group actors, dressing them in duck costumes, then having them kick all who enter the restaurant in the shins.

Overall Protest Rating: 7

Though I was disappointed that sinks weren't clogged with cement or that cars weren't vandalized, the kindness and organization of the protesters won me over.

PROTEST NO. 3: NEIMAN MARCUS ANTI-FUR DEMONSTRATION

The ad reads:

> This is a weekly anti-fur protest that happens rain or shine. Signs and leaflets are provided. Please also do not wear or bring anything leather or that looks like leather. [An obvious problem in the past.]

This is a classic. It's the granddaddy of them all—a lovable, old-school fixture in the world of animal rights protests. I can't wait. I hope there will be blood thrown on shoppers!

Level of Adorableness of Animal at Hand: With Fur, 9. Without Fur, 0.

One woman, like a lone Don Quixote, protests on her own in front of the downtown Neiman Marcus. She has a slew of gruesome signs secured to a newsstand, and she is smiling.

Quality of Protest Signs: An Intense 10

What abortion protestors achieve with the classic bloody fetus shot, fur protestors achieve with the bloody, skinned dead animal signs. The signs sell the protest.

An adorable cat, if granted the power of human speech, seems to be saying, "I Am Not a Coat."

A fox, with the ability to form human sentences, is made to say, "Does Your Mother Have a Fur Coat? My Mother Lost Hers."

"The Real Face of Fur," features a bloody animal carcass.

"Fur. No Skin off My Back," features another bloody animal carcass.

The funny "Neiman Carcass" features, you guessed it, a bloody carcass.

(My idea for fur protest signs: "My Parents Went To Neiman Marcus And All I Got Was This Lousy Fur Coat," with a picture of a bloody animal carcass. Or the funny "Got Fur?" with *two* bloody animal carcasses.)

"Ewww," a shopper remarks, peering at the sea of signs. Another woman teams up with the lone protestor. Then a guy joins (who, I assume, is protesting in order to get busy with one of the two anti-fur women). Holding signs, smiling, they casually chat like any huddled group of three friends catching up. This is utter bullshit. Where's the angry blood-throwing? The newly arrived woman, still chatting away, despondently extends her hand filled with flyers (which people react to with the same avoidance as they would to Scientology literature). I stand there for several seconds. Finally, still waiting to be handed a flyer, I mumble, "I, too, am against fur." She doesn't acknowledge my presence.

Quality of Flyers: An Equally Intense 10, but 2 Points Taken off for Too Much Rhyming!

All the flyers, like the posters, say, "Neiman Carcass." (Good thing they're not picketing Macy's—they wouldn't have a rhyming slogan!) The flyers state that the department store is responsible for cruelty, suffering, and death. Instead of the standard unhappy animal-in-a-cage photo, it goes for a cute cat image.

"We speak for those who can't," says the flyer.

Protest Extras: 9

Genuine steel-jaw traps are a nice dramatic touch. Another great addition is actually stringing up some animal pelts to the light post like they were a South American president during a rebel El Revolución!

Quality of Protest Video: 0

More bullshit! There's no video to speak of! Serious points are subtracted.

Down the street, I notice a leather shop goes completely unprotested. The goods inside could be an animal protestor's equivalent to Ed Gein's psycho workshop. I'm sure they could come up with some bloody signs against skinning cows. But then again, leather makes for good wallets, not to mention shoes.

Suggestions for a Better Protest

- Instead of signs with slogans that rhyme, how about signs with anagrams, haikus, or limericks?
- Hire those naked, hot supermodels, who would actually live up to their saying, "I'd rather go naked than wear fur." Yeah!

Overall Protest Rating: 3

No videos, no chants, a small turnout, and protestors smiling? Much like the TV show *Friends* when it was in its ninth season, this protest has gotten lazy.

What I've learned is harming animals is bad—really bad! But I also learned that getting good help to make effective protests these days is harder than finding a supermodel who *really* doesn't wear fur.

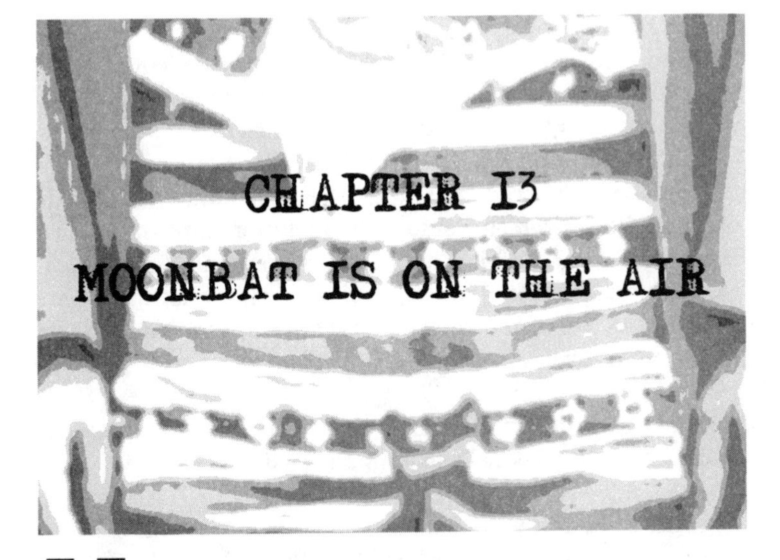

CHAPTER 13
MOONBAT IS ON THE AIR

Hark for the love of those right-wing talk radio shows, where the hosts end up screaming at their invited guest like an irate child with a broken Xbox on a disappointing Christmas morning. Be it Bill O'Reilly, Rush Limbaugh, or Michael Savage, a specific set of rules and strategies of right-wing punditry are followed on their shows to prove to faithful listeners that their opinion is faaaaar superior than that of their puny guests. What better way to infiltrate the machinery that is conservative radio punditry than by learning their rules from the inside? As Fortuna takes a lucky spin, recently I was asked to be a guest on right-wing talk radio shows, in order to spout my croissant-eating views. That's right, Bubba, I got booked as the "Bay Area moonbat liberal," with hosts ready to extend their claws and *tear me a new one*. It was like entering Dante's radio purgatory.

My virgin foray into conservative punditry was a debutante debut on the *Michael Medved Show*—a movie review guy and Orthodox-Jew-turned-extreme-right-winger talk radio host. (Where the hell do those lines intersect?) But that was merely conservative radio light compared with "Michigan's Most Listened to Christian Talk—the *Bob Dutko Show*" on WMUZ–The Light. OK, imagine Rush Limbaugh but with a Jesus twist—that's what I was up against. I remember it distinctly.

Other guests on the *Bob Dutko Show* bill: a guy who's going to give "scientific" proof that the Earth is only thousands of years old, not billions, which would make evolution impossible. Host Bob Dutko states, "Which, by the way, *scientifically*, I agree with. Not just because the Bible says so, but that's what the *science* actually says. We're not going to deal with emotion—we're going to deal with *fact* and *science*!"

Rule of Punditry #1: An "I don't take shit from anyone" catchphrase. "Fearlessly Defending the Faith!"

Rule of Punditry #2: Hard-rock intro music—further showing you don't take shit from anyone! The show's theme, a Christian band's version of Tom Petty's "I Won't Back Down" plays. I diligently wait on hold while the Fearless Defender of the Faith spouts matter-of-factly, "Why don't we see the kind of religious diversity in television programming that we do in ethnic diversity? Look, I'm all for ethnic diversity, but if we really want to show a representative of American culture, don't you think 80 percent of the characters on TV ought to be calling themselves Christians? It seems to me we should be judged by the content of our character and not the color of our skin. It sounds familiar to me a little bit. Does it to you?"

Then my introduction: "Right now, let's get to a guy who is not shy about criticizing President Bush, or any other Republicans or conservatives, for that matter," Dutko says. "He's a flaming liberal. I can't give you the subtitle of his book. It has a cuss word in it, and I'm not going to do it!"

The word, by the way, is *ass* (*Republican Like Me: Infiltrating Red-State, White-Ass, and Blue-Suit America*). In the imagination of the Christian listeners, phrasing it as such I'm sure they're thinking the cuss word is *motherfucker* and are immediately already plotting for this "flaming liberal's" eternal damnation. One pundit point for Dutko!

Rule of Punditry #3: Immediately get your guest on the defensive, working up his emotions so he'll come across as a blathering idiot.

"I think you got a double standard going here," the Fearless Defender of the Faith rants in regard to Target store employees saying, "Happy Holidays" rather than "Merry Christmas" to include other religions' shitty little holidays in order to cash in on their non-Jesus-believing consumer dollars. Yup, I made the rookie mistake of immediately criticizing Bob Dutko's asinine view of his supported boycott of Target stores.

The nature of his tone: I'm going to take my football and go home if I don't get my way. "You're saying that's leaving out the poor Jew or atheists or whatever," he adds about other religions' Grinch-like stealing of little Cindy Lou Who's last can of Who-hash.

My response to their inclusion: "Why not give the little guy a shot?" It might be Bob Dutko fears that saying, "Happy Holidays" will somehow lead the trajectory course to back-alley abortions being performed in Target store dressing rooms.

"Why not educate the Jews and the atheists and everyone else that there *is* in fact a holiday called *Christmas*. And it *is* a national holiday. That it *is* based on a historic figure named Jesus Christ who was born," he lectures like a red-faced high school principal. "It *is* a historic holiday based on historical events. What's wrong with educating people on that reality?"

My response: "I think people are aware that Christmas takes place."

"If I go into a store, and it's run by a Jewish person, and they put up 'Happy Hanukkah,' the cross around my neck is not going to melt. I can handle somebody saying to me, 'Happy Hanukkah.'"

Summary of applied punditry tactic: Jews got that crappy animated Adam Sandler Hanukkah movie, didn't they? That should be plenty for those greedy bastards.

Rule of Punditry #4: Use an unrealistic extreme and compare it to the guest's argument. This is becoming like talking to a guy who thinks Spider-Man really exists and can point to all the exact issues of Marvel comics to back up his claim. The Fearless Defender of the Faith argues against homosexuality being taught about in schools—especially in a positive light, explaining why Christians shun them. "You want a Hindu to be a good Hindu? Do you want Hindus to now start eating cows?"

The nature of his emotions: disgusted.

"I'm sure you don't see anything wrong with Hindus not eating cows. I'm sure you don't see anything wrong with Muslims praying to Mecca five times a day. If you respect other people having their beliefs, why not respect Christians having their beliefs as well?"

Summary of applied punditry tactic: shoving a hamburger at a Hindu is much like shoving a penis toward a Christian man.

Rule of Punditry #5: Only read the press release, book jacket, and a few highlighted paragraphs to significantly know what the author is all about before formulating your knee-jerk arguments.

"We're continuing our talk with author Harmon Leon. His book is *Republican Like Me*—kind of targeting and attacking, if you will, Christianity, conservatism, republicanism, but in a humorous type way, satire and that type of thing."

I jump in.

"Was there anything in the book that you found funny?"

"Uh . . . yeah." His voice cracks. "I mean . . ."

"So, what did you specifically find funny?"

"I haven't read . . . I can't point that out specifically. . . . I just kind of skimmed through parts. So I know that you take kind of a sarcastic approach, to, uh . . ."

"Irony," I clarify, fearlessly defending the literary device. "I use irony!"

"And I'm a guy who enjoys sarcasm . . ."

"No, no! Irony often gets mistaken for sarcasm. They're two different things."

"Yeah, OK, all right," he says sarcastically (which is different from irony). "You know what? I can point out both of them. I got no problem recognizing irony, and I got no problem enjoying humorous satire."

Summary of applied punditry tactic: the Fearless Defender of the Faith, though strident on his political views, is surely a man who enjoys a good laugh as much as anyone!

Rule of Punditry #6: Act like the group you represent, no matter how massive and powerful, is actually the poor victim of the opposition.

"I guess, since you talk so much about irony, let me bring up something I consider to be one of the ultimate ironies in the liberal-versus-conservative debate."

The nature of voice: outrage.

"That's the use of the word *censorship*," he spews. "It amazes me that liberals in the country will point their fingers at conservatives and accuse conservatives of being the book burners and the censors and the ones denying free speech." He bellows about evil liberals being the ones censoring the poor ex-gay voice, the anti-condom-using abstinence educator, the Ten Commandment displays, and the intelligent design theory in schools. "Those people are silenced!" boils the Fearless Defender of the Faith. "You talk about irony!"

My response: "Yeah." Pause. "That's pretty ironic!"

My argument: "Do we let Scientologists come into our schools and teach that we all evolved from volcanoes?"

"Teaching that we all evolved from rock and sand, you don't think that's mythology? 'Cuz that's what's being taught in our schools right now. We all evolved from rocks. Rocks and sand! Do you think that's mythology, or do you think that's sound science?"

Summary of applied punditry tactic: There's nothing pretty about Christian sarcasm.

Rule of Punditry #7: It shows weakness if the host gives in to any points of the opposition. Combat this by being really patronizing while cutting off the guest by trying to shout him down.

"Would Jesus want his message to be told through people being hit in the back of the head with chairs?" I ask about the Christian Wrestling Federation (which body-slams for Jesus).

"Let me answer the question. I don't have a problem with that as long they don't get into too much gore . . ."

"What about Christian black metal—the heaviest of heavy metal?"

"I'm not a fan personally." Dutko worries Christians may cross over to mainstream devil-worshiping heavy metal.

"So would you not see the satire and irony and humor in that?" I ask.

"Weeeeell, see now, I don't *get* the irony, 'cuz . . ."

"You just mentioned the irony."

"Hold on a second here . . ."

"What about Christian hard-core punk? Punk originated as anti-establishment, anti-religion. Now it's used to spread the word of Jesus. Would you find anything funny in that?"

"No!"

One thing Bob Dutko *does* find funny: "I've poked fun at the Promise Keepers from time to time." Explanation: "Sometimes it gets around to guys in a circle of five crying on each other's shoulders. I've poked fun before saying, they turn into 'Promise Weepers.' That's not a good rally if somebody doesn't cry."

My response: "So you're saying Promise Keepers are the only Christian arena I'm able to poke fun at?"

"I don't have a problem with you poking fun at it."

Summary of applied punditry tactic: Promise Keepers cry like girls, so it's OK to satirize them.

Rule of Punditry #8: Pose a large, extreme question in the last few seconds that can't possibly be answered articulately with time running out, thus making the guest seem incompetent at the closing.

"Let me point out something though. You will poke fun at the Promise Keepers. And that's fine, poke fun," Bob Dutko says with sixty seconds left, adding, "Why should the Promise Keepers be criticized for their supposed oppression of women when, in Islam and throughout the Middle East, women are treated far worse than anything the Promise Keepers do."

Level of his voice: raised and angry.

"Actually teaching that you are to beat your wife if she doesn't listen to you and you can't get her into submission. Do you find it *ironic* that Promise Keepers is made out to be this anti-women group?"

"So wait, you're giving me thirty seconds to give a little sound bite on that?"

Screaming: "I'm curious how you can look at Islam and their treatment of women and then put a bulls-eye on Promise Keepers?" More screaming: "What I'm telling you what I find ridiculous about a lot of liberal arguments and claims of irony is that they can point the finger at Promise Keepers and ignore radical Islam in the Middle East!"

My response: "Since I didn't mention radical Islam in my Promise Keepers story, it's liberal hypocrisy?"

"What I'm saying, what I'm saying, is don't make Promise Keepers out to be the bad guys when you got people a hundred times worse and you just ignore them." (And hell, they're towel heads to boot.)

Summary of applied punditry tactic: The only things that are funny to satirize are groups one doesn't belong to and groups who wear different types of clothing.

"Mr. Leon, I know we don't see eye-to-eye, but I do appreciate your willingness to come on and go 'round and 'round on some of these issues."

"I would suggest, before you have someone on as a guest, maybe read something they've written!"

And now, a biting conclusion heavily borrowed from *My Antonia,* Willa Cather's novel set in nineteenth-century Nebraska, which follows the tale of the spirited daughter of a Bohemian immigrant family planning to farm on the untamed land: "For Bob Dutko, the other right-wing pundits, and myself, this had been the road of destiny. Now I understand that the same road was to bring us together again. Whatever we had missed, we passed together the precious, the incommunicable past."

CHAPTER 14
SCAM OUTSOURCING

If only I could be considered upper-class, then I could be part of the 17 percent of the population who get those fabulous tax breaks. As it stands now, I have to dish out a good portion of my yearly income to Uncle Sam for the soul sin of being poor. There has to be a better answer.

Everyone has received one of those pesky e-mails from some official-sounding person in Nigeria, who, for one reason or another, has specially contacted *you*—random person on the Internet—in order to get millions (sometimes billions) of dollars out of Nigeria. There are always dire circumstances involved, and you're always promised you'll be rewarded with a hefty percentage. It's just that easy!

Welcome to the world of Nigerian e-mail scamming!

Believe it or not, e-mail scamming is Nigeria's third-largest industry. Business-wise, if the government cracked down on this scam, it would be equivalent to forcing Nevada to close its casinos. Now, America is even outsourcing our scams. This racket has been emptying the pockets of its hapless victims for decades in various incarnations—first, it was worked through letters, then through faxes, and, in this age before the jetpack, via e-mail (unless you have really good filtering software). What really pisses me off is that we should support scams that are American-based. (USA! USA! USA!)

Things a Nigerian E-mail Scammer Needs

1. An urgent-sounding letter.
2. Foreign-looking documents.
3. The Internet.
4. An explanation for why he can't get $40-odd million out of Nigeria.
5. A claim that he is the son of the president of Nigeria or someone else important.
6. You.

How the Nigerian E-mail Scam Works

Picture this scenario: some wealthy foreigner needs *your* help to move millions of dollars from his homeland to yours. He will reward you with a hefty percentage of his fortune if you agree to assist him. All you have to do is pay a "transfer fee," something in the vicinity of $16,000.

Scammers have purchased a list of thousands of random e-mail addresses, and, just your luck, yours is one of the ones they hit on. They write you a letter, in formal yet broken English, posing as a member of a very wealthy Nigerian family who is in a serious bind. The "wealthy foreigner" spins a sob story. You're hooked.

You pay the "transfer fee" and dream of untold riches. Then come the "complications." (There are always "complications.") You're required to shell out even more money. Eventually, your bank account is drained dry. Then you cry.

Nigerian Scam Fun Fact

According to special agents of the Secret Service Financial Crimes Division, in the United States alone, during a mere fifteen-month period, over $100 million was sucked up by Nigerian e-mail scammers! No kidding.

Me and Mr. Bakare

One morning I receive a Nigerian scam e-mail. It begins, "DEAR FRIEND." The author explains that his name is Mr. Hassan Bakare from Nigeria, "chairman of the contract review panel." He needs my help (me!) in assuring the smooth transfer of billions (yes, *billions*) of dollars. All I have to do is provide my full name, bank account number, address, telephone number, and fax number. The billions will flow through my account into America, and for my assistance I will receive 30 percent of the billions!

Are these scam artists heartless monsters who will stop at nothing to get their hands on the contents of our bank accounts, or do they still possess a shred of humanity, while I'm trying to dig myself out of my own financial hole? Hmmm—I want to find out. So I answer the scam e-mail right away. I say that I'm a very sick old lady named Gladys who is hooked up to a kidney dialysis machine. I add that I require a lot of medication.

The Correspondence

Dear Mr. Bakare,

Jesus has sent you to me! Thank you for contacting me! God bless!

I've been trying many business ventures lately and have lost a lot of money. Your plan seems like the type of thing that might work for me. My hospital bills are piling up, and my insurance money is starting to run out. Tell me what I have to do to get started!

Your new friend,
Gladys

Mr. Hassan Bakare quickly writes back and explains that he and his three partners met earlier in the day (this very day!) and decided to take me (sick old lady) on as their foreign partner. Well, sodomize me with the rusty hook of scurvy-infested pirate! Then Hassan gets a little spiritual on my ass. He shows sympathy for me, a poor sick old lady. He struggles with his spelling and grammar.

MY DEAR FRIEND,

I MUST LET YOU KNOW AT THIS POINT THAT GOD ALMIGHTY HAVE HIS WAY OF DOING THINGS FOR HIS PEOPLE. I BELIEVE YOU HAVE NEVER THINK OF GETTING THIS LIFETIME OPPORTUNITY WITH YOUR CONDITION BUT I MUST EQUALLY LET YOU KNOW THAT ME AND MY PARTNERS FASTED FOR SEVEN DAYS FOR THIS VERY TRANSACTION FOR GOD ALMIGHTY TO BRING SOMEBODY WHO WILL HELP US.

I AM USING THIS OPPORTUNITY TO INFORM YOU THAT GOD ALMIGHTY HAVE OPEN THE WINDOWS OF BLESSING FOR YOU AND WE TOO, I AM AS HAPPY AS YOU. WITH GOD ON OUR SIDE THIS TRANSACTION WILL NOT ONLY BRING GOOD FRIENDSHIP BETWEEN US BUT INTERRELATIONSHIP BETWEEN YOUR FAMILY AND MY FAMILY.

FINALLY I HOPE YOU ARE MARRIED, FOR I HAVE THREE CHILDREN AND MY BEAUTIFUL WIFE. PLEASE SAY ME WELL TO YOUR FAMILY . . .

BEST REGARDS,
HASSAN

Mr. Hassan Bakare ends by promising me that the billions of dollars will be in my bank account within fourteen working days. (Hurrah!) In my reply, I again emphasize that I'm a sick old lady.

Dear Mr. Hassan,

Today I threw up blood. I've never seen so much blood in all my life.

I also got horrible news from the doctors about my health. I need major surgery that will cost a lot of money. Your investment opportunity sounds like it could be the answer to all my prayers. Without the surgery, I might die, but if I could afford it, my life will be saved.

Can you assure me that your plan works? Even though I might die, I want to make sure that I have money to leave my granddaughter. She has a rare immune-system disease and is required to live in a plastic bubble.

Are you people good Christians who believe in Jesus Christ our Lord and Savior?

I don't have a bank account, so please advise me on what to do.

Praise Jesus!
Gladys

It worked! Mr. Hassan Bakare collapses under my sob story and shows compassion—complete and utter human compassion!

MY DEAR FRIEND,

HOW IS YOUR HEALTH? I HOPE YOU ARE GETTING BETTER. WE ARE REALLY WORRIED BECAUSE TIME IS NO LONGER ON OUR SIDE, WE JUST HAVE TO COMPLETE THIS TRANSACTION WITHIN THE SHORTEST POSSIBLE TIME.

I MUST EQUALLY MAKE YOU KNOW THAT WITHOUT YOUR BANK ACCOUNT THERE IS NO WAY WE CAN PULL THIS TRANSACTION TO A SUCCESSFUL END.

I UNDERSTAND THAT YOU HARDLY E-MAIL ME WITH YOUR FULL NAME AND I DO HOPE I AM DEALING WITH A GOD FEARING PERSON LIKE ME BECAUSE THIS TRANSACTION IS ALL ABOUT TRUST AND HONESTY . . .

Now I feel like the bad one. But then Mr. Hassan Bakare finds a way around the whole bank-account issue.

> I ADVISE YOU TO LOOK FOR A PERSON WHO CAN HELP US WITH A BANK ACCOUNT, SOMEBODY WHO YOU CAN TRUST THAT WILL NOT RUN AWAY WITH OUR MONEY.
>
> THANK YOU,
> HASSAN

I decide to get snippy with Mr. Hassan Bakare for doubting my loyalty.

> Young Man!
>
> I do not like your tone and attitude. I'm beginning to think I'm not dealing with Christians. IS THIS TRUE? Of course I have a bank account! I run a very successful home-assembly business making "upper-scale country angels." But I have found NO trust in you. If we're going to be business partners then I need to trust you. I would like to see a photo of you and your family. I can tell by looking at a person whether or not I can do business with him.
>
> Thank you very much.
>
> Mrs. Gladys McDonald

He responds:

> MY DEAR FRIEND,
>
> I RECEIVED YOUR MAIL AND THE CONTENT WELL UNDERSTOOD. I AM VERY SORRY IF I HAVE OFFENDED YOU IN ANY WAY. THE PROBLEM IS THAT WE HAVE VERY SHORT TIME TO CONCLUDE THIS TRANSACTION.
>
> NOTE: I ONLY ASK IF YOU HAVE AN ACCOUNT WHERE THE MONEY WILL BE TRANSFERRED TO. I WAS AFRAID AT FIRST THAT IF YOU CANNOT PRIVIDE AN ACCOUNT THAT MEANS NOTHING CAN BE DONE BUT SINCE YOU HAVE ONE I THANK GOD FOR HIS MERCY AND SURPORT.

MAY THE ALMIGHTY GOD BLESS YOU AND YOUR FAMILY,
BAKARE

Lo and behold, Mr. Hassan Bakare actually does send a photo. I wait several days before answering him.

Dear Balky,

Sorry I haven't written sooner, but I was in the intensive care unit of the hospital all week. I had a stroke that paralyzed half my face. I was throwing up a lot of blood. Now it's temporarily stopped. I have to go back tomorrow for some more tests and a CAT scan.

And thank you for the picture. Was that taken with a digital camera? What is the little one's name? Is it Petey? Do you have any other pictures so I know that you're telling the truth?

The medicine has made me tired. I must sleep now.

Gladys

I think Mr. Hassan Bakare is beginning to like me, for he now uses the lowercase in writing his letters.

My Dear Lady,

I receive your mail and am very sorry for your sickness so far, I know that with God all things are possible so just put God first and he will surely heal you from your sickness.

Furthermore I have sent you my family pictures as requested but if at this time you are still not convince I am sorry. My pictures are not important now. If you are not satisfied with what you saw then forget about this business and let me look for more serious person who will not delay. You are delaying this transaction and as you know we have little time to conclude this.

May the Almighty God take good care of you and your family.

Hassan Bakare

That bastard! He's willing to sell me out even though I'm a sick old lady with a half-paralyzed face! I wonder if I can get him to send me money?

LISTEN YOUNG MAN!

I am a very sick woman with a half-paralyzed face! Having you pressuring me is not good for my health! I am serious about the transaction, but I have to know that you are serious too.

Now, if you have all the money that you say you do, as a token of trust could you send me some so I can pay my hospital bill? Then we can proceed with the transaction as requested. We are talking about doing a large cash-flow transaction, so $1,000 shouldn't be a problem between partners. I would also like you to send me a monkey—something about chimpanzee size.

If it is, then I should tell you that I got another e-mail today from one of your countrymen who can be my partner. And he even sent me several pictures of him and his family, in various poses, as requested!

God bless good old Jesus,
Gladys

This doesn't sit well with Mr. Hassan Bakare—especially the monkey part. In fact, he's pissed!

My Good Friend,

I think I understand your problem, you don't even trust yourself because if you do and you have that Godly mind you will learn how to trust another human being like you. If at this point paying your hospital bill and sending you a monkey will make you believe that this transaction is real then forget it, I will still pray to my heavenly father to send me somebody who is God fearing and who will help me pull this transaction to a successful end.

You are not even grateful to God that at your sick period such opportunity came knocking at your doorstep. Am sorry I have to stop here.

Bye,
Hassan

Mr. Hassan Bakare has pitted the Almighty against me! How dare this scam artist say I don't even trust myself! I decide to ask him for a second chance.

> No, Hassa!
>
> You got me all wrong. Please! I *am* grateful, very grateful. Please don't do this to me! Hassa, look into your heart and give me one more chance. Please! I am on a lot of medication and my judgment isn't always good. Just tell me what you need. Pleeeeeeeeeeeease!
>
> Yours in Jesus,
> Gladys
>
> PS: You asked for a photo and I finally got one taken with one of those digital cameras. Aren't they amazing! Here is the photo.

I include a picture that I lifted off the Web of a very old woman being tended to in a hospital bed. Mere hours later I hear back from Mr. Hassan Bakare. Surprisingly, he's had a spiritual change of heart.

> Dear Gladys,
>
> I received your mail dated 13th of August 2005. I must tell you that God will not allow me to denied you this opportunity after such an apology from you. I will always pray for you, and I believe that God will once heal you from any afflition that you are suffering from, because with him anything is possible. (I advise you keep your faith and trust in God.)
>
> I am in receipt of your photograph and I cannot but confess that you are very beautiful, even on a sick bed. I wonder what you must have looked like in your teens, you must have been an angel . . .

Our moment is short lived. Hassan Bakare goes on to stress that he needs my bank account information. I decide to act like he's granted me a second chance at life.

Dear Hassa,

In the name of Jesus, thank you! Thank you, Hassa, thank you! I couldn't be happier. Now I'm so happy that the pain of my serious medical ailments doesn't seem so unpleasant (but I do throw up blood often and frequently). God bless!

Hassa, thank you for saying I looked like an angel as a teen. Oh, Hassa, please—you make me blush like a schoolgirl! Please, you're a married man!

To help speed up the process, could you send me the same bank account information about yourself? But please hurry, for just today, I received this e-mail from a Dr. Bello Yusuf of the Nigerian National Petroleum Corporation, which I've included below.

God bless us and look over this transaction.

Gladys

Yes, I turn the tables and include an e-mail from another Nigerian scam artist in order to pit the two against each other. It works.

Dear Gladys,

How are you today, I hope you are getting better as me and my family joined hand in prayer for your quick recovery.

I wish to inform you that scamers whom I do not know got access to my e-mail box, which you and I knows the implication of such thing in this business endevour.

In the first place, I want you to understand that I do not know this person who claimed to be Dr. Bello Yusuf. I know all the top officers of NNPC. Our senior officer in the person of Oba Seki has been my good friend since our university days.

You have just received mail from my country's scamers, impostors and fraud stars. Beware! This scamers are always in the air with their systems, hijacking peoples mail, calls and faxes, seeking for whom to defraud. Once again beware! Me and you will not be their vitims. I want you to tell me when you received the mail from the so called Yusuf. I pledge you not to ever in your entire life reply to their mails.

My wife told me that she is looking forward to seeing you as I have explained everything to her this morning.

Yours faithfully,
Hassan Bakare

Craftily, Mr. Hassan Bakare forwards his new e-mail address in order to divert the scammers.

Dear Hassa,

Dear me, you are a good man! Your heart is filled with nothing but good. You remind me of my late husband. Will you be coming to America for the transaction? I'd love to meet your wife. We can go shopping together and do each other's hair—you know, women's stuff.

Who are these scammers and what do they do? Oh my! This sounds serious. I have never heard of this before. Are they bad people?

I do not believe that my nice Dr. Bello Yusuf is one of them, for he sent me some money for my hospital bills (and I must remind you that you didn't!). So please tell me.

God bless!
Gladys

He writes:

Woman,

Please I am not for a childs play. If you are not competent for this transaction, I sincerely grant your endulgence. I am beginning to suspect you, because you do not even trust your self. Common particulars (which I already gave you my) for the registration of your good self is taking you all these time, I wonder where your faith is.

Dr. Bello Yusuf is a scamer. If you dont know the meaning of scamer, then it means a pretender, someone who copy other people and his fake. If you are not satisfied with my explanations you can go ahead and follow him but I assured you that the end will definitely be regrets as the government has always warn us to abstain.

Lastly, had I know scamers by face I would have get them arrested and jailed them for the rest of their life. We only hear that they exist in this country and other part of the country also.

To enable me to register your good self with the concern ministry as time is no longer on our side. If you dont send me the above mentioned particulars, I am sorry, I will have to find someone else.

Yours faithfully,
Hassan

This is getting intriguing. If I can't get the scammer to give me money, then I want to learn how the whole operation works. I'll use the angry approach.

MR. HASSAA!

LISTEN AND LISTEN GOOD! I am sensing something in your tone I do not like. DO NOT refer to me as "Woman." I am old enough to be your grandmother. In fact, you must now refer to me as Mrs. Gladys Knight or I will NOT continue with this. How dare you say I do not trust myself!

I think I made it clear that my faith is in Jesus Christ, and I do what he tells me. Furthermore, DO NOT talk that way about my beloved Dr. Bello Yusuf. He has already proven his trust to me by putting money in my bank account. AND YOU HAVE NOT!

If he's a scammer, how does he scam money? Huh? If you can at least answer that question then maybe we can get this thing on the road and transfer the money ASAP.

Let's get it going! Woo!

All you need is to give me straight answers, and no horse pucky!

Mrs. Gladys Knight

Mr. Hassan Bakare seems slightly sad and sentimental in his next e-mail.

Dear Mrs. Gladys Knight,

We do not have to get temperamental having gone this far. It only breaks my heart when I go out of my way to completely open up to someone I confide in, only to become an object of suspicion. It hurts. You will feel the same way if you were in my position.

I first introduced you to this transaction. Do you ever ask yourself how come the so called Dr. Bello Yusuf managed to know about this transaction and to get your contact address when he was neither told by you nor me? This is the handy work of a scamer. They have the facilities to intercept peoples mails and calls, work on them and pretend to be what they are not. They usually start by being very nice because they know that ignorant people hardly resist nice people, but their ultimate goal is to use and defraud their victims. You asked me "How do they scam money?" They usually do this in so many ways, but the most common one that I am aware of is that they eventually ask you send them your bank account to enable them transfer funds into it, heaven made you to believe in them like "Dr. Bello Yusuf" is doing. But they turn around to defraud your account of vitually all the money already inside. Some even get you into trouble by sending you money from stolen/forged foreign credit cards and ask you to send it back to them, etc. I strongly advice you to discontinue any forms of communication with Bello Yusuf and his likes permanently. "To be for warned is to be for armed." They might even adopt tricks which I do not even know because they are very crafty skimers.

Thanks and God bless. I remain your good friend.

Kindest regards,
Hassan

I respond:

Mr. Hassa,

I'm sorry I didn't get back to you sooner, but I had a serious relapse and had to be in the hospital for many nights. The doctor didn't think I would pull through. In fact, I was pronounced clinically dead. But what pulled me through, when all seemed darkest, was the thought of your generous offer. If I didn't have that to think about, I certainly wouldn't be alive right now.

The doctor told me that any type of agitation would be too much for my heart to take. Once I get a little bit of my strength back, which should be in a few days, I will be able to begin the transaction. I already began my transaction with Dr. Bello Yusuf. He was so nice to send me an assortment of flowers and a fruit basket when death was knocking on my door.

Yours in Jesus,
Mrs. Gladys Knight

I include in my e-mail my fax number, which is actually the fax number of a local copy center. Now he's faced with a dilemma: he can either demonstrate his humanity and stop this scam, or he can push on using this new key piece of information—the precious fax number. Mr. Hassan Bakare chooses the second option.

Dear Mrs. Gladys Knight,

Kindly accept my apology for the delay in response. I was choked up with official responsibilities. I do not have any reason to be mad at you please. I only advise you to stay away from Mr. Bello Yusuf. He is not genuine. Time will prove me right if you insist, but you must have been hurt. That will break my heart. My comment about your beauty was not meant to flatter you. It is the truth. You are simply beautiful.

I will not be sending you faxes immediately. But I will do so as soon as I conclude with your registration, incorporation, and other preliminary works necessary to the smooth and successful conclusion of this project.

I will provide you with the details of this transaction and our master plan for success as soon as I receive these information from you in your next mail.

Please take good care of your health. You are very important. I wish I was a medical doctor, I would have taken over your case. I wish you speedy and perfect recovery. Awaiting your prompt response.

Kindest regards,
Hassan

OK, I'm dealing with one of the most coldhearted bastards on the planet. All I want is an ounce—a mere ounce—of real human compassion. I want some small sign of remorse for trying to rip off a sick old lady. Time to lay it on thick.

Bakare,

You were right. You were so right. I trusted Mr. Bello Yusuf and he ended up cheating me out of a lot of money. You were so right! It got me so upset that I ended up having another stroke and now the other half my face is paralyzed. How can a person do such a thing and look at himself in the mirror every day? Please tell me.

Now I trust you, for you told me about this and I didn't listen.

We need to do this transaction quickly or else I'm going to be kicked out of the nursing home. If there's any way you can help me out, please let me know. I can pay you back when the transaction is complete.

The pain is unbearable. I must sleep now.

Mrs. Gladys Knight

Well, I thought it would work.

Dear Mrs. Gladys Knight,

It breaks my heart to hear that your health have degenerated to partial stroke as a result of Mr. Yusuf Bello's cheating. I wish I had been able to prevent it. How can a beautiful woman like you suffer such. This is so sad. The fact that I will not be able to send you some money to alleviate your health problems hurts me more but I just have to tell you the truth. Firstly, I and my colleagues had practically committed all our funds towards the financing of this investment to ensure a smooth and successful completion. Secondly, it is presently difficult for individuals to send money from my country to a more developed nation like the U.S.A. and Europe because such cases are very rare. The reverse is usually the case. Nevertheless, I will see what I can raise or do.

Better still, I would suggest that you send me those informations I requested for in my last mail to you as a matter of urgency. This will enable us start up and finish this project as soon as possible. Then you will have more than enough funds to take care of your needs.

I wish you God's protection and speedy recovery. Awaiting your prompt response.

Kindest regards,
Bakare Hassan

I'll give it one last, desperate effort. I'll lay it on *extremely* thick and see if I can get any money out of him.

DAer Mr Haasennn

SORRry my tuping is not good buttt I"M in GREeat pain and my strOOKE HAS leeesen the mobiltiy in my aaaarm. DO YOU MEEEAN IT!!!! dID YOOOu reeely thinkk YOOOu can senD+ mee mooney? THatt wooouldd be greeat. YoU could jjuuust seenD it regualr mail. Thank! YOU! THANNK YOOUU!

MRS G;ladyss Knight

Strangely, I never heard from Mr. Hassan Bakare again. I often stare out the window and wonder what he's doing right now. Maybe he developed compassion for his fellow human beings and that's why he stopped. Or perhaps he's encountered another Mrs. Gladys Knight who gladly sent him all of her kidney dialysis money, and he's now sailing on a shiny new boat. I guess I'll never know!

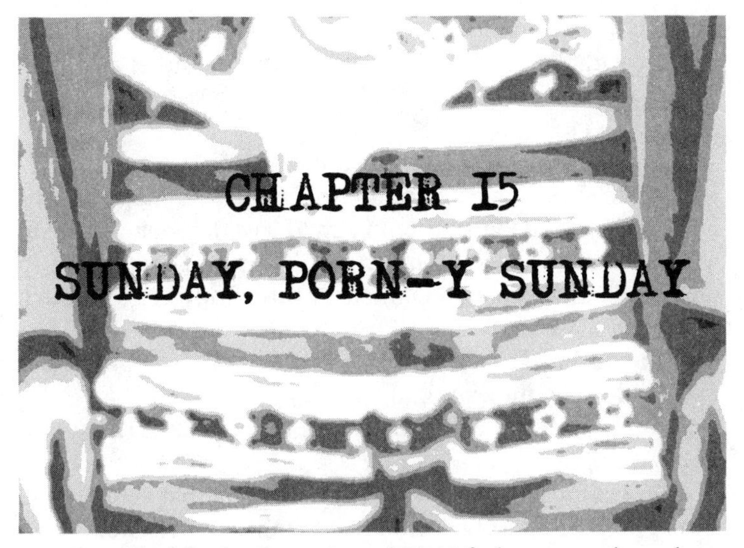

CHAPTER 15

SUNDAY, PORN-Y SUNDAY

Note: *The following chapter is rated PG-13 for language and sexual content. Those under eighteen must read this while accompanied by a parent or legal guardian.*

Essential glossary. To write a successful PG-13 rated chapter about porn, it is *essential* to create and use the following conversion glossary:

Porn Term	**PG-13 Conversion**
the male genital apparatus	any American president
the female genital apparatus	Mrs. Butterworth
poo, or something the color of poo	Justin Timberlake
the act of intercourse	to shake hands
male climax	praise Jesus

"Porn is the hate literature of our time!" I read from *Think before You Look*—a book regarding America's porn addiction and how it can be cured through, yes, of course, Jesus. As I page through the publication, I remark to the large, highly repressed woman with glasses in a matching tweed suit jacket and skirt, who is manning the table, "Today's sermon was nothing short of, how do I say, powerful!"

"So it hit home," she says with unblinking eye contact.

"Yeah," I remark with an ultrasolemn face, adding a jerking hand motion as if I were gripping my *Thomas Jefferson*. "I used to work it about a dozen times a day." Pause. "Sometimes two dozen." I add with a guttural moan, continuing to page through *Think before You Look*.

"My husband's testimony is in that book," she points out matter-of-factly, almost proud.

I read, "'Internet porn soon made me sexually disinterested in my wife . . .'"

How surprising. Who would have thought that her husband would become sexually disinterested in this piece of work? Welcome to Porn Sunday.

That's right, it's Porn Sunday. Hurrah! Seventy churches around the country are hosting the event in order to *address the porn epidemic in our country*. First, the avian flu, now this! Apparently Christians, like everyone else, enjoy looking at naked women. What a shocker! Except now it's time to shield their eyes and feel shame. Orchestrated by Pastors Craig Gross and Mike Foster, who run XXXChurch.com (the number-one Christian porn site), their intent is to "bring America out of the porn closet."

I personally don't think that porn is so bad. First of all, it provides people with hands-on work—people like me, for example, who get to write about it. If the Christian Right had its way, I wouldn't be on assignment for *Hustler* magazine writing about how churches want to eliminate porn. It seems a little self-serving, but thank God for porn for providing me work!

I decide to spend my Porn Sunday at the Arcade Church in Sacramento. (Where did you spend yours?) Outside, the parking lot spills over with cars as a big pink "Porn Sunday" banner waves proudly in the wind. No kidding. I've taken it upon myself to attend Porn Sunday undercover in order to fit in with the demographic that they're trying to reach and perhaps to become a role model for others.

Pseudonym: Dirk Saddler (slightly porn star–sounding name).
Outfit: Slacks that fit too tight. Pimp shoes.
Back Story: Former porn addict who lost it all, *everything,* but has redeemed himself by now becoming addicted to Jesus Christ.
Approach: In order to pose as a former porn addict, I must think like one.

Inside, the pews are sweltering with *the hottest* churchgoers who are whiter than white, facing toward the pulpit (especially the churchwomen with their supple, heaving breasts). Wait! Must. Not. Think. Like. That!

The words "Dirty Little Secret" are projected on a large screen.

"Welcome. Many of you who haven't been here before," proclaims *the cool pastor,* Pastor Jake, casually dressed in jeans and untucked shirt. He leads the Porn Sunday festivities from the pulpit as I take my place between a guy sweating from the brow and a military jarhead sunk deep into his Bible.

"Take some time to self-reflect," the cool pastor addresses the congregation, which comprises old people, couples, and a few rows of smirking teens—all of whom put hands on their foreheads and close their eyes as a guy onstage softly plays guitar.

Dirty Little Secret.

Then, a skit. (Who doesn't love amateur dramatics?) Executed with the wooden acting finesse of a driver's safety video, a husband and wife sit at a kitchen table on the pulpit along with a prop refrigerator and some children's toys.

"How was your lunch today?" woodenly asks wife character.

"Great," replies the husband, telling of overseeing a new building project and leading Bible study.

Excellent skit if it ends there—but there's more. The wife fumes about an incident at work.

"Jeff, that sleazy computer tech that sits next me, you know what he said when he gave me the new computer? 'Don't let your husband visit any dirty Web sites.'"

"Hey, will you slow down for a second," barks the husband character, shifting uncomfortably. "You said you took the computer in?" There's a dramatic pause. "I have something to tell you. I visited a porn site."

The wife gasps along with the congregation. "You used my work computer to look at naked pictures?"

Bad already, it gets a whole heck of a lot worse.

"If I have to be brutally honest, it's not just naked women I look at," says the husband character, not saying exactly what. My guess? Brazilian monkey porn, guy-on-guy action, or German scheizer movies.

"You prepare Bible study on that computer!" cries the wife.

More crying. Curtain. The skit ends in pure shame. Surely their stage marriage is now over. (Might there even be an offstage theatrical suicide?) To think it was all because of porn.

Dirty Little Secret!

* * *

> **Porn Fun Fact:** Have you ever thought about a career in porn? Men earn $250 to $450 per sex scene, while women snag $400 to $1,000. Porn is the one field in which women's salaries outstrip men's. You surely can't say that for corporate America!

It's fine to preach against porn on Porn Sunday, but do these people know what porn is really like? Porn is a billion-dollar industry, so someone must be liking it. To be fully prepared for what I encounter at Porn Sunday and the XXX Church ideology, I sojourned a few months earlier smack right to the heart of the fornicating beast, to find out firsthand about *the hate literature of our time.* That's right, I went to an industrial section of beautiful North Hollywood, directly across from a sheet-metal shop, in order to become a clothed extra in a porno movie. (Clothed extras are sometimes needed in porn during the *plot parts.*)

The first scene is on the roof. Mariachi music blares from the restaurant next door. Planes descend in the background. "What's the movie about?" I ask the jaded boom-mike operator, hoping to prepare for my role. "I'm really not sure," he mumbles.

Ron, a veteran director of some five hundred porno films (including *The Sopornos I, II,* and *III*), explains the two-day feature shoot of *The Contortionist,* penned by Raven Touchstone. "This one's about a codependent woman who becomes everyone she meets," philosophically elaborates Ron, who's clad in stylish suspenders and thick black glasses. "She becomes the victim and the rescuer."

Not to mention that she gets her *hand shaken* a lot.

Ron gets serious now, even evincing a bit of nostalgia. "Nowadays, people don't want to see features. There's no style, no nothing! The actors used to be responsive," the director says. "Now they're a whole different breed."

"Let's hurry, I got to get home to my wife," barks Harv, who's wearing a police uniform and will portray Officer Dick Husky. Harv is best described as one ugly mofo.

After some small talk about Harv's kids, everyone's ready to roll. I'm wearing a trench coat and a hat for the clothed extra role of detective. I've chosen to go by the clothed porn extra name of "Harm-on-Hammer!"

"What's my motivation?" I ask the director, who's been kind of oblivious to my presence.

"You walk from this side of the roof to that side," he mumbles.

I think about it for a moment.

"This side of the roof to that side," I repeat. "Got it!"

Action!

Cameron, the blonde porn starlet with huge fake ta-tas, sprinkles a canister of ashes, supposedly the result of cremation, off the roof.

"More tit," directs the cameraman. "More drama."

I walk from one side of the roof to the other.

"You're under arrest," cries Officer Dick Husky, grabbing Cameron by the waist and exposing her upper body as she struggles and squirms. "You're under arrest for scattering ashes in a public place, indecent exposure, and . . . AROUSING AN OFFICER!"

"Aroused?" coyly shrieks Cameron.

Raven Touchstone can write some mean dialogue.

The morning drags on. The set inside is now inhabited by large quantities of older, unintimidating men and sleazy father figure–types. One guy looks about a hundred; he pages through porn magazines with a very old woman who could pass for a worker at a craft-fair booth. (Could she be Raven Touchstone?)

Being very careful where I sit, I set up camp at the food table. I'm sad to learn that I'm being relieved of my role as a clothed extra—not fired, but by no means am I asked to be in the upcoming scene. (Maybe I shouldn't have smiled and waved at the camera!)

"Just let me know if you want me to walk from this side of the room to that side," I tell the director as I put a heap of salsa on a chip.

It's a reality that male readers probably won't believe, but after a relatively short time, a porn set actually does become boring. At least, this one's boring—until the shotgun masturbation scene starts.

"Harv, what are you doing?" bellows the suspender-clad director to help the actor find his motivation.

Like Brando, Harv thinks for a moment.

"She's playing with the gun and her *Mrs. Butterworth,* and I'm encouraging it," Harv answers.

Cameron, naked, places the firearm between her legs.

"Action!"

"That's it, Precious. There's your new best friend. Get intimate with it now!" commands Harv, referring, not to his *Rutherford B. Hayes,* but to the shotgun.

Cameron cocks the gun and diddles her *Mrs. Butterworth* with it.

A group of big leering guys and gramps around the set get real quiet and start breathing heavily in unison. It sounds like they just ran a 5K.

* * *

XXX Church Fun Fact: Did you know Porn Sunday founder Pastor Mike Foster got the idea for the XXX Church (the number-one Christian porn site) when he was in the shower praying? He said, "God, I want to do something huge for you." God came back to Foster and said one word: "Porn!"

Back at Porn Sunday, it gets really quiet after the skit of the married couple's confrontation at the kitchen table, as a low murmur runs through the church and sweat runs down the brow of the sweaty guy's brow.

"This is just a glimpse of the many stories impacting our community," remarks the cool pastor as those around us shake their heads. "What you don't see in this story is the children."

"Uh-huh. Yes," spontaneously blurt members of the church.

"And it's coming to a home near you!" he sternly warns. "I'm not talking about a little bit of porn. I'm talking about a lot of porn." (Really! When?)

An old guy with cane gets up with a big "Hurumph," assisted by a blond uptight woman, and makes a big, drawn-out exit.

The cool pastor tells of an e-mail he claims to have received from a twelve-year-old girl who's struggling against porn. It was written while she cried, with alcohol and a bottle of sleeping pills in front of her, because Satan gave her nightmares. Another e-mail is from a man in his fifties who claims to have spent $500 per month on porn, went to jail because of porn, and now asks, "Please pray for me and keep me from porn and fornication."

"Sexual impurity is the number-one thing keeping us from following Jesus!"

A big-haired lady gets up and walks from the church, shaking her big-haired head. The cool pastor's voice quivers, "Porn gives an image of sexuality which isn't what God created. It's an unfair image of women that you can't live up to." (I've said it before—what about amateur porn? That makes even the myopic Bank of America receptionist seem sexy.)

Clapping and a chorus of "Amen."

"A little porn's OK," the cool pastor says this twice with distaste, almost sounding like he's about to cry. "Porn is destroying. Porn is destroying." He explains of the clear trajectory from glancing at a Victoria Secret catalog to soon becoming a child-porn addict. He then proposes a McCarthy-era solution to parents: "When you get home, say 'Let's look at your MySpace account together.' When you think your kids are sharing music, it's porn," he confirms. (Apparently pirating music is OK.) "Wives, it's time to talk to your husbands. And husbands, it's time to talk to your wives. If you don't go public now, I'll speak to you twenty years in the future when it's ruined your lives. Go public!" he says four times, telling how one wife found out her husband was looking at porn, not because she looked on his computer, but because God told her. "Go public!"

Steps should be taken. Accountability software should be installed on all computers, which will e-mail a friend if you look at questionable Web sites. Also appoint one person in your house to erase the history on your computer, thus checking which Web sites are looked at. Of course, the obvious solution: "Get rid of your computer. You can check your e-mail elsewhere . . . or ruin your life," the cool pastor stresses. He continues, admonishing us to block TV shows, since pornography is now on basic TV. (Will *Entertainment Tonight* and everything on MTV now be considered pornography?) "Spend more time with God's word, less time on TV," he offers as an alternative. The cool pastor turns to the row of giggling, disinterested teens: "I'm really messing you guys up today, but I'm saving your life."

—clapping—

"Today is a great day because the secret you kept so long is rising to the surface," the cool pastor says with a glowing smile.

* * *

Porn Fun Fact: Did you know that *Contortionist* script writer Raven Touchstone has penned more than six hundred porn scripts in her twenty-year career? She was also a child actress and was the voice of the doll at the end of the original *Planet of the Apes* movie.

It's time to move to hard core. Harv appears solemn, almost meditative. He's a fifteen-year veteran, yet still nervous. His fingers are pinched around his nose. He occasionally stares intensely off into space. He's getting into character, or waiting for the Viagra to kick in, as if he were Laurence Olivier transforming into Richard III, only with a boner.

"We need water on the set," the production assistant announces.

"OK, we're rolling here," says Rob, the producer of *The Contortionist* and the Milton Berle of porn-set humor. "Cameron, get a *Gerald Ford* in your mouth."

The director, with cigarette in his mouth, yells "Action!" Harvey removes Cameron's shirt.

"Hand on her breast again, Harv," a cameraman directs. "Arch your back again."

My stomach loudly grumbles. The jaded boom guy shoots me a look. Naked Harv is now at full attention. I don't find this pleasant.

"Play with the breasts, Harv!"

The camera crew dances around, dramatically switching camera angles as Harv gets down to tongue exercises. Cameron grunts and groans as if she's having a tooth pulled.

"Guys, let's move this coffee table!"

The actors momentarily stop the monkey dance as the crew removes the piece of furniture.

"Harv, can you turn your head so the shadow doesn't fall on her *Mrs. Butterworth*?" spouts the suspendered director, taking another drag off his cigarette.

"We got six minutes of tape!" declares the rotund sound guy. "Let's roll out to hard core!"

Harv and Cameron start going at it with monkey-in-heat fervor, loudly grunting and using various descriptive, declarative sentences. Gramps breathes heavily over my shoulder. I move across the room and nibble on a doughnut from the food table.

"These are good doughnuts," I tell the other porn actress, who's twenty, has huge fake ta-tas, and goes by the name "Honey."

"Weren't you on the *Gush II* shoot?" Honey asks me.

"No," I reply, telling her I'm pretty sure she's mistaking me for Harmon-the-German, my evil porn twin.

On the set, the tempo builds. It builds! It builds! It builds! Then the rotund sound guy barks, "Let's change the tape!" Everything comes to a grinding halt. Harv dismounts. Still fully aroused, he takes time for a cigarette and shares his mainstream aspirations to be a stand-up comedian.

Being in the comedy industry, I offer advice to nude, aroused Harv.

"When at a comedy club," I advise, "be sure not to hump anything onstage!"

Harv takes this in, then pulls out a tube of lube and lotions up his *Calvin Coolidge*. I could really do without watching this.

"OK, guys, we're back to work again!" commands the director.

Cameron starts bouncing away like she's riding a crazed pogo stick.

Again, the moment is short-lived. The production assistant rushes in. "If anyone is not parked in our spots, they're towing cars!"

Everything is brought to a halt.

"Am I good across the street?" inquires Harv with a naked woman mounted on top of him. The worried porn starlet dismounts.

"Can you make sure my car is safe?" she asks. Much talk about parking and moving cars ensues.

When the parking situation is cleared up, the director shouts, "We're going into reverse combo." Harv lubes up again, repreparing his *Andrew Jackson*. Must he do that?

"You guys are doing great!" says the cameraman. "Look over your shoulder, Cameron."

The tempo builds. It builds! It builds! It builds!

"I got a muscle cramp!" Cameron suddenly cries.

Once again, everything is brought to a dead halt.

"Kind of walk around and put some weight on it," yells the director.

Apologetic, Cameron hops around naked. The boom guy takes time to read the paper. One of the grips naps on the couch.

* * *

> **XXX Church Fun Fact:** Did you know that Porn Sunday's anti-porn billboards and advertisements were rejected by Clear Channel and *Rolling Stone* magazine because of the sexy motif and the prominence of the word *porn*?

Here comes Jack! Jack—a large, goateed man wearing shorts and a red picnic-table-patterned shirt—is brought up to the pulpit of the Arcade Church. Jack is a former porn addict ("Hi, Jack!"). Jack uses today's hip-hop language to make an impact—yes, using the cool language of today here in church, in order to get through to the kids.

"Yo! Pornography went into my home and destroyed my marriage," the goateed man says, telling it like it is—with *today's* language. "Satan is pimpin' this generation, and the first stop is the church," Jack, the hip former porn addict, continues. "We've chosen the role of the ho. The devil's a pimp. Don't be his ho."

"That dawg is not talkin' shizzle about porn," I share with a sweaty bro, who fails to acknowledge me.

"Parents think 50 Cent is talking about Snickers bars when he's talking to you about taking your daughter to the candy shop."

This is true. The rapper 50 Cent (whose real name is Curtis Jackson) has no Snickers bar intentions at the candy shop. (But why is a good Christian and an *ex*-porn addict listening to 50 Cent?) He then spouts his new mantra.

"*Let Jesus be your pimp*. Will you continue to be used by the devil and be his ho?" Adding, "Say no to porn. No porn."

Nonplussed, the row of dudes with baseball caps nod their heads. With all this religious guilt laid on them today, these kids will be way too scared to ever masturbate. And if they do, they will live in shame because it's *wrong*!

"I know whole families who didn't come to church today because of this," shares a tense mom in a sparkly church outfit, after the sermon, as a line of people wait to thank Pastor Jake. "They thought that porn should not be talked about in the church on Sunday."

"Well, what did you think of the service?" I ask.

"His language was pretty harsh," she says.

"What language do you speak of?" I ask in order to hear her repeat it.

"You know all the *pimp* and *ho* stuff."

I get defensive, "Hey! He's speaking *today*'s language, and that's what the kids respond to," adding, "That *be-yotch* Satan needed a little smack talkin'," I confirm, using more of *today's* language.

Moving on, I approach a table where a large, smiley manly man is giving out pamphlets for a weekend men's prayer encounter camping retreat. It will be geared toward those with porn addiction. The manly man shoves a pamphlet into my paw.

"Today's sermon was, how do I say it, powerful!" I exclaim. "I could tell you firsthand how porn has affected my life."

"Has it been something you've been struggling with?" the manly man asks, making creepy eye contact that shifts as I explain my faux porn addiction.

"Yes," I say, licking my dry lips, explaining that I was addicted to gay porn, most specifically photos of men in the outdoors doing very compromising things. His creepy eye contact becomes stronger. I wave his brochure. "Yeah, I'll have to check out this men's prayer retreat. We'll be camping, right?"

* * *

> **Porn Fun Fact:** Did you know the average career span of a porn actress is two years? But remember: porn years are like dog years, only more so. Each year in porn is fifteen years of regular life!

Things suddenly turn really depressing. Looking closely at the monitor, the director in suspenders shouts, "Jim, we need a courtesy wipe!" He points to the monitor, right at the insertion point. "I think I see some *Justin Timberlake*!"

The porn starlet stops monkey grunting. She freaks out. "What's wrong? What's wrong?"

"Nothing," the director says, cigarette still in mouth. "Can I get some baby wipes, please!"

"It's just the lube!" she stretches for an excuse.

"I thought I saw something you could wipe off," explains the director. "Sorry to stop the momentum."

The freaked porn starlet storms off the set. Porn isn't as glamorous as it looks.

With the lead actress nowhere to be found, we have no other choice but to break for lunch. The entrée: greasy chicken. While I try to eat my greasy chicken, the director and the rotund sound guy watch the *Justin Timberlake* footage as if it were the Zapruder film.

"Have we done anything illegal? No!" the director in suspenders rationalizes. "Have we done anything to stop getting this sold? No!"

What they have done is ruin my appetite.

"That separates the professionals from those who want to be; they can't handle the pressure," notes the philosophical Gino, the seven-year porn vet who is in the next scene.

I ask Gino to pass the coleslaw. He rambles on, making eye contact strong enough to go beyond my comfort level. "When I 'pop,'" Gino explains, "I don't want a lot of guys hanging around, but I still do it. I block it out. I truly go into a zone."

I can't take my eyes off of Gino—winner of last year's Adult Video News award for best oral sex scene—mostly because of his obvious hairpiece. I ask a burning question: "Why do you like porn?"

"I'm kind of an exhibitionist. I get turned on having people watch and guys thinking, 'I want to be in his shoes.' I like acting," Gino says as Honey walks by; he points to her. "And I get to have sex with that beautiful woman."

Rob, the producer and Milton Berle of porn, interrupts. "I made him do this scene where he's *shaking hands* with a sixty-year-old woman."

I have another heaping serving of coleslaw as Honey and Gino, who'll soon be having sex, meet for the first time.

"What have you heard about me?" asks Gino.

"That you have a big *Woodrow Wilson*!"

"Any notes?" Gino asks.

Honey thinks for a moment. "Don't stick your finger in my *Justin-Timberlake-place*." She says, pausing. "Unless you ask!"

* * *

> **XXX Church Fun Fact:** Did you know the Porn Sunday founders often get harangued and dismissed by both sides of the ideological fence, from customers at porn conventions to a hellfire-and-brimstone clergyman who's equipped with a bullhorn outside?

Porn Sunday extends into the evening with a special movie presentation of a documentary on the XXX Church called *Missionary Positions*, followed by a prayer session held in the church's gym. For this I've enlisted the services of a busty stripper friend of mine to pose as Sapphire, Dirk Straddler's beautiful new Christian wife. Dressed in a very tight, almost see-through belly shirt that would make any guy get down and pray, Sapphire will be the true test for the men at Porn Sunday.

Entering the gym, filled with either young people or really old people, it's apparent many have had *the big talk*. One couple sits tensely in silence: he's a guy with beard and mullet who shifts uncomfortably picking his teeth, while his wife sits rigidly upright. A girl pats her boyfriend on his back for comfort. A girth-challenged mom in yellow and her teenage daughter stare straight ahead, looking very uncomfortable, as a zitty-faced guy on his own, slumped in his chair, makes an unhappy face.

A stone-faced fireman-type turns to two poodle-headed ladies and says, "Was it just me, or was the sermon this morning really full of passion?"

"I was addicted to porn," I interject into the conversation. "But I don't need porn anymore, 'cuz look at my new wife. I mean *look* at her," I say, as Sapphire sways from side to side. "Why would I need porn when I could come home to that every night, if you know what I mean."

I poke him in the ribs.

Pause. "OK."

"You know, we have a pool. We're new to the area, and if you ever want to come over and go swimming, just let me know," I add with a wink, gesturing once again to Mrs. Dirk Straddler.

Pause. "OK," he utters again, quickly making his excuses, then leaving our presence.

"I already got phone calls from couples who were here and opened up about porn," says the cool pastor before introducing the *Missionary Positions* documentary. "We're thrilled about what God is going to do to you through this movie." Then, explaining more about *Missionary Positions*, "You might see a few things you might not desire to see—but this is real."

Missionary Positions follows the plight of Porn Sunday founding pastors, Craig and Mike, whose XXX Church (number-one Christian porn site), does such zany things as operate a booth at Erotica LA where they give out T-shirts that say *Jesus Loves Porn Stars.* Surrounded by a sea of porn stars and sellable items such as big black dildos—as well as one of their wives in a bunny costume (who is constantly groped)—the two come off as funny, likable characters.

The film starts out with the dynamic anti-porn duo traveling to the hedonistic red-light district of Amsterdam. The mere mention of that city of sin creates groans from the crowd. When the words *Animal Sex* appear on screen, some old lady lets out a loud, "Oh, my God!" An old man's face in the audience cringes when a porn star at Erotica LA pushes her huge meat pillows together. My fake wife Sapphire gets up and leaves only because she's really hungover.

"She's easily offended," I whisper to the old woman next to me.

* * *

Porn Fun Fact: Did you know that, due to a boycott by the American Family Association (AFA), a growing number of Holiday Inns are now discontinuing their in-room pornographic movie service? AFA has been

> encouraging churches and Christian organizations to boycott Holiday Inns until a policy change is made concerning pornography. Along with that, the organization has declared a call to action for grocery stores to remove such magazines as *Cosmopolitan, Glamour,* and *Redbook* from checkout lines because they claim that these publications feature pictures of half-nude women and contain descriptions and tips on casual, social, and noncommittal sex.

The day drags on like it were high school. Right after the director screams, "I don't know where she took off to, but she better be back by 6:00!"

Fortunately for the production of *The Contortionist,* Cameron reappears, looking as if sudden noises would incite screaming.

"Are you OK?" asks the director in a sleazy/fatherly sort of way.

She nods weakly, like a wounded deer. It's a tender, fatherly moment that's only interrupted by, "OK, let's get some soft-core coverage!"

"God, it's good, baby!" shouts Harv as the camera rolls. From this angle I notice that Harv, in my estimation, has a very visually unappealing, if not floppy, ass.

The rotund sound guy reads tech cues from a clipboard. "We got five [minutes of film] hard and three plus on soft!"

There's a brief discussion on where Harv should *praise Jesus.* Several of Cameron's body parts are mentioned.

"Can we get it down her *Mrs. Butterworth,* or is that illegal?" asks a concerned Harv.

It's finally agreed: her bottom. Harv shall *praise Jesus* on the bottom! Hurrah for all!

They assume the *praise Jesus* position. Once again, direct, descriptive, declarative sentences are shouted.

I feel a bit nauseous. The greasy chicken, Harv's visually unappealing, if not floppy, ass—it's all turning me off. The producer walks around with dollar signs in his eyes.

"I have four minutes of tape left, do you want him to *praise Jesus*?" asks the rotund sound guy.

"All right, let's bring it home!" barks the director, captain of a copulating ship.

While being captured from all camera angles, Harv finally *praises Jesus*. The moment is faked several times for facial close-up purposes.

"And cut!"

I thought there might be some sort of applause or celebration. Instead, the director, with cigarette in mouth, snaps, "Give her two pieces of toilet paper to wipe the *Jesus praise* off her *Mrs. Butterworth*!"

Without fanfare, Cameron is quickly clothed for the next scene. With that, I retire from being a clothed porn extra. I think back nostalgically that, if my dad had brought me to a porn set when I was but a lad, he could have effortlessly explained to me the beauty behind the facts of life.

* * *

But in the meantime, it's that moment of prayer back at Porn Sunday, and *praising Jesus* in entirely another way.

"Everyone who comes in this room, the voice of God is stirring in your heart," the cool pastor says after the film as the lights in the gym stay dimly lit.

"If you want to come up and pray, please feel free to do so," the cool pastor offers. He also suggests we could write down our prayer requests and put them in a straw basket onstage next to a large wooden cross. Two guys slowly make a move. I make a beeline toward the cross, first placing a prayer request in the basket that reads, "Please, God, if I look at porn again, be sure to cut off my *thing-y*." I get into get a prayer position next to a man lying on his stomach with his arms spread out (no kidding).

When finished, I maneuver to one of the prayer counselors stationed against the side wall, confessing my porn addiction to a chunky woman who will pray for me.

"What are you still struggling with?" she asks, putting her hand on my shoulder as I speak in low tones.

"Since I quit looking at porn, I'm now highly turned on by

Redbook. I also have impure thoughts about Oprah, which I act upon. Please pray for me!"

Trying to track down the fictional Mrs. Dirk Saddler, my Porn Sunday sadly comes to a close, as I remember the words of novelist Salman Rushdie, who once called porn a litmus test for defining the bounds of a free and open society. Yes, a free society where one can start an exciting and lucrative new career filled with a bunch of fun-loving folks, living out their lifelong dreams in Van Nuys, California.

CHAPTER 16
I EXPOSE THE ILLUMINATI!

On the back of the dollar bill, the all-seeing eye perched atop the pyramid is an ominous symbol of the Freemasons. Its grim and deadly secret: that America is covertly run by a shadow government called the Illuminati, a.k.a., the Freemasons. Whispered discussions on my part with a Freemason expert—the guy who sells my friend weed—confirm my suspicions.

The Freemason society is the oldest, most powerful organization in the world. Our founding fathers were Freemasons. So were numerous signers of the Declaration of Independence, presidents (selected, of course, by the Illuminati), oil company CEOs, senators, astronauts, and even Walt Disney. They all boast membership in this exclusive club. Even the Statue of Liberty was built by Freemasons. A symbol of liberty? Or of *the Illuminati running this country*? You decide.

David Icke, the world's most controversial writer, writes (controversially) in books like *Children of the Matrix* that the Illuminati are descendents of an insidious reptilian Anunnaki race that came to Earth to wrest control in what is called *the reptilian agenda*. By inserting themselves into all levels of our human government, once they've broken down our society from the inside, they will reveal themselves as our crocodile overlords. And while admittedly dog-barkingly insane, these theories may *just be crazy enough* to explain the Freemason's motto, *Ordo Ab Chao*—Out of Chaos, Order.

I have decided to infiltrate the Freemasons in order to rub elbows with the powerful Illuminati. My hope: to find solid proof of their satanic rituals and maybe some blueprints lying around outlining their vicious reptilian agenda to take over the country—if not the world!

Into the Secret Society

To become a Freemason, I discover, one must first be invited. It's an age-old tradition that the fraternal organization never solicits new members: Men—and only men—must seek membership on their own initiative. (It's sort of like reverse Scientology, minus the E-meter but adding in world domination.)

To break into the inner sanctum of the Illuminati, I choose the appropriate undercover elitist persona:

Pseudonym: Chad Rockefeller.
Occupation: Banking (Freemasons run all the banks).
Preparation: Learning all the Freemasons' secrets I can muster off the Internet.
Catchphrase: "I'm mad with power!"

I call a number listed on the Freemason Web site and talk to Jerry, an elderly Anunnaki descendent who sounds like he was just awakened out of a deep sleep. (He must have just come out of his pod.) Explaining that I come from several generations of Masons, I tell Jerry its high time I got into the "family organization." Just like that, I'm in.

"Why don't you come down to a lodge dinner," invites Anunnaki descendent Jerry.

"Do I need to wear a tuxedo?" I ask, guessing cunningly how a world-enslaving Illuminati scion might dress.

"If you wear a sport coat with a string or bolo tie, you wouldn't be out of place."

"How about a top hat?"

"No."

Just like that, I have a dinner date with the Freemasons. Time to touch rings!

Bring on the Reptiles!

As the fog rolls in like a blanketed ghost over San Francisco, I enter a Masonic Lodge that is plastered with the odd-looking yet familiar Freemason compass symbol. I am ready to begin my Illuminati rendezvous. Making my way up a wooden staircase, I pass ancient photos with serious men, some of whom wear tuxedos and top hats (the Illuminati) and others decked out in strange Masonic aprons (perhaps these are the cooking staff). A nearby glass case displays tools and swords—presumably for the human sacrifice portion of the evening, which I'm looking forward to. Overcome by a surge of mystical unholy power—similar to the end of *Raiders of the Lost Ark* when all the Nazis melted, but minus the melting—I find myself muttering, "This is where world events are manipulated and influenced!"

I follow noise—manly chitchat and bellowing laughter—erupting from a large echoing dining room. My pulse races, since I know that inside will be the local chapter of the Illuminati: direct descendants of the superior reptilian race who are plotting to carry out the New, and perhaps even Interplanetary, World Order.

Hesitantly entering, I'm taken aback by their subversive nature. These clever reptilian bastards have taken the human form of good-natured elderly gentlemen, most of whom have chosen to disguise themselves with old-fashioned suspenders. What manner of savage beast puts on this guise of an old guy telling dirty jokes about traveling salesmen, I think, when in a mere hour they will be commencing a satanic ritual—most likely sacrificing a young virgin to the owl-god Moloch or something!

"We got a prospective member," announces elderly Anunnaki Jerry, dressed in a suit jacket and periodically hacking into a handkerchief (a symptom of the human/reptilian manifestation, I surmise cannily). Jerry gestures to several tables of old guys in suspenders. "We were talking about you earlier. These are the lodge brothers. They're very friendly. Anyone you want to know, just walk right up and introduce yourself."

"What did you say your name is?" a reptilian lodge brother asks with a smile.

"Chad Rockefeller!"

"Well, unfortunately, we're not roasting anybody tonight," he laughs, arrogantly hinting at past fiery, robed satanic rituals.

Shaking hands with the group, I give the third in line—a red-faced guy—the Boaz Grip (thumb pressed against the top of first knuckle joint), which I learned from a Secret Freemason Handshakes Web site. A pretty bold maneuver on my part, given that the penalty for divulging a Masonic secret would involve plucking out my heart, then feeding it to wild beasts. Red-faced guy, in return, gives me a non-Illuminati handshake and makes a face like someone just did a bad smell.

"One thing Masons do is eat good. You won't see a Masonic Lodge that doesn't move on its stomach," Jerry states, patting me on the back. "Let's grab some *grub*," he announces as I catch his subtle Freemason use of the word *grub* (clearly a euphemism for *world power and plotting global domination)*.

"Yes, let's grab some *grub*," I repeat, locking eyes, as we stand in front of a spread of sandwiches cut in fourths, chicken wings, and potato chips. "I'm sure Freemasons really like *grabbing grub*!"

Jerry points out, as I contemplate how many sandwich fourths to put on one's plate, "Freemasons date back to the days of King Solomon when they worked building the pyramids." He then hacks a large cough into his handkerchief, making me think he's one of the original members.

"Now, the pyramid on the dollar bill, would that symbolize the stonemasons of the pyramids?" I ask, handing Jerry a pair of tongs.

"Yeah, sort of." Pause. "Something like that." He quickly

changes the subject as if I stumbled upon something. "One does not realize how much Masonry there really is until they learn about it," he exclaims, unaware of my knowledge that the Great Seal of the United States and the Dairy Queen emblem are both evil Masonic symbols.

"Believe me, I'm aware!" I utter.

Joining the table of *outwardly* kindly old men in suspenders, I sit between Jerry and the chapter historian, directly across from the Inspector, who reports back to the Grand Master. (Is the Grand Master's name Flash?)

"How long have you been involved with the lodge?" I question the historian while picking at my potato chips.

"Since the Civil War," he replies with a diabolical laugh. (Obviously Freemasons' satanic rituals provide eternal life.)

"So, Chad, what brought you down to the lodge?" questions a bearded man who occasionally spits food while he talks (obvious difficulty adapting to his human tongue). "Do you have family in Masonry?"

"Yes." I explain, "I want to carry on Freemason traditions and history," adding with a wink, "if you know what I mean."

"Then you probably knew that Benjamin Franklin was a Mason."

"I'm aware of Ben Franklin and his Mason activities," I mutter with disgust, biting into a sandwich fourth. Obviously, I'm being tested on my knowledge that he and Thomas Jefferson practiced satanic sexual occult rituals, proven by the remains of ten bodies found buried beneath his home (covered up by the Freemasons, of course). "You could *dig up* a lot of history about Ben Franklin! Am I right?"

"He'll give you an hour and a half about that," a lodge brother joshes the historian, snickering with a "Ha-ha-ha!"

Setting the lodge brothers up to spout more Masonic lies, I inquire, "Weren't most astronauts Masons?"

"Some of them," Jerry curtly replies, letting out a hacking cough.

"The Masons flew up to the moon," laughingly adds the bearded man who occasionally spits food, perhaps tickled by the

Apollo 13 moon landing hoax. (It was staged and filmed on a Walt Disney soundstage in order to show the arrogance and contempt in which the Illuminati holds the common man.)

"Yeah, we know what *really* happened with *Apollo 13*," I snort knowingly, poking Jerry in the ribs. "*Apollo 13*," I repeat, shaking my head, chuckling as I slap the table.

"What kind of work do you do, Chad?" a lodge brother at the end of the table inquires.

"I'm a banker."

"Any free samples?" he cries jokingly to big laughs, arrogant laughs that prove that the Freemasons run all of the world banks anyway (along with the oil companies).

"Who do they think I am, the Knights of Templar?" I mumble, referring to the medieval Mason sect that created the bank loaning system.

"I used to work at the Bank of America headquarters," the guy who spits food adds (confirming my theory). "At the turn of the century, a banker left a lot of money to the Freemasons," he says, smiling. "We use it for *fun*."

Reading between the lines, I interpret that his usage of the word *fun* actually means *the Freemasons own banks that financed all wars up until the present day.*

"Some people don't like *fun*," I scornfully declare to more blank stares. Pushing a sandwich fourth with my thumb, I ask, "How long will it take for me to become a member?"

"How good are you at memorizing things?" Jerry answers a question with a question.

"What do I have to memorize?" I query, hoping it has nothing to do with the Anunnaki elite destroying society in the year 2012—on the date they've set for restarting the earth clocks.

"What happens to you during the evening of your first degree? A new member has to go through three different degrees," clarifies Jerry.

I pipe in. "Aren't their also *three* branches of government?!" (The subtlety, concerning the Illuminati controlling the government no matter which party is in power, goes over his head.)

The red-faced man eerily offers, "It's like going down a corridor with a bunch of different doors, and each door you open expands the picture," hinting it might involve the great owl's blood-letting ceremony, witnessed via closed-circuit TV by world leaders at Bohemian Grove.

"The third degree is as good of a Mason as you will ever be," the bearded food-spitter confirms.

Jerry gestures to the room of old guys in suspenders. "In all the degrees, every one of these men have gone through exactly the same degree."

"Was it the same for Freemason John Wilkes Booth?" I inquire, as my comment goes ignored.

"It's been the same since way, way back. Since the stonemasons," adds Jerry as new initiates start clearing our plates. "Masonry is in every country all over the world. In a few countries it's sort of underground and it's sort of secretive."

My jaw falls after hearing one of the countries.

"That would be Iraq," boasts Jerry with a broad smile. "We're spreading all over the world."

I'm horrified to the point of dropping a sandwich fourth. All this time I thought the Iraq war was over oil. Now I'm realizing it's instead to establish a Freemason stronghold in the Middle East.

"The lodge isn't open yet, but I'll show you around." Following at Jerry's heel, I'm taken from where the sandwich fourths were served, past glass cases with ancient mason tools.

"Wasn't the captain of the *Titanic* a Freemason?" I ask as Jerry unlocks the main lodge door.

"Yes. He was going to retire, so they let him be captain for his last voyage."

"The unsinkable ship," I state with a smirk, cleverly referring to the Freemason plot that turned the unsinkable ship into a floating tomb for the wealthy that opposed the Federal Reserve Banking System.

Putting on a horse-and-pony show, Jerry feebly tries to clarify, "The captain had to stay on schedule so they would arrive in New York for newspaper photos. That's why they were going eighty knots through a field of icebergs."

"Newspaper photos?" I sarcastically repeat with bemusement, wondering if next I'll be told that Lady Di was killed in a car crash (instead of the Masonic-orchestrated murder via forces embedded in a single spoken word due to her knowledge that the royal family is part of the reptilian agenda).

Inside the Freemasons' sacred hall looks like the Mad Hatter's playroom.

"Masonry is very high on symbolism," Jerry points out to randomly placed objects scattered across the large room—pillars, a ship, a square, a compass, a globe (a symbol of what they control). "These are things explained to you in your degrees. If you ask a question, I might be able to answer it, and I might not."

"Here's a question," I ask Jerry while looking around the room. "Who really killed JFK?"

"I'm not sure what you mean."

"Wasn't Lyndon B. Johnson a Freemason?"

"Yes."

"That's all I really need to know."

Flustered, Jerry points to a large G mounted on the wall. "These are all instruments of geometry. Geometry, you see, is in the east."

"I'm aware what G stands for," I cry for humanity, knowing full well it actually stands for *Good God, We Control the Globe*!

"Oh, yeah."

"Is there anything you can say about that?"

"Not really, no!"

Of course he can't speak of it. Pointing to an altar placed in the center of the room (this must be for the satanic sacrifice to the owl-god Moloch), I remark, "I'm sure you can't say anything about that or the initiation?"

"No, not really. But it's nothing that will embarrass you," he blurts, adding, "One rule of Masonry, you can't talk about religion or politics." Jerry stresses. "Freemasons believe in the Supreme Being referred to as *The Great Architect of the Universe*." (Is it a reptilian architect?)

Why follow a particular religion when Freemasonry has a kick-ass ancient Anunnaki religion from galaxies away!

Before he can answer, we're interrupted by the arrival of the master of the Masonic temple. With a long, dark coat, he's a good thirty years younger than the majority of Anunnaki here tonight. And I know why—he's been drinking virgin child blood to obtain his fountain of youth.

"This is Chad Rockefeller. He works as a banker. He's interested in becoming a Freemason."

Feeling growing repulsion for these Illuminati reptilian elite, I defiantly shake the master's hand with the Jachin secret handshake (pressing the top thumb hard on the second knuckle). A cocky move given that the penalty for exposing that secret is having one's heart ripped out.

The master mason makes an unhappy face. He asks if he could have a word with hacking-cough Jerry. They periodically look over at me, as I flash a broad smile. Certainly they think I'm a prime Freemason candidate who can provide them with the lost Word of God quested by the Anunnaki Illuminati (if pronounced correctly, it can provide the possessor virtual control over the entire world and hold any nation ransom).

Suddenly, like the Bat Signal, a large G on the wall lights up. Abruptly, all the old men upstairs in suspenders eating sandwich fourths slowly start assembling in the sacred lodge room, except now they're all wearing very silly-looking Freemason aprons tied around their waists.

"The Illuminati really has got to get their shit together if they plan on world domination with this collective bunch," I mumble toward the kindly elderly gentlemen in aprons.

"You'll have to come with me now," solemnly states Jerry. I'm whooshed into a room filled with numerous portraits of decades of masons on the wall. They seem to stare at us with piercing eyes, as the door to the sacred hall is firmly closed, the better to worship the Satanic Black Pope, who holds a secret position in the Vatican.

"I know what you're thinking. But it's not true," I clarify to the Tiler, wearing a Masonic apron with a small sword dangling from it like a tiny phallus. He guards the meeting room door. Surely he, too, assumes I'm the Freemason candidate who can provide the lost Word of God.

"Brother Tiler!" announces a Freemason, emerging from the closed sacred room now wearing a large, silly purple cape, holding a long staff with a Masonic compass on top of it. "Your brethren request that the meeting is about to begin."

He goes back behind the closed door. A strange, loud hissing noise erupts from the sacred room—a noise that a reptilian race makes when removing their *human* faces and shape-shifting into their scaly lizard true selves as on their home star ZA-OS. I try not to panic.

As the meeting commences without us, Jerry shares about those who misread Freemason secrets. "In the past, we've always taken the high road and have not disclosed certain allegations and responses."

"Is it true the penalty is death if you divulge the secrets of the Freemasons?" I ask, a bit concerned, being this is the group that murdered Lady Di, as the New World Order is plotted behind closed doors. "Such as having your throat cut and your tongue torn from its root?"

Annoyed Anunnaki Jerry shakes his lizard-hidden head in annoyance. "Just about everything there is to know about Masonry is on the Internet. Do yourself a favor and don't read about it ahead of time." (I'm sure that's what he would have told the captain of the *Titanic* if the Internet was around back then!)

"Would I be able to find the Grand Hailing Sign of Distress on the Internet?" I ask, testing his coverup plot by raising both hands toward the heavens, with each arm forming a square at a ninety-degree angle.

"They're secrets, but it would spoil it for you to be ahead of it!"

"What about secret passwords like Mor-bon-zi?" I spout, continuing the Grand Hailing Sign of Distress. "Will my bowels be taken out and burned to ashes?"

Jerry and the Tiler both make unhappy faces.

"Brother Tile-er, the third degree is about to begin," sinisterly announces the reappearing guy with a purple cape, who shoots me a piercing stare that makes my heart jump, before going back into the sacred room. (Do I hear chanting?)

"I'm mad with power!" I cry, waving my arms wildly at various angles like I was doing the Safety Dance. Suddenly the room starts spinning out of control, in a whirlwind sea of pyramids, large eyeballs, and compasses. I find myself crying, "Mor-bon-zi!"

"I wish you wouldn't do that," Jerry expresses with a frown and voluminous hacking cough.

He and the Tiler roll their eyes, as I unexpectedly feel the ghostly presence of Ben Franklin ritualistically sodomizing Thomas Jefferson.

Their newfound repulsion suddenly hits me. It's all clear now—the sandwiches, the chicken wings, the potato chips.

They didn't invite me here to be a prospective member; they're fattening up the calf. They plan to sacrifice me to the owl-god Moloch in order to solidify the New World Order. No wonder they wear aprons—the blood will spout everywhere!

Almost knocking over a glass case of compasses, I quickly make excuses (I have to attend a Scientology meeting), I bolt out of the Masonic Lodge, fleeing in terror with more proof of their Illuminati plot than Lady Di had right before her "mysterious" car crash. I make one last Grand Hailing Sign of Distress, but this time it's for real—you never want to see a room full of pissed-off Anunnakis!

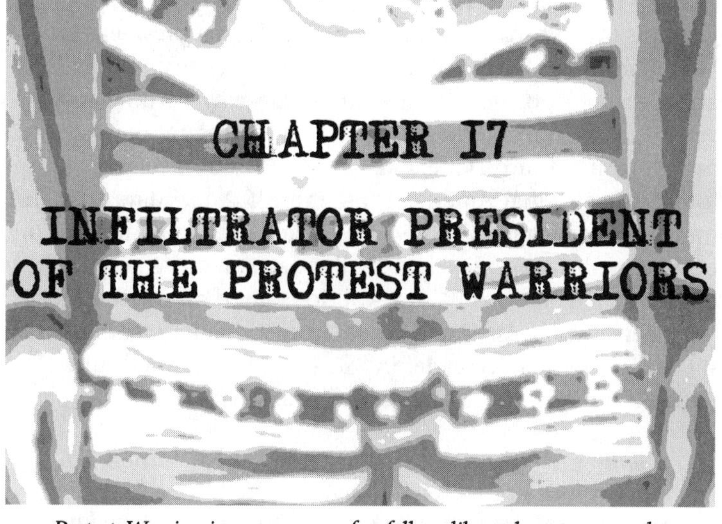

CHAPTER 17
INFILTRATOR PRESIDENT OF THE PROTEST WARRIORS

Protest Warrior is a new way for fellow liberty-lovers across the planet to mobilize against the left within their own cities. As you know, those on the left usually carry the loudest microphones . . . but they go silent quickly when truth is thrown back in their face.

—from the Protest Warrior Web site

I want to meet these truth-throwers. With the cunning motto "Fighting the Left—Doing It Right!" the main objective of Protest Warrior is to organize counterprotests to liberal protests. Isn't protesting a protest kinda like trying to parody a parody?

Their plight would make sense if they were the weak taking on the powerful, except, as this book has mentioned (with the subtlety of baseball bat to the back of the head), their boy Bush is in the White House, a Christian Right surge is sweeping America, and Republicans control the three branches of government. In this case, it comes across like schoolyard bullies on the wrestling team picking on the kids in the theater department.

Going to the Protest Warrior Web site, I log in to the Sacramento chapter. To my astonishment, under the position of chapter president, it reads, "Leader Not Assigned." A button prompts me to consider running for the chapter president office. With lightning speed, I push yes. In order to consider this lofty and esteemed position, I must first write why I would make a good Protest Warrior chapter president. Going by the patriotic pseudonym "Monroe Jefferson," I quip, "It's time to show those loony-liberals what America is all about!" A few days later the inauguration begins. I receive an e-mail congratulating me on becoming the new president of the Sacramento chapter. They refer to me as "Sergeant." This will look good on my resume.

There's more. An e-mail arrives from a chapter member, with the ledger reading, "A leader in Sacramento. It is about time!" A patriotic guy named Steve enthusiastically writes:

> It is time to get the Sacramento-area Protest Warriors out again! Looks like the World Can't Wait folks are back. The Sac/Yolo Peace goons have an event planned. This should be the one to attack.
>
> Care to make a mission out of it?

Since Steve looks up to the new president, that's just what I do—*fight the Left—doing it Right!* I send out several e-mail battle cries to my entire Sacramento Protest Warrior chapter—191 members—to protest the upcoming rebuttal of Bush's State of the Union address:

> OPERATION DROWN OUT THE LIBERAL MOONBATS TRYING TO DROWN OUT BUSH
>
> Sacramento Protest Warriors—
>
> I'm your new chapter president. I'd like to declare a liberal MOONBAT WARNING!!!! MOONBAT WARNING!!!!!
>
> Let's stick it to the Liberal Moonbats! Let's prove they can't push our President around who has really neat stuff to say on Tuesday night. Who's with me? Let's all dress in red, white, and blue and bring signs.
>
> Email me if you want to make a difference. Or do you want to be eating croissants in France?

Fighting the good fight!

Sgt Monroe Jefferson
Protest Warrior Chapter President

The few Protest Warrior responses are a bit lackluster:

I can't make it because it is during my work hours. Too bad Liberals don't seem to have jobs.

* * *

We have NOT left the Democratic Party, THEY LEFT US!
Defending GOD and Country.
Defending the Boy Scouts.
Defending the Right, Against Gay Wrongs.

* * *

Good luck with counter protesting the moonbats—carry garlic as they are the same bloodsucking a-holes in protest as they are when picking up welfare checks with the other dhimmi. God bless you and America!

Steve e-mails back requesting that I—the chapter president—call him. When I phone, the woman who answers screams with a sense of excitement, "It's the Sacramento Protest Warrior leader!"

When Steve first inquires why I wanted to become chapter president, like the leader I am, I proclaim, "I want to show those loony liberals what America is all about!"

Then, suspicion starts: "You know, the national Protest Warrior leader has been e-mailing me some of the missions you've been posting lately," he says. "He was really baffled on what was going on."

"What's the problem?" I state in a defensive manner.

"Some of the wording was just kind of strange. He just didn't understand what was going on."

"Is it wrong to get overenthusiastic about showing loony

liberals what America is all about!" I justify with patriotic passion.

"Jason should have been the leader of Sacramento years ago," he mumbles. "I thought Jason was going to apply."

I don't know who Jason is, but speaking the Protest Warrior jargon, I ask with a sense of authority, "Is anyone else from *our unit* coming down to the liberal-loony protest tomorrow so we can *fight the Left—doing it Right*?"

Protest Warrior Steve proudly declares, "No, I do this stuff by myself." He elaborates on his tactics against the "local goons." "Last time, I went down there and flew the Communist flag over their heads. The Russian USSR flag!" he states with pride. "Those people there really hate me because I've been going there for ten years."

"Ten years!" I exclaim. "Really? That's insane!" I catch myself, then clarify, "—an *insane* amount of dedication for the cause!"

"They call me 'commie' because I'm carrying the flag, but every single car that drives by thinks I'm with them." Laughs. "I don't go to debate, I just go to laugh at them, and they can't take it." More laughs. "Someone gets in my face and starts talking crap, I look at them and go 'Have you washed today? You stink!'" He sniffs. "Woo, man!" Big laughs. "You know that kind of stuff. Ha-ha! I smile and laugh, smile and laugh, and call them stupid."

"Yeah, those liberal dummies should take a shower using soap!"

"And I tell them, 'Oh! Are you talking again? Your breath stinks, bitch!'"

Restatement of Fact: This guy has been doing this alone for ten years!

"Will you break out the Communist flag tomorrow?" I ask with a glimmer of hope to witness this spectacle, which would have had more of an impact during the cold war. (Steve's dream gig is to wave a Communist flag over "Cindy *bin* Sheehan's" head, in order to show what he thinks of the mother whose son died in Iraq.)

"If I see a big enough crowd, I'll bust out the big red Russian Communist flag!"

"What do you suggest to write on my sign, slogan-wise?" I inquire. "How about, 'Fight for the Right!'" I throw out, explaining the use of the word in this case applies to both correctness and conservative politics.

"See, they don't get those signs. They don't understand irony," he says (clearly not understanding *my* irony). Steve riffs on. "Like, I have a sign of a hippie shaking the hand of a Nazi, and it says, 'Come Together for All Our Common Goals—Peace, Love, Harmony, and Killing Jews.'"

"Yeah." Pause. "And it goes right over their heads," I remark (wondering where he's going with this one).

"All they see is the swastika on the Nazi's arm, and they call me a Nazi," Steve barks with disgust. "I'm like, 'Hey, read the fucking sign.'" He laughs. "Is this over your head? Do you have *any* idea the subtlety of this sign?"

A Nazi with a swastika now equals subtle?

"Yeah!"

Steve is also an infiltrator. "Last year in November, I pretended to be interested in World Can't Wait. I e-mailed and said I wanted to lead a chapter and that kind of crap, and they totally bought into it," Steve enthusiastically explains. "So I was made the leader of the World Can't Wait chapter of Sacramento!"

"No, way," I cry with disbelief. "You *infiltrated* the opposition? I would never think of doing that!" *This is becoming like Spy vs. Spy!*

"I was giving them all the jargon like, 'power to the people,' 'direct action,' and all this bullshit that I just made up."

"You really were *fighting the Left—doing it Right,*" I commend him (utilizing Protest Warrior jargon).

Steve explains his grand scheme for tomorrow's loony-liberal protest. "I wanted to do a fake World Can't Wait rally. I e-mailed them and they posted my rally on their Web site. So here's the thing—there's two World Can't Wait rallies tomorrow in Sacramento. One is real, and one is completely 100 percent bogus, and that's mine!" With a huge snort: "I'm going to be at the one across from the capitol, of course, getting some covert video of loony leftists showing up to a big empty nothing. So that's what I'm doing."

Pause. "OK." Pause. "So no other Protest Warriors are showing up?"

"It's a tough turnout on the weeknights," he explains. "Here's the big difference between our side and their side: we work, they don't!"

"Exactly!" I proclaim with passion. "Those loony liberals spend all day eating their croissants and watching their Susan Sarandon movies," I venomously spew. Since it's a weeknight, and he has the time to capture covert video, I ask Steve what he does for a living.

"Yeah, well, me, I'm actually unemployed right now," he sheepishly admits. "I have all the time in the world to plan this crap," he says. "If two people show up, scratch their heads so I can take pictures and laugh, then it will be worth it!" the schoolyard bully states. "I'm just there to piss them off anyway." A sad lilt suddenly overcomes Steve's voice—as if his days of making fun of the underdog are numbered. "Protest Warrior is starting to fall to the wayside. Here's the thing to understand about Protest Warrior. We don't start protests—we just attend other ones and toss a wrench into their gears."

"Right. To make fun of them and their un-American opinions!" I summarize their obvious purpose.

"That's the core essence of Protest Warrior—it's mocking these people."

"Yeah, they're just commies," I cry. "They should be eating a bowl of borscht in Cuba or something."

"Mocking them is fun, and that's what we do. That's the whole original basis of Protest Warrior. I go right up in them, I infiltrate and mess with them!"

"Let's show the liberals what America is all about!"

Moonbats Unite!

On the eve of Bush's State of the Union address, about twenty protestors, mostly kindly old hippie-types, are perched on a busy street corner in Sacramento, with signs reading everything from "Bush Is in the Matrix!" to the more blatant "Bush Is an Asshole!" Some have brought noisemakers, while others bang on the bottom of pickle buckets, trumpeting for passing cars to honk their anti-Bush support.

But the big question is, where the hell is Steve—my Yoda? Where is he and his big, stupid, red Communist flag to show me the ropes on how to mock the loony Left for sport and personal amusement, you know, as he's done for the last ten years? Like the ending of *It's the Great Pumpkin, Charlie Brown,* I stand on the outskirts, still waiting for him to arrive so I can watch his big song-and-dance display. Is he maybe a liberal infiltrator, posing as a Protest Warrior, in order to dupe me (a Protest Warrior infiltrator)? Is he a double-agent? Getting to the bottom of this, I approach the protestors (forgetting I'm in a "I Support Desert Storm" T-shirt Protest Warrior disguise).

"Have you seen a guy with a big Communist flag?" I ask an old lady with deep crevices in her face, who's intensely pounding on a plastic bucket—looking like she might do this for a living.

She stops bucket-pounding and replies, "He's usually out here, but I haven't seen him. He only comes by the bigger protests now."

Bigger protests? I thought he was content with two people scratching their heads.

"What does he look like?" I question, in case I run across someone fitting his description, perched in the bushes, getting covert video and laughing his head off.

Weirdly describing him, she tilts her head and reflects, as additional protestors arrive with more elaborate drums. "He's very tall and handsome. Sometimes he brings a friend with him."

Cars continue to honk as I'm taken aback, and frankly confused, by her almost schoolgirl crush. "So do you get along with him?"

"No, he hates us!" she says. Looking at my "I Support Desert Storm" T-shirt, she adds, "Why? Are you his friend?"

"No, I'm just a fan of large, red Communist flags, and I heard he had a really nice one." Pause. "I'm a collector!"

She scoffs. "Waving a Communist flag around in 2006? Come on—isn't that a little bit dated?"

Secretly agreeing, I ask myself whether this woman—pounding on the pickle bucket—is the sole voice of sanity in this insane world. My contemplation is soon interrupted when she suddenly segues into how 9/11 was orchestrated by the Bush administration.

"Do you really think the planes were hijacked by so-called Arab gentlemen?" she says intensely, making finger quotes. "How come there's video footage showing the plane's windows were blacked out?"

I shrug my shoulders, looking at her sign that reads: "Exposing the 911 Inside Job!"

"All the passengers who were 'supposedly' onboard have been popping up in other parts of the world!" (Are Freemasons behind this?) As she goes on describing eyewitnesses accounts of small, planned explosions occurring inside the World Trade Center, I believe this old lady probably isn't the best representative for shedding the loony-Left stereotype.

Before leaving, I use Steve's Protest Warrior tactic and blurt to one of the hippie guys playing the drums, "Have you washed today? You stink!" He, in turn, looks sad and confused that I would be such a mean-spirited prick. (Being a Protest Warrior makes you feel like a complete asshole.)

On the way out of town, past the capitol building, there are, to my amazement, several dozen passionate protestors stationed outside, holding anti-Bush signs as cars honk as they drive by. Since Steve organized this event, he must really be laughing his head off—or maybe not!

LONE VOICES MUST BE HEARD

The harder the conflict, the more glorious the triumph.
—Thomas Paine
(a quote posted on the Protest Warrior's Web site)

With the poor turnout of the Protest Warriors, leaving red, white, and blue egg on my face, I decide it's time to reorganize my chapter and its members. I—the chapter president of my Sacramento unit—call forth a Protest Warrior meeting (which I will lead).

> Sacramento Protest Warriors—
>
> In my latest chapter president address, I'd like to declare, LOONY ALERT!!!!!!!!!! Hey, it's time to get the chapter going again and take action against the loony left and let our voice be heard. Who's with me!!!!!!! One thing I'd like to start is monthly meetings where we can plan various missions against traitors to our country (you know those who should be singing the French national anthem).
>
> ATTENDANCE IS MANDATORY!
>
> Fighting the good fight!
>
> Sgt. Monroe Jefferson
> Protest Warrior Chapter President

For the meeting, I request that people "dress patriotically." This will enable us to spot each other in public as fellow Protest Warriors. Remembering what Steve said in our phone conversation, I'm sure to expect that my meeting will be infiltrated by the Left. (Oh, I guess that's me!)

Those who answer my *call to arms* are The Few, The Proud . . . The Conservatively Pissed Off! So pissed off, in fact, that they drove from all points in the region to bond with like-minded pissed-off patriots. As long as liberals protest the politics of beloved George W. Bush, society hasn't given them a fair shake.

Before the meeting, I first need a little Protest Warrior preparation.

Outfit: American flag bandana; patriotic red, white, and blue tracksuit top; and T-shirt that says, "We Love the USA!"

My Objective: As chapter president, to go completely *mad with power*.

"In the Next War the *Losers* Get France!" reads the bumper sticker of the car in front of me. Is this one of my chapter members? Heading toward my mandatory Protest Warrior meeting, I look forward to the whole affair with the same enthusiasm as one receiving shady back-alley dental work.

Upon arrival, at the reception area of Carrow's Restaurant—the Denny's of northern California—I spy a blond woman and a man with a receding hairline who wears a T-shirt emblazoned with a large Ronald Reagan. They sit awkwardly, eyeing people as they enter.

Adjusting my American flag bandana, I take a stab in the dark, "Are you here for my Protest Warrior meeting?"

"I am!" the man proclaims.

"So am I," adds the blond woman.

With two clenched fists, I cry, "It's time to show those liberals what America is all about!" When their lackluster reaction dies down, I snottily declare, "I'm Monroe Jefferson, the Protest Warrior chapter president. Did you two come together?"

Gesturing toward the large cranial Ronald Reagan likeness, the man says, "No, she spotted me because of my shirt."

"That shirt is fantastic!" I respond, waving my finger, adding with a respectful nod, "You just might make a good Protest Warrior chapter vice president!"

I turn toward the blond woman dressed in unauthorized civilian clothes. "Didn't you read my e-mail about dressing patriotic!" I bellow, reprimanding her for not following my Protest Warrior chapter president orders. (I should make her drop and give me ten push-ups.) She makes an unhappy face.

"There's going to be a group of us." I boastfully tell the hostess, puffing out my chest to emphasize my "We Love the USA" T-shirt. "We're a right-wing political organization. I'm the president!" Since she's clearly unimpressed, I add, "We *fight the Left—doing it Right*!"

The hostess steers us toward a table where we make rigid, uncomfortable right-wing small talk. Because I'm the chapter president, the pair leans in, listening intently to what I have to say. "The harder the conflict, the more glorious the triumph," I state, quoting Thomas Paine (certainly not for the last time tonight), which helps break the ice.

As we're handed menus (that chicken-fried steak looks good!), the rest of my "unit" slowly files in—each arriving on his own.

"Is this the Protest Warriors?" asks a man with glasses, who claims to be a schoolteacher.

"It is!" I bark. Then with abrupt anger, "And you're late!" I give him something to think about, "What if you were late for an operation? That just won't do!" Like an authoritative dick, I lean far back in my chair, adding, "Pull up some table!"

He's followed by a guy in a white shirt and tie, who is the Republican Independent candidate for Congress in District 5. I know this because his business card and bumper sticker, which he hands everyone, say so. (Schmoozing *my* Protest Warrior chapter for his vote—what nerve!) Then comes a gung-ho guy with mustache and glasses (another lone Don Quixote for the Right). So gung-ho, in fact, he wears a Protest Warrior T-shirt.

"Where did you get your awesome T-shirt?" I ask, planting him a patriotic high five.

"I ordered it right off of the Web site!" he proudly proclaims. His shirt features an angry, shirtless muscular guy wielding a large sword and sign that reads "Protest Warrior Now!" Politics aside, I have to say the Protest Warrior emblem is . . . kinda gay—in every sense of the word.

"You just might make a good chapter vice president," I state, slapping him on the back, eyeballing the guy in the Ronald Reagan T-shirt (keeping him on his toes). "For those of you who came late, let me bring you up to speed. The harder the conflict, the more glorious the triumph." I'm met with utter blank stares.

"How was the counterprotest last week?" meekly asks the schoolteacher.

"Not so good," I recount, fumbling with my cutlery. "It was only me and my mom. It really sucked 'cuz I misplaced my big, red Communist flag I normally wave." And then, "How come you weren't there? There's really no excuse for not attending," I stress, laying down my authority on my suspected first choice for liberal infiltrator.

"It was the night of the State of the Union address," the schoolteacher rationalizes. "That's my Super Bowl!" he proclaims.

I reprimand the entire group, giving the thumbs-down for their lack of attendance. Their reaction: sad faces. "It just won't do! We need your commitment next time there's a liberal loony fest." I then describe the festivities. "Their moonbat protest was crazy. No one was wearing shoes. Eight people were on stilts! Someone served sushi. They burned over five American flags!"

Everyone gasps.

"It's during the day. We're all working," spits the man with the Reagan shirt. "They're probably on welfare." (Funny, the skinheads in Georgia said the liberals were the rich kids!)

After handing out the last of his bumper stickers, the Republican candidate for Congress takes a picture of the group and leaves abruptly, as the lone Goliaths taking on an army of Davids tell of their solo plights.

"I was the Protest Warrior team leader for Vacaville," the gung-ho guy in the Protest Warrior shirt says with an enthusiastic smile. "There're a lot of patriotic people there," he says, mentioning the turning point was two years ago. "We got the main street corner in Vacaville with some signs and some flyers, and we just stood out there."

"Inspirational! How many Protest Warriors turned up?"

"It was mainly two guys and myself," he boasts. "Yeah, just two guys—but very passionate."

Pause. "OK."

Suddenly, the entire mood shifts. The meeting takes a serious right turn. We meet the professional Protest Warrior.

"Are you Monroe?" utters a large, unsmiling Protest Warrior in a blue shirt and military haircut, extending his huge hand, in a firm, no-nonsense grip. (I, in turn, give him the Freemason Boaz Grip.)

"Yes, I'm Monroe Jefferson—chapter president. I'm glad you could make it," I say, hoping he won't see through my bullshit. I have an uneasy feeling that this man is going to whip my hat and bandana off and expose me—that's why he was sent! Will I be outed as the infiltrator? "Pull up some table!" I remark with a nervous laugh.

The very large, humorless, intimidating man who arrives with his girlfriend (who doesn't speak during our entire Carrow's Protest Warrior meeting) stresses his military background. He is much more intense than my other chapter members.

"'The harder the conflict, the more glorious the triumph,'" I quote yet again, adding, "Thomas Paine said that!" This utterance impresses him less than the others.

As the large, intimidating man and his silent girlfriend take a spot at the end of the table, the blond woman suggests, "Why don't we go around the circle and say our names, what we do, and why we want to be part of Protest Warrior?"

"Listen, *I'm* the chapter president!" I stress, offended she went over my head without my approval. "I'll be the one to suggest that." Pause. "Why don't we go around the circle and say our names and what we do?"

As we work around the table, the man in the Reagan T-shirt says, "I grew up ready. I knew I was a Republican at the age of seven!"

"I didn't consider whether I was liberal or conservative until 2000 when a high school friend was trashing Bush," explains the gung-ho guy, who had then joined the military. (Once in the Army, he thought, "This is the place for me. These are my people!")

"The Left has become sooo left," the blond woman declares.

"And the Right is sooo *right*," I interject, again clarifying my use of the word *right* (big nods follow).

After she mentions being an electrical engineer, it's my turn.

"I work as a salesman for a company that manufactures American flags," I announce to enthusiastic reactions.

"Is someone going to take notes?" interrupts the large man, bucking my authority. He almost rolls his eyes, scoffing at the lack of professionalism at my meeting.

"As chapter president, I will do the note-taking!" (This will also enable me to record every detail.) "Has anyone been to other Protest Warrior events?" I ask, taking charge. "Let me see a show of hands!"

The large, intimidating Protest Warrior pipes in from his end of the table. "We went to crash an Islamic workshop in San Francisco held in a public school. It was an Islamic workshop to raise money for a group of terrorists and fund their cause," he says, providing his spin on the event. "Since it was in a public school, we had the right to be there as well. So the Protest Warriors ended up getting a police escort into the building." He adds, "We're private citizens! We're here to see what's going on!" Once the Protest Warriors got inside, they were appalled with what they found. "There were pictures of kids learning how to fight!" he says of what he interpreted as a budding terrorist cell in the making. Here in broad daylight—inside an American public school!

With that, our Carrow's food arrives. The blond woman stops our meeting by bowing her head and praying out loud over her quality budget-priced food. It's awkward. The rest of us look uncomfortably at each other, unsure if we should also bless our budget-priced meals we are about to eat, here, at Carrow's.

"One of the big things is the liberal-loony fest on March 18 down in *Frisco*," I stress when the prayers wrap up, referring to the third anniversary protest of the Iraq War (and annoyingly calling San Francisco "Frisco"—which would make any local citizen's blood boil). "This is our Super Bowl," I declare, looking at the schoolteacher/potential infiltrator. "So what can we do to make a Protest Warrior presence in *Frisco*? For this event, I'd like to hook up with the *Frisco* Protest Warrior chapter. Attendance is mandatory!"

"We need five or more to crash an event," interrupts the intimidating, large man, again leaning on my meeting-leadership parade. "There's two types of events," he commands like a war-torn vet. "One is a pro-event—we go out and support a cause. The other is we try to crash an event."

"I knew that," I arrogantly blurt.

"The anti-protests are the ones we crash. They're really fun, but it can get real dangerous."

"Now what would also be fun?" I throw out. "A bake sale!"

After momentary dead silence, next comes some serious Protest Warrior brainstorming, when I put our collective brainpower together, here, at Carrow's, and come up with bright ideas on how to *fight the Left—doing it Right!*

"Bullhorns!" I adamantly stress. "We need lots of bullhorns!"

"No bullhorns," nixes the large guy. "We should nominate one person to speak that knows all the issues. If the media's going to show up, we don't want to seem like babbling idiots."

"As president of this chapter, that will be my duty!" I declare, pounding my fist on the table.

"No weapons," adds the blond woman.

"No fighting. Unless it's one-on-one in an alley," contributes the gung-ho guy, miming a headlock/punching motion. Then, as an aside, "I got a friend who wants to join, but I can't get him to abide by the nonviolent rule."

I laugh, poking him in the ribs, also miming a headlock/punching motion. "Everyone should start going through physical training for the event. Start jogging three miles a day. Start doing a hundred sit-ups!"

Other suggestions: "It costs about fifty dollars to put a sign together," instructs the large, intimidating guy with his arms folded. "The Web site tells you how to do it. The signs they have are really funny and sarcastic," he adds, actually breaking a chuckle.

"Yeah, they have a kid training at a terrorist camp with an AK-47," explains the Reagan-T-shirt-wearer with a girlish laugh. "It says, 'Family Values.'"

"There's a Saudi family with a T-shirt on that says, 'I Just Blew Up a Bus and All I Got Was This Lousy T-shirt,'" adds the gung-ho guy with a smirk.

"I have a great sign," I announce as everyone directs their

attention toward me. "It has a hippie and a Nazi. They're shaking hands. Get it?! Do you have any idea of the subtlety of that sign?"

The table seems a bit unclear.

Breaking a momentary uncomfortable silence: "I made a big 'United We Stand' sign. People just loved it," shares the intimidating guy. "How can you roll your eyes at 'United We Stand' with an American flag!"

Rolling my eyes, I ask, "Has anyone ever attacked you and taken your sign?"

"I'm a big guy, so no one touches them!" he confirms without smiling.

As the ingenious ideas keep rolling, the gung-ho guy commends me. "You got balls to get this going!" (These are my people, and they look up to me and my balls!) But the moment is short lived.

"At the next meeting, we should nominate president, vice president, and secretary. It should be a person who's on the ball and who will keep coming," the large, intimidating guy says as the waitress starts bringing our checks. With a stern expression, he looks around the table to solemn faces.

I become outraged at his suggestion of a chapter president coup d'état.

"Helloooo! We already have a president, thank you!"

"In all fairness, I didn't see you at the last meeting," he firmly states (while his girlfriend still doesn't speak). "I didn't see anyone here."

"The chapter decided you're the man who stepped up," jumps in the gung-ho guy, taking my side (and looking more like vice presidential material). "Keep it rolling. I'm glad you did this."

"You organizing this meeting is a huge step," commends the Reagan T-shirt wearer with a big smile. I could feel guilty for reawakening this group and gaining their loyalty, except for the fact that it's utterly ridiculous.

"The whole thing is recruiting," stresses the gung-ho guy.

"You should e-mail the members from your Vacaville chapter [all two of them] and let them know," I respond, wanting to really get the hell out of there.

"They're your members now, too," he says, patting me on the back, as we do a cool-guy handshake. "This will double! It will blow up!"

"That's when we'll get infiltrators," the large guy with the silent girlfriend warns. "When we get big, you can expect that from the other side."

I suspiciously eye the schoolteacher who hasn't spoken the entire meeting, and sinisterly say in his direction, "Maybe we have some infiltrators here tonight?"

The large, intimidating guy makes an angry face. "We had someone on *the other side* who came in and infiltrated the group, then he would write shit on the Protest Warrior Web site. We found out who it was. He showed up at the next meeting, and it was not good." I shift uncomfortably, as he makes an expression like he would kill his own mother.

"Did he dress like our side?" I uncomfortably ask, adjusting my bandana, adding, "I can guarantee no one will infiltrate this chapter under my command!"

As we prepare to leave, the gung-ho guy in the Protest Warrior T-shirt shares how he infiltrates at protests. "Dress like them and bring a video camera. Proclaim you're with a college paper. Preplan some questions. 'How do you feel about killing unborn babies? How do you feel about Republicans?' You say, 'Hey I'm on your side,'" he explains adamantly. "Let them speak their mind! They're loonies!"

"I'd loooove to infiltrate the opposition and make them look real stupid," I say, wiping crumbs off my "We Love the USA" T-shirt. "Yeah, I could dress like them!"

As we collect money for the bill, he concludes, "It's all about exposing them for who they are and making them look like jackasses."

"Exposing and making them look like jackasses," I repeat, nodding my head.

"Was anyone concerned that the guy was taking pictures?" pipes up the schoolteacher, referring to the Republican candidate who left ages ago (probably only saying this to create a diversion from the others believing that *he* is actually the liberal infiltrator).

The large, intimidating guy suddenly hovers over me. "I'm with Protest Warriors for one reason, to give our side a good fight!" Why does he have the crybaby "poor us" attitude? The forces of his political party have all the power—they're all in charge!

"Yeah," I blurt, giving my presidential final word. "It's time to show the liberals what America's all about!"

Leading My Troops to Battle

Earlier, Steve was looking forward to the March 18 war anniversary protest, which he dubbed "Operation Broken Record." He said that the only people who show up now are the "hard-core Commies, jokers, anarchists, legion of scum, and all those fuck heads."

But there's soon trouble in *fighting-the-Left—doing-it-Right* Protest Warrior paradise.

"I can't go on Saturday. I cannot," Steve repeats, sounding defeated on my voicemail. "I can't go. I know this is the big one." Pause. "I just can't go on Saturday." Heavy sigh. "God dang it!" The horrible monkey wrench in Steve's plans is his wife, who had twins the previous day by emergency C-section. "I'm going to try and go down to the Sacramento protest because I got to do something!" Yes, even though his wife just had twins (via emergency C-section), Steve still needs to mock loony lefties and have a good laugh—that's dedication!

A big blow to Operation Broken Record. We're now minus one big, stupid Communist flag, sure, but I, Monroe Jefferson, will "step up and lead the group." With cringing apprehension, I grab my hand-scrawled sign that reads, "What Part of 'American' Don't You Understand?" (what does that phrase even mean?), dreading the prospect of getting pummeled by the very peer group who is reading this book right now. Suited up for game day, I'm in my Protest Warrior costume: a red, white, and blue track top; military aviator shades; a T-shirt that reads "I Support Desert Storm"; an American flag bandana; and a camouflage hat and fatigues. On the very day after the largest US/Iraqi coalition attack on insurgents, I must now face ten thousand impassioned liberal protestors foaming about the Bush administration's failed WMD search and the screwed-up results thereof.

As I'm purposely a half hour late, the blond woman (the one who prayed over her meal at Carrow's) is truly freaking out. "Monroe! We were setting up our signs, and we're already getting hassled," she exclaims over the phone. "We need more Protest Warrior support down here!"

"The harder the conflict, the more glorious the triumph," I assure her.

Of course she's freaking out! This is no suburban Sacramento, with its Outback Steakhouses on every corner. No, this is SanFranfreako at its freakiest. Perched on city hall steps, a handful of hardened men, who look like refrigerator repairmen, make up the small conservative posse hoisting American flags. Shoved into an obscure out-of-the-way corner, the right-wing group is segregated from the war protestors in a designated area that is grouped together with the pro-Israel supporters. (What if you're pro-Israel but against Bush? There's very little middle ground at war protests.)

Grabbing a large American flag from a pile, I make my way over to my stressed out Protest Warrior chapter. "The harder the conflict, the more glorious the triumph!" I trumpet again upon my arrival to the blond woman; the large, intimidating guy; and his nonspeaking girlfriend (continuing her run of silence), who fumbles with assembling a stack of homemade signs.

"Dude! Dude! The flag," the large, intimidating guy urgently remarks, gesturing toward the corner of Old Glory that accidentally draped against the ground.

I quickly make the solemn adjustment as a sudden blast of "George Bush is the reincarnation of Hitler!" erupts from the direction of the protest.

"That's *so* disrespectful, period!" exclaims the blond woman with disapproval.

"You're really negative today," I mention.

With an air of concentrated determination, the large guy approaches one cop in the sea of police officers. "Why do we have to be over across the street and not over there," he demands, gesturing toward the American-flag-toting crew, whose nonseismic impact is limited to those occasionally strolling by to look at our conservative freak show spectacle.

"A lot of people's emotions are worked up, and we're just trying to avoid conflict," the cop patiently explains.

"Is it illegal to go over there with an American flag?" the large guy asks, pointing unhappily toward the sea of "Impeach Bush" signs.

"You can go any where you want with the flag," the officer says with a smirk, giving off an "I'm on your side" vibe.

"Just thought I'd ask. I didn't want to break any laws." The large, intimidating guy, sticking out his potbelly, turns to me. "Grab a flag. Let's go for a walk."

"Where should we walk?" I ask, praying it's safely with the rest of the hardened refrigerator repairmen.

"Right through the crowd," he stresses with a look of determination, aiming toward the mass of worked-up protestors.

"OK." Shit! Well, I guess this is what I signed up for. "Let's go for a walk!" I proclaim.

"You guys are brave," a man with an Israeli flag interjects, patting me on the back. "Be careful, they're crazy!"

"A Protest Warrior knows no fear!" I state with chest puffed out (fully knowing what follows is going to be, at best, unpleasant).

Leaving the womenfolk behind, we march like a scowling duo of determined misfit conservative crime fighters—American flags poised—ready to face roughly ten thousand irate protestors. Passing a hooded Abu Ghraib prisoner impersonator with difficulty adjusting his mask (thus causing him to periodically break character), I follow at the heels of the large, intimidating guy as he drags me toward the liberal lions worked up to devour the right-wing.

Like a big burning pit of bitterness in the middle of the peace festivities, we park ourselves close to the stage, proudly displaying our American flags. As a man descends upon us with a "Bush = Hitler" sign, I try to stay focused straight ahead, yet keeping my peripheral open for angry anarchists. Getting into character, I stand with a permanent scowl, feeling beams of hate projected in our general direction. My huge, oversized Denny's parking lot American flag drapes over everyone in the vicinity whenever the wind blows. Some people walk by, "accidentally" pushing into us. Other protestors openly laugh. An old hippie dude stops, salutes me, then, moments later, gives me the finger.

A photographer whispers in my ear, "You should really be across the street."

"As *true* Americans, we have the right to be here!" I scornfully declare.

"I'm just worried about your safety," she stresses to my unease.

"Can you lift your American flag higher? I can't see the stage," a woman with hemp clothing insists as an African American dance troupe performs. My chain-smoking, fellow Protest Warrior reacts by raising his flag even higher and prouder over his head with his arm fully extended.

The press, on the other hand, treats us like media darlings. Along with an old guy holding a Bush doll hanging from a noose, we're the most popular photo ops! The media swoops down upon us as a *New York Times* photographer snaps a photo of two idiots brandishing American flags—namely, us. I play it up big for the cameras, scowling with my mouth gaped and an I-can't-even-believe-what-I'm-hearing expression.

For the rest of the protesting crowd, our efforts of pushing the flag in their face—to not-so-subtlety say that they're *un-American* for voicing their political opinions (which is a *very* American thing to do)—elicits scorn.

A protestor gets in my face and sarcastically says, "Your flag is drooping on the ground."

"Seriously, you should be a little more mindful of the flag!" remarks the blond Protest Warrior woman, who rejoins us, holding a very tiny handheld American flag. The large guy's passive, silent girlfriend stands with her arms folded and a big, how-did-I-get-dragged-here look on her face.

"Thank God, we got some reinforcements," I declare as the blond Protest Warrior woman becomes a virtual abyss of bitterness, leaning in close to make negative comments about everything said on stage. (The silent girlfriend continues her reign of silence.)

Onstage in front of a large banner proclaiming, "Bring the Troops Home Now! End Colonial Occupation," a man in a suit addresses the crowd: "I represent hundreds of members of Iraq vets against war." He adds, "I am also a gay vet!"

"The only guy in the military they can find against the war is a faggot!" the blond woman spews.

"I wish I had earplugs!" I spout (not referring to the speakers but to her inane ranting) as a big gust of wind almost blows off my hat, exposing that I'm in disguise.

We venture back. I notice that the refrigerator repairmen, who are shoved in an obscure corner, are now joined by loud frat guys who hold a large "God Bless America" banner—one of whom loudly rants into a bullhorn, "Why are they whining about the war? That's negative, people. It's a beautiful day out here."

Before I can even catch my breath, the large, intimidating guy commands, "Grab a sign. Let's walk," wanting to make another insurgent attack.

"Where are we going?" I ask, hoping he doesn't mean through the crowd with his moronic sign blaring: "Except for Slavery, Communism, Socialism, War Never Solved Anything."

"Through the crowd!" he says, now holding both the moronic sign and the American flag.

"OK." Do I really have to?

We walk toward the protestors like two floppy-shoed right-wing clowns.

"If you're so smart, why are you walking around with a sign and an American flag at a peace rally?!" rants an older, enraged man wearing an "End the Occupation" T-shirt, blocking our path. (Great! I sense direct, screaming face-to-face confrontation.)

"Who's more brave?" I demand. "Me, walking around for what I believe in, or you, being like one of the sheep?" I quickly add, "That's as brave as the soldiers fighting in Iraq!"

"Who's a sheep?" the man cries, veins popping out of his neck. "Am I a sheep? You're the sheep. Why aren't you over there fighting? Why are you here carrying a goddamn sign?" he stresses, adamantly pointing his finger. "You want to fight? Why don't you go over there and fight."

"I would if I could," the large, intimidating guy jumps in, trying to maintain his composure.

"So would I!" I blurt.

"What are you, a big pussy—you can't go over there and fight?!" the angry man fumes, waving his hands madly.

"Let me ask you a question. How did you get your freedom?"

"I got my freedom because moral people took on moral causes to get it." The angry guy then turns on me. "You look like a brave guy. Why aren't you fighting there? You got that hat and that American flag bandana. Why aren't you fighting there?"

I get defensive. "Sir, first, don't criticize my American flag bandana. Second, I'd fight if I could stick to the don't ask, don't tell policy!" I make a dreamy look. "I bet the next thing you're going to tell me is it's a war for oil."

He jumps in: "No, it's a war for Israel. That's what it's all about. It's a war for Israel!"

OK, we liberals really got to get our shit together with these conspiracy theories. (I'm almost ready to argue out of character.) I'm beginning to see why our country is so Red State/Blue State divided—those at the polar extremes are both complete assholes, except the Red State assholes have all the power.

As the march swelters and commences, we abruptly wrap things up. The bitter blonde and the nonspeaking girlfriend (with the folded arms) take their right-wing song-and-dance on the protest march route. I become diverted by a woman with sunglasses, covering the event for a Latino radio station. "Can I ask you a few questions?" she asks, holding a tape recorder.

"Sure!" I express with increased flag waving, as I watch my conservative crew slowly walk off into the distance, which will allow me to be the PR spokesman for the PW organization—now every single listener will think I'm a Protest Warrior! Wasn't it all about making the opposition look like jackasses?

"Will you tell me who you are and where you're from?" she says, putting the microphone under my chin.

"I'm Monroe Jefferson. President of the Protest Warriors—Sacramento chapter."

"Do you support the war in Iraq?"

"Absolutely! One hundred percent!" I then throw out my catchphrase, "What part of 'American' don't you get?"

She nods her head vigorously to encourage my whacked rhetoric. "How do you feel about the hundred thousand people already dead?"

"It's more like thirty thousand," I coldly correct. "You're getting facts from the liberal media!"

"Well, that's still thirty thousand people dead."

"Yeah, but that's seventy thousand more people still alive!" I angrily roll my eyes and sniff, "Liberal media!" Then I add, "We won in Vietnam, we'll win in Iraq!"

She clarifies, "Vietnam was not considered a winning situation."

"Liberal media!" I spout again, with more huffing and eye rolling. As the leadership representation of Protest Warrior, I conclude the interview with a sound bite that will resonate through the airwaves: "As a Protest Warrior chapter president, I safely speak for all us when I say, KILL 'EM ALL, LET GOD SORT 'EM OUT!" I give another vigorous wave of the American flag. "Remember," I add, "I represent the Protest Warriors!"

To the Streets of San Francisco!

With the massive march underway, I realize I've lost my fellow Protest Warriors! Now I'm just a lone "patriotic nut" holding an American flag and wearing an "I Support Desert Storm" T-shirt within a sea of peace protestors (not a good feeling). Lurking in the shadows, I'm frantically searching for any liberty-lovers wielding American flags.

Turning several street corners, I spot the underdogs (except these underdogs are right-wing frat guys). Regardless, I join forces with the small group of pumped-up Young Republican frat boys and their annoying bullhorn. Whipping out my homemade "What Part of 'American' Don't You Understand?" sign, I file in inconspicuously with the ten guys sporting military haircuts and wearing camouflage like mine.

"Oh, my god! Stop the war. Stop it right now!" the frat leader whines, affecting yet another stereotypical gay voice into the bullhorn. These are the bullies; they came to throw spitballs at the peace protestors' heads—that's their sole purpose.

"What part of 'American' don't you understand!" I scream, as taunts of "This is the stupidest group of people with no brains!" ring from those marching around us.

A protestor on a bike wheels by to shout, "You guys are definitely idiots because you have no connection to what is real in the world."

"There's a lot of cops around—don't get too worked up!" taunts a guy sporting a "Got Freedom?" T-shirt, carrying a "Peace By Any Means Necessary" sign. He fires another verbal spitball. "I'm marching for imperialism." He sarcastically makes a peace sign.

As the march concludes at the civic center, the Young Republicans take up a remote street corner, far from the majority of protestors. The leader gets real cocky and confrontational with his bullhorn, since there are few people around to confront him and a large line of cops on bikes.

"How can Bush be a mastermind and the dumbest president ever?" the leader spouts into his bullhorn, mostly for the benefit of his smirking buddies. "He can't be both." (Isn't that what Cheney's for?) "It does not add up," he says with a proud, smug smile as if he's discovered some great epiphany. "Does anyone want to come over and answer the question? No one? There are thousands of people here, and no one can answer that question?"

"You're egging people on," declares a guy with dark sunglasses and a baseball cap, emphasizing his point by tapping the ringmaster's shoulder.

"Whoa! Whoa! What are you pushing me for?" the Young Republican declares, then threatening him like a big future pussy CEO of Enron, "Do you want one of these guys to take you downtown! If you touch me again I'm going to have that guy right there haul you downtown." The frat guy points to a police officer, much like Bush would point at his father to get him out of a DWI conviction. "Do you understand what I'm saying to you?"

"Fine, I won't touch you," remarks the guy with the sunglasses. "All I'm saying is you're an asshole. You're the one egging people on!"

"'I made it all the way through the fourth grade, and I have the right to be here!' Uh-huh, uh-huh," heckles a pudgy guy wearing a "Peace Through Superior Firepower" T-shirt, holding the largest American flag of the day.

"This is why our country is divided," remarks a skinny guy with glasses who suddenly appears, carrying a stack of antiwar literature. "It's because our two sides can't sit down and talk."

"You're not going to corrupt my sanity with your delusionalism," spouts the "Peace Through Superior Firepower" bully.

"Why are you out here?" the guy with glasses questions the pudgy bully and me.

Turning to the pudgy bully, I speak for both of us. "It's about letting *our* side voice *our* opinion," I state as the frat leader does another mock, sarcastic gay voice into his bullhorn.

"It's about people coming out for a parade," the skinny guy clarifies. He points to the other protestors. "They don't think they can change anything. Because they are not actually asking a question of how they're going to create that change."

The bully laughs at him. I crudely join in, then abruptly stop. I question, "What do you mean?"

The guy with glasses is surprised I'm taking interest in what he says.

"Your group can say, 'We're standing up for America.' But you have to admit this administration has created a lot of bullshit, and they're trampling on the very institution. That's something that any leftist or any Republican can't deny!"

"That's an interesting point," I say with astonishment, nodding my head. "I never thought of it that way."

I turn to the bully. "Maybe he has a point here! Maybe we do need to think about it on a larger societal scale. Maybe we should get a dialogue going with the liberals instead of mocking them? Maybe listen to each other. Interesting," I add, nodding my head.

The bully retorts with, "Every person can do their part to be responsible and self-sufficient."

Before he can finish, I hand the bully my "What Part of 'American' Don't You Understand?" sign. "I don't think I need this anymore," I say, as I grab the skinny guy's antiwar literature. Removing my American flag bandana and letting my dreadlocks fly, I make my way toward the other protestors, with echoes of: "Which is it folks, is Bush an evil mastermind, or is he a dumbass?" erupting from the smug Young Republican's bullhorn.